D1330091

Monetary Regimes and Inflation

History, Economic and Political Relationships

Peter Bernholz

Professor Emeritus of Economics, Centre for Economics and Business (WWZ) University of Basle, Switzerland

Edward Elgar
Cheltenham, UK • Northampton, MA, USA

Published by
Edward Elgar Publishing Limited
Glensanda House
Montpellier Parade
Cheltenham
Glos GL50 1UA
UK

Edward Elgar Publishing, Inc.
136 West Street
Suite 202
Northampton
Massachusetts 01060
USA

A catalogue record for this book
is available from the British Library

Library of Congress Cataloguing in Publication Data

Bernholz, Peter.
  Monetary regimes and inflation: history, economic and political relationships/by Peter Bernholz.
    p.cm.
    1. Inflation (Finance)—History. 2. Monetary policy—History. 3. Economic stabilization. I. Title.

HG229.B485 2003
332.4′1—dc21   2002034659

ISBN 1 84376 155 6 (cased)

Typeset by Cambrian Typesetters, Frimley, Surrey
Printed and bound in Great Britain by MPG Books Ltd, Bodmin, Cornwall

Contents

Preface   ix
Acknowledgements   xi

1   Introduction   **1**

2   Inflation and monetary regimes   **3**
2.1   Inflations: long-term historical evidence   3
2.2   A description of different monetary regimes   5
2.3   Monetary regimes and inflation   7
2.4   The inflationary bias of political systems   11
2.5   The influence of monetary regimes   14
2.6   Some other characteristics of monetary constitutions   15
2.7   Conclusions   18

3   Inflation under metallic monetary regimes   **21**
3.1   Inflation caused by an additional supply of the monetary
        metal   21
3.2   The debasement of metal standards by rulers   24
3.3   Reasons for the introduction and maintenance of stable
        metallic monetary regimes   30
3.4   Price and exchange controls   32
3.5   Consequences of inflation for the real economy   34
3.6   Conclusions   36

4   Moderate paper money inflations   **40**
4.1   The introduction of paper money   40
4.2   Paper money inflation in Sweden during the 18th century   41
4.3   Paper money inflation in Massachusetts, 1703–1749   45
4.4   Inflation during the American War of Independence   47
4.5   Paper money inflation during the American Civil War   50
4.6   Chinese paper money inflation under the Ming regime   52
4.7   Conclusions   61

5   Characteristics of hyperinflations   **64**
        Introduction   64
5.1   Some characteristics of the French hyperinflation   66

v

5.2	Hyperinflations are caused by government budget deficits	69
5.3	Real stock of money and currency substitution	74
5.4	Undervaluation and currency substitution	82
5.5	*Undervaluation as a consequence of currency substitution: a simple model	90
5.6	Other characteristics of hyperinflations	92
	5.6.1 Consequences of high inflation for capital markets	92
	5.6.2 The development of prices	95
5.7	Economic activity and unemployment	101
5.8	The political economy of high inflation	104
5.9	Social and political consequences of hyperinflation	107
5.10	Conclusions	110
6	**Currency competition, inflation, Gresham's Law and exchange rate**	**114**
6.1	Introduction	114
6.2	Empirical evidence for periods one to three	116
6.3	*The model	118
6.4	*First period: introduction of paper money	121
6.5	*Second period: fixed exchange rate and loss of official reserves	122
6.6	*Third period: Gresham's Law at work	123
6.7	*Fourth Period: The return of good money	126
6.8	Conclusions	131
7	**Ending mild or moderate inflations**	**135**
7.1	Conditions favouring the stabilisation of moderate inflation	135
7.2	Restoration of stable monetary constitutions after wars at the old parity	136
7.3	Preconditions for returning to a stable monetary regime at a new parity	138
7.4	Further discussion of historical examples	146
7.5	More recent historical examples	151
7.6	Conclusions	157
8	**Currency reforms ending hyperinflations**	**160**
8.1	Introduction	160
8.2	Political-economic preconditions for initiating successful reforms	162
8.3	Sufficient economic and institutional conditions for successful currency reforms	163

8.4   Characteristics of most successful currency reforms:
       empirical evidence   166
8.5   Less and least successful reforms   175
8.6   The influence of wrong evaluations of reform packages by
       the public   189
8.7   Conclusions   193

Appendix   Sources for historical data not identified in the text and
              literature relating to different cases of hyperinflation   197

Index   207

Preface

Many good books and a huge number of articles have been written on inflation. As a consequence, a new book on this subject can only be justified by looking at events from a different perspective. This has been done in several respects. First, a comparative historical analysis going back to the Roman currency debasement in the fourth century and ending with the hyperinflations (that is high inflations with a monthly rate of 50 per cent or more during at least one month) of the 1990s has been used. Second, all 29 hyperinflations in history (which all occurred, with the exception of the hyperinflation of the French Revolution, in the 20th century) and the currency reforms ending them have been included in the analysis. Third, the political forces responsible for inflation and for ending it by adequate reforms are discussed, together with the conditions under which they can be expected to operate. Fourth, the importance of monetary regimes for the stability of money is documented. Fifth, it is shown that certain qualitative characteristics of inflations and of their consequences are stable traits over centuries. Finally, a clear distinction has been made between the differing traits of moderate and high inflations and the reforms necessary to end them.

Chapter 1 offers a very brief historical overview. In Chapter 2 the importance of monetary regimes for monetary stability, given the inflationary bias of political systems, is documented and discussed. Chapter 3 analyses inflation if commodity standards in the form of metallic monetary regimes are present. In Chapter 4 moderate paper money inflations are studied, whereas in Chapter 5 all historical hyperinflations are extensively analysed. Chapter 6 provides a formal analytical framework for a complete inflationary cycle from the introduction of paper money to its total substitution by stable metallic money or foreign currencies. In Chapters 7 and 8 the political and economic conditions for successfully terminating moderate and high inflations respectively are described with the help of comparative historical analyses.

In writing the book formal mathematical analysis has been kept to a minimum. Still, some exceptions have been made for a deeper understanding. They can however be left out by the reader without losing the general thread of the argument, and have been noted with an asterisk *. To enliven the reading of the book, short personal experiences of contemporary observers have been inserted into the text, especially in Chapter 5. They are observations by people like Ernest Hemingway and Stefan Zweig, who did not have any knowledge

of the economics of inflation. As a consequence, the evidence provided by
them is often more convincing than any econometric analysis would be.

The literature on inflations is huge, so that only a part directly relevant to
our argument will be quoted in the references. But to allow the reader to delve
more deeply into the discussion concerning the different experiences with
hyperinflation, some additional works will be mentioned in the Appendix
together with the sources of the data presented.

I would like to express my gratitude to Pieter Emmer, Leiden, Hans
Gersbach, Heidelberg, and an anonymous referee for reading all or part of the
manuscript and for providing important advice on how to improve it. I am also
grateful to the Wissenschaftskolleg (Centre for Advanced Studies) zu Berlin,
where I stayed as a Fellow for the academic year 2000/01, and was able to
draw upon the generous support of the library staff when working on the
manuscript. Above all, I would like to thank my wife, Elisabeth Bernholz
Homann, for her patience with a husband embroiled for long months in writing this book.

Acknowledgements

The author and publishers wish to thank the following who have kindly given permission for the use of copyright material in Chapters 2, 4 section 6, 5 section 3, and 6.

Bernholz, Peter (1983), 'Inflation and Monetary Constitutions in Historical Perspective', *Kyklos*, 36, 397–419.
Bernholz, Peter (1989), 'Currency Competition, Inflation, Gresham's Law and Exchange Rate', *Journal of Institutional and Theoretical Economics*, 145 (3), 465–88.
Bernholz, Peter (1997), 'Paper Money Inflation, Gresham's Law and Exchange Rates in Ming China', *Kredit und Kapital*, 30 (1), 35–51.
Bernholz, Peter (2001), 'Monetary Constitution, Political-Economic Regime, and Long-Term Inflation', *Constitutional Political Economy*, 12, 3–12.

Every effort has been made to trace the copyright holders but if any have been inadvertently overlooked the publishers will be pleased to make the necessary arrangements at the first opportunity.

1. Introduction

Inflation presupposes the existence of money, which evolved as an unplanned social institution by a number of inventions and innovations during a period of perhaps 2500 years. It was fully developed with the introduction of coins in Lydia and Ionia about 630 BC, and in China at about the same time.

It follows that inflation cannot be older than money. But it seems that especially rulers soon detected the potential to increase their revenues by tampering with its value. Already in antiquity we know of many cases of lowering the intrinsic metallic value of coins for this purpose. Examples are the minting of bad coins by Athens during the Peloponnesian War (Aristophanes, *The Frogs*, 719–37) or by Rome during the Second Punic War, especially from 217 BC (Heichelheim 1955, p. 503).

The damage and suffering caused by inflation during the course of history are enormous. Still, the worst excesses of inflation occurred only in the 20th century. This development was a consequence of the further technical development of money from coins to paper money and book money together with changes in the monetary regime or constitution ruling supply and control of money.

The use of the word *inflation* for an expansion of the money supply or an increase in prices, quite in contrast to the first occurrences of inflation as historical events, is of rather recent origin. The term derives from the Latin *inflare* (*to blow up or inflate*) and was first used in 1838 in the context of *an inflation of the currency*, according to the Oxford English Dictionary (1989). During the following years until 1874 it was also employed for an *inflation of credit* and an *inflation of prices*. This meaning of the word seems to have been strengthened during the American Civil War (1861–65), when the gold dollar was supplanted by the *greenback*, a paper money issued by the Government, which soon lost part of its value.

We will use the term 'inflation' only for an increase of the price level extending over a longer period, usually several years, as measured by one or several price indices. It follows that we do not consider the increase of the prices of a small group of goods like that of oil and its derivatives or of food caused by a bad harvest as inflation. In an inflation all or at least most prices rise according to this definition.

History has seen inflations of very different magnitudes, ranging from the so-called *price revolution* of the 16th century, which was caused by the inflow of gold and especially silver looted and mined by the Spaniards in Latin America, to the biggest paper money inflation of all times in Hungary after World War 2. Whereas the former implied only an average annual increase of the price level by about two per cent over a period of nearly one hundred years, the latter led in a limited period of six years up to rates of inflation of about 350 per cent per day in the summer of 1946. Because of these different orders of magnitude it has become customary to speak of *creeping* or *mild inflation*, of *galloping* and *accelerating inflation*, and of *high* and *hyperinflation*, though mostly no clear delimitation of these terms has been offered. An exception is the definition of *hyperinflation* introduced by the American economist Philip Cagan (1956), which is present in all cases in which monthly inflation has reached in at least one month 50 per cent or more. It is convenient to adopt this somewhat arbitrary convention, which is arbitrary since many other *high inflations* show the same qualitative characteristics, as we will see. In this book, therefore, *hyperinflations* will be seen as extreme cases of *high inflations*. We will also employ the term *moderate inflation*. The borderline between this type of inflation and *high inflations* will be defined with the help of the real stock of money, as given by the stock of money divided by the price level and corrected by the growth of Gross Domestic Product, GDP. Whenever this corrected real stock of money declines during an inflationary process, *high inflation* begins according to our definition. It is true that this definition does not provide a clear dividing line in terms of a percentage inflation. But it has the advantage that it points our attention to the time from which the public tries to escape the loss of value of their money by reducing its use by a flight into other currencies or commodities.

The following chapters of this book will turn first to the description of empirical historical facts concerning inflations. In doing so we will especially analyse the qualitative characteristics of high inflations. By looking at these facts it will be relatively easy to explain political and economic causes of inflation, and to present a macroeconomic model of the latter relationships. A study of how inflations can be successfully ended concludes the book.

REFERENCES

Cagan, Philip (1956), 'The Monetary Dynamics of Hyperinflation', in Milton Friedman (ed.), *Studies in the Quantity Theory of Money*, Chicago: University of Chicago Press.
Heichelheim, Fritz W. (1955), 'On Ancient Price Trends from the Early First Millennium BC to Heraclius I', *Finanzarchiv*, 15(3), 498–511.

2. Inflation and monetary regimes[1]

2.1 INFLATIONS: LONG-TERM HISTORICAL EVIDENCE

We turn first to the long-term development of inflation since about 1800 in several countries belonging for decades to the most highly developed economies of the world (Figure 2.1). On the vertical axis the logarithm of the cost of living index, CPI, is depicted, whereas time is denoted on the horizontal axis. We have used the logarithm of CPI since CPI itself would not fit on the page.

As we can see from the figure, the price levels of the United States, Great Britain, France and Switzerland do not show an upward or downward trend

1790 = 2

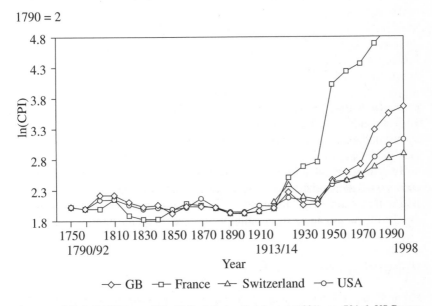

Sources: Mitchell (1976), pp. 735–47. Statistisches Bundesamt (1981), pp. 704–6. US Bureau of the Census (1976), *Historical Statistics of the United States: Colonial Times to 1970*. Bicentennial Edition. Statistisches Bundesamt (2000), pp. 230f.

Figure 2.1   Development of cost of living indices in four countries (logarithms)

3

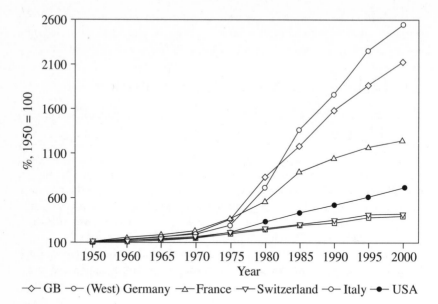

Sources: See Figure 2.1.

Figure 2.2   Development of cost of living indices in six countries,
*   1950–2000*

before 1914, but only long-term swings. The situation changes, however, after 1914 and at least from 1930, since a pronounced upward trend, that is a long-term inflation, can be observed after this time for all these countries, including Switzerland.

The empirical evidence just presented leads to the question, how the difference in inflation performance before and after 1914/30 can be explained. Before trying to answer this question it is however advisable to take a closer look at the development of inflation in some developed countries from 1950 to 1998 (Figure 2.2). Note that in this case no logarithms of the cost of living index have been used on the vertical axis.

The figure draws our attention to three facts:

1. an inflationary development can be observed for the whole period;
2. inflation has accelerated since about 1970;
3. after 1970 two groups of countries show different inflationary developments. The first group consisting of Italy, France and Great Britain shows a higher rate of inflation than the second consisting of Switzerland, (West) Germany and the United States.

In Section 2.3 we try to answer the question why these different paths of inflation could happen before and after 1914/30 and since 1950. Before doing so, we have however to describe the main characteristics of different monetary regimes.

2.2 A DESCRIPTION OF DIFFERENT MONETARY REGIMES

By a *monetary regime* we understand the set of rules governing the institutions and organisations which finally determine the amount of money supplied. If we turn our attention to the laws and decrees containing all such formal rules we speak of a *monetary constitution*. Subsequently we consider the following monetary regimes:

1. *Metallic standards* like the *gold, silver* or *copper standard*. In such standards gold, silver or copper coins circulate, whose nominal face value corresponds to the value of the metal contained in the respective coin. This does not preclude token metallic coins also being used, whose metallic value is less than their nominal value. But such coins have been at least in modern times convertible at their face value into the coins with full metal value. If banknotes exist they are also convertible at their face value into such coins. The same is true for chequing accounts of the public held at the banks. The gold, silver or copper content of the full-valued coins is usually determined by law and is called the gold, silver or copper *parity*. In such monetary regimes everybody has the right to exchange banknotes or money held in chequing accounts into the metal and vice versa any time they wish to do so. They also have the right to melt down coins or to bring the metal to the mint to have it transformed into coins at the parity, with a fee covering the costs of minting.

These rules ensure that the price of the metal in the market corresponds to the parity. Observe also that the amount of money in such a system is regulated by the actions of the public which keep the parity in line with the market price, and thus finally by the supply of gold, silver or copper. Since this amount is limited, a long-lasting inflation can only occur if new deposits are found which can be exploited. And this inflation is limited by the additional amount brought into circulation.

If several countries are, let's say, on a gold standard, their currencies are connected by fixed exchange rates, the parity of which is determined by the ratio of their gold parities. The exchange rates can only fluctuate around this ratio within a narrow band determined by the transportation and insurance costs of gold. These relationships are not determined by official interventions in the exchange markets, but by gold arbitrage undertaken by private businesses or individuals.

2. In history several *weakened metallic standards* have existed. For instance, after World War 1 several countries returned to the gold standard without allowing the circulation of gold coins. In this case the right of citizens to convert banknotes was limited to a conversion into gold bullion at the parity. A further weakening of the gold standard could be observed after World War 2 in the so-called Bretton Woods system, when convertibility was limited to the right of foreign central banks to convert dollar notes into gold at the American Treasury at the dollar parity. The system lasted until 1971, when President Nixon abolished even this limited convertibility. Note that in the latter system nearly all other nations were on a discretionary paper money standard (see below), but with a fixed exchange rate parity to the US dollar.

3. A third monetary regime is given by the *discretionary paper money standard*, which is usually but not necessarily combined with a central bank holding the monopoly to issue banknotes. In such a system chequing accounts with banks are denominated in the units of the paper money and the owners have the right always to convert the amount held in these accounts into banknotes at the fixed one-to-one parity. The paper money standard is called discretionary since the monetary authorities have the right to determine the supply of base money at their discretion, sometimes vaguely limited by the law. Base money denotes the amount of banknotes issued and of deposits by the banks at the central bank. In this monetary regime no 'natural' limit for the expansion of the money supply, like a scarcity of monetary gold or silver exists.

Discretionary monetary standards differ in two important characteristics from each other: namely whether the monetary policy is run by a central bank which is independent from the political authorities, especially the government, or whether this is not the case. The second discriminating characteristic is given by the foreign exchange regime. Here it is important whether the currency is linked by a fixed exchange rate (a *foreign exchange parity*) to another currency or whether this is not the case. In the former case of a *fixed exchange rate system* the central bank is not independent in its monetary policy, whether it is institutionally independent or not. This is different from a *flexible* or *floating exchange rate system*, where the monetary authorities have full control of their monetary policies. Note that in fixed exchange rate systems usually a small band around the foreign exchange parity is determined by law, within which the exchange rate can fluctuate, and which is maintained by central bank intervention.

If several currencies are linked by a system of fixed exchange rates only one country can follow an independent monetary policy. This is a consequence of the fact that only n – 1 independent exchange rates exist among n currencies. If for example the Deutschmark (DM) and the French franc have a fixed exchange parity with the US dollar, then the parity between these two currencies is also fixed. Assume now that the German and French central banks maintain their parities with the dollar by interventions, that is by buying and selling dollars, in the foreign exchange market. Then the monetary authorities of the United States need not intervene at all and are free to follow a monetary policy at their discretion. But this is not true for the other two countries. For selling and buying dollars is done by buying and selling DMs or French francs respectively. But this changes the monetary base. Consequently, these countries have to follow a monetary policy in tune with that freely selected by the United States.

Historically, foreign exchange rates have been mostly fixed in relation first to the UK pound and later to the US dollar. The Bretton Woods system was in this sense fully based on the dollar. The franc was used less, and also the DM in more recent years: the former by countries in the *French franc zone*, the members of which had been French colonies, the latter especially in the *European Monetary System* from 1979–1998 (Bernholz 1999), but also in some other smaller European countries. On the whole, these *reserve currencies* belonged usually to countries experiencing the lowest rates of inflation and enjoying well-developed money and capital markets.

2.3   MONETARY REGIMES AND INFLATION

> *Experience with paper money until today proves at least that it is possible . . . to give value to a paper money, which cannot be exchanged any time* [at a fixed parity] *at will into another money. This may not . . . be at a permanently equal value with some metal money; but this would not by itself result in a disadvantage. . . . The obstacle . . . for maintaining an equal purchasing power . . . is the impossibility to fulfil the requirements for the strength of this belief. One would have to introduce the most reliable guarantees to prevent that paper money would ever be used for financial purposes to create artificial purchasing power for the issuing agency without labour out of nothing; and to secure that it would be increased only according to the true necessity of the economy. . . . These guarantees are relative to the first point only given by the absolute impossibility to increase the money arbitrarily without effort. . . . Men would first have to be capable of unlimited self-discipline to resist any temptation to increase money arbitrarily, even if their very existence, or that of the state, were at stake. . . . A somewhat greater security against the abuse of the right to issue money might perhaps be provided by one or the other constitutional form. But this certainly does not amount to a big difference.* (Adolph Wagner, German Professor of Economics, 1868, pp. 46–8)

Let us now turn back to the historical facts about inflation contained in Figures 2.1 and 2.2 and analyse them from the perspective of monetary constitutions. Then it is at first striking that from 1800 to 1914 the monetary regimes of the respective countries were based on silver or gold standards, with exceptions during the Napoleonic wars. But even the suspension of the gold and silver standards during this period was removed afterwards with a return to the old gold or silver parities. Similarly, after World War 1 Britain and Switzerland returned to the gold standard at the old parity, which had not been left by the United States. France also returned to the gold standard in 1927, but at a lower gold parity. In the crisis of the Great Depression the gold standard was abolished from 1931, but by France, the Netherlands and Switzerland only in 1936. Since then all countries were and are on a discretionary paper money standard, though Switzerland stuck to the gold standard, but only legally (and as a curiosity until 1999).

It follows that the change from a non-inflationary to an inflationary long-term development depicted in Figure 2.1 can be explained by the change of the monetary regime from 1914 to the 1930s. This hypothesis is supported by two additional pieces of empirical evidence. First, all hyperinflations in history occurred after 1914 under discretionary paper money standards except for the French case during the Revolution of 1789–96 (Table 2.1), when a paper money standard was introduced with the *assignats*. This contradicts the hypothesis put forward by Capie (1986), that wars have been responsible for

Table 2.1   Hyperinflations in history

Country	Year(s)	Highest inflation per month %	Country	Year(s)	Highest inflation per month %
Argentina	1989/90	196.6	Hungary	1945/46	$1.295* \ 10^{16}$
Armenia	1993/94	438.04	Kazakhstan	1994	57
Austria	1921/22	124.27	Kyrgyzstan	1992	157
Azerbaijan	1991/94	118.09	Nicaragua	1986/89	126.62
Belarus	1994	53.4	Peru	1988/90	114.12
Bolivia	1984/86	120.39	Poland	1921/24	187.54
Brazil	1989/93	84.32	Poland	1989/90	77.33
Bulgaria	1997	242.7	Serbia	1992/94	309 000 000
China	1947/49	4208.73	Soviet Union	1922/24	278.72
Congo (Zaire)	1991/94	225	Taiwan	1945/49	398.73
France	1789/96	143.26	Tajikistan	1995	78.1
Georgia	1993/94	196.72	Turkmenistan	1993/96	62.5
Germany	1920/23	29 525.71	Ukraine	1992/94	249
Greece	1942/45	11 288	Yugoslavia	1990	58.82
Hungary	1923/24	82.18			

Note: Moldova may also be a candidate for inclusion. Producer prices rose by 64.5% in April 1994. But the data are insufficient to verify this for consumer prices.

Sources: See Appendix.

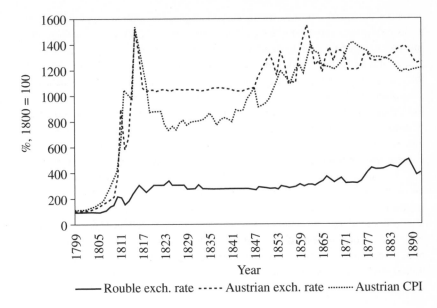

Note: CPI = Cost of living index

Sources: Muehlpeck *et al.* (1979), Soetbeer (1886), Zielinski (1898)

Figure 2.3 *Russian and Austrian exchange rates and Austrian cost of living index, 1799–1892*

hyperinflations. Though this is true for many of them, given a discretionary paper money standard, those of Bolivia, Argentina and Brazil in the 1980s and 1990s occurred during conditions of peace. Moreover and more importantly for our argument, except for the French hyperinflation no other such event took place before 1914 even during devastating wars. Second, all countries moving to inconvertible paper money standards in the 18th and 19th centuries experienced higher rates of inflation than those on gold or silver standards (Figure 2.3). Note also that the French hyperinflation occurred during the rule of a discretionary paper money standard based on the *assignats*.

In Figure 2.3 the inflations in Russia and Austria (later Austria-Hungary) are reflected in the developments of the Austrian cost of living index and the Austrian and Russian exchange rates vis-à-vis the Hamburg Mark Banco (MB) and the French franc and the British pound. Both countries suspended the convertibility of their currencies into silver in about 1795, and tried to restore it several times, first after the end of the Napoleonic wars. This met with more success in Russia than in Austria, as one can see from the graph.

Anyhow convertibility was again suspended several times, especially at the outbreak of wars, since the military efforts were then partly financed by issuing more paper money. Finally, both countries succeeded in introducing the gold standard in the 1890s, which held until the outbreak of World War 1. If we compare Figures 2.1 and 2.3 we see that inflation was present in these two countries which were on a discretionary paper money standard at least part of the time, whereas this was not true for those on metallic standards. A similar picture could be drawn for instance for Brazil, Argentina and Italy (Spinelli and Fratianni 1991). In these countries inconvertible paper money circulated sometimes for decades and the rate of inflation was higher than in the countries enjoying convertible silver or gold currencies. Since their citizens were however aware of the example of the more stable, more 'civilised' nations, their governments tried several times during the 19th century to return to convertible silver and later gold currencies. As a consequence, monetary policy was not as inflationary as in the 20th century even in the weaker countries. Argentina, too, succeeded in moving definitely to the gold standard in the 1890s. Italy kept its allegiance to the Latin Monetary Union with France, Belgium and Switzerland and restored convertibility of its notes after some time.

In all these cases inflation was less pronounced than in the 20th century. No hyperinflations like those in Table 2.1 occurred, with the exception of the French hyperinflation during the Revolution.

We conclude from the historical evidence presented that the long-term tendency of currencies towards inflation depends mainly on the monetary regime or constitution:

1. Metallic standards like the gold or silver standard show no or, as we will see in the next chapter, a much smaller inflationary tendency than discretionary paper money standards.
2. Paper money standards with central banks independent of political authorities are less inflation-biased than those with dependent central banks.
3. Currencies based on discretionary paper standards and bound by a regime of a fixed exchange rate to currencies, which either enjoy a metallic standard or, with a discretionary paper money standard, an independent central bank, show also a smaller tendency towards inflation, whether their central banks are independent or not.

Our results seem to cast doubt on all explanations which try to explain inflation by non-monetary factors, for instance a cost-push and demand-pull inflation. In the latter theories it is asserted that inflation is a consequence of excessive wage increases reached by unions or by excessive demand. The hypothesis according to which inflations are a consequence of public budget deficits seems also not to fare well. To draw such conclusions may however be premature, in spite of our results. For we have still to answer the question, why and under which conditions inflation-free monetary constitutions come about and can be maintained. Moreover and more fundamentally, we have to ask why the tendency towards inflation is smaller with metallic standards or with independent central banks than with discretionary paper money standards with dependent central banks and flexible exchange rates. It is this last question to which we turn in the next section.

2.4   THE INFLATIONARY BIAS OF POLITICAL SYSTEMS

In addressing the question why different monetary regimes show such remarkable differences in their inflation performances, the hypothesis is advanced that governments have an inherent bias towards inflation. This bias is strengthened if they are operating under adverse conditions, like wars or revolutions, though some of these conditions may themselves be consequences of government actions. If this hypothesis is true, it follows that the inflationary bias of governments can only be limited or fully checked in the long run by monetary constitutions restraining them. In this section we will explain why governments have an inflationary bias; we will return to the monetary constitutions binding their hands in Section 2.5. Section 2.6 will turn to some other characteristics of the different monetary constitutions discussed.

Democratic governments will be considered first. In a democracy parties compete to gain and maintain government power. As a consequence the party or parties in power have to try to gain as many votes as possible in the next election to secure at least a majority in parliament. However, voters are rationally uninformed about matters which are not very important to them, since the negligible chance that their individual vote would make a difference to the outcome of the election does not warrant more than very little effort and expense to inform themselves about party platforms and their possible consequences. It follows that they are only reasonably well informed about what is important to them, usually their and their relatives' job security, their wages and incomes, and the availability of not too expensive housing. They are thus usually ignorant about monetary policies and their future consequences. Moreover, these matters are complex and not easily understood without a specific education. On top of this, the positive though usually short-lived consequences of an expansionary monetary policy, namely an upturn of the economy and a decrease in unemployment, follow more quickly than its negative consequences in the form of higher prices. As a consequence, because of the complexity of the problems and of their rational ignorance voters will judge the performance of the government mostly by the results of former policies and even events which have not been caused by measures of the government.

The fiscal and monetary policies preferred by the party or parties in power, given this rational ignorance of voters, are the following. The government usually has to concentrate the benefits of its actions on small segments of the population, so that they are perceived, whereas the costs have to be spread widely so that they are not felt. This is especially easy in a growing economy where even with an increasing share of public revenues in gross domestic product disposable incomes of individuals are still growing. Additionally, expenditures can be increased without burdening anybody through higher taxes by taking refuge in borrowing. It is true that government must pay interest on a rising debt, but this lies in the future, after the next elections. Also, additional expenditures spent at the right time before elections will stimulate the economy and reduce unemployment, leading to better re-election chances. This gives rise to the so-called political business cycle, much discussed in public choice theory (Frey 1978). But with the passage of time interest payments on a higher and higher debt consume a rising share of government revenues and lead to higher interest rates in the markets, crowding out worthwhile investments. Finally market participants may even believe the government to be an insecure debtor and demand a risk premium on interest.

Given these relationships it is tempting for the ruling party (parties) to finance part of the public deficit by creating money, that is by taking refuge in borrowing from the central bank. This prevents, at least for some time, higher short-term interest rates and allows the positive effects just mentioned. Inflation follows only with a time-lag after the election, which may be fought immediately afterwards, and has the appealing side-effect of reducing the real public debt. But measures taken to reduce inflation after elections have negative effects on economic activity and employment. Consequently they have to be abolished in time to allow a new stimulation of the economy before the next election. As a consequence there exists an inflationary bias of democratic governments in peacetime.

It should be obvious from the above arguments that the forces for inflationary deficit-financing are strengthened if economic growth is slow or absent, because under such circumstances any increase of the tax burden will reduce disposable per capita income. In case of wars or of international tensions inflationary financing will be practised for the same reason. It is then justified by the government by pointing to the danger existing for the nation, and will be of a much greater magnitude. It should be mentioned in this context that there has never occurred a hyperinflation in history which was not caused by a huge budget deficit of the state. As an example consider the case of Bolivia (Figure 2.4).

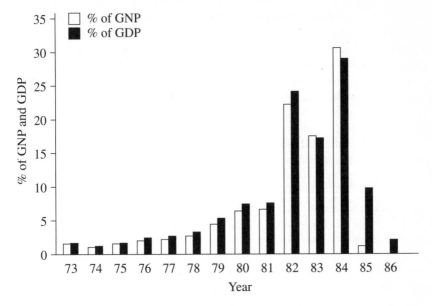

Note: Budget deficit as % of GDP based on GDP in prices of 1980

Source: Machicado (1986)

Figure 2.4   Bolivian budget deficit as % of gross national and domestic products

The economic historian Capie was, as mentioned, led to state that hyperinflations only occurred in the wake of wars or revolutions because of the reasons just given. Though, however, wars are certainly an important factor, this is not generally true, as can be seen by the recent hyperinflations in Argentina, Bolivia, Brazil, and Peru (Table 2.1).

Are autocratic governments less prone to deficit-financing by inflationary money creation? Obviously not, as can be seen by looking at the countries mentioned in Table 2.1, since many of them were certainly not democratic during the relevant periods. This is for several reasons. First, dictators are often interested in securing their power by all means and spend considerable resources on the military, police, and secret service. Second, they often try to safeguard their own future wellbeing against the hazards of a coup d'état by transferring resources to foreign countries. Third, they are often bent on expansion of their state. Fourth, because of irregular interventions in the economy the latter may not be very efficient and thus productive in terms of tax revenues. Finally, since dictators want to preserve their power, they may not want to increase the resistance in the population to their regime by excessively high tax burdens. There are, of course, exceptions. In some cases, because of ideological belief or benevolence on the part of the dictator, he may even restore a sound monetary and market regime, as was done by the Pinochet regime in Chile. But even then, in an autocratic regime there is no guarantee at all that the next dictator will follow the same policies.

2.5   THE INFLUENCE OF MONETARY REGIMES

As soon as only the principle has been accepted that the state is allowed and has to influence the value of money, be it even only to guarantee its internal stability, then the danger of mistakes and exaggerations emerges at once again.

These possibilities and the memories of the financial and inflationary experiences of the recent past have pushed into the background the unrealisable ideal of a money with an unchangeable intrinsic value as compared to the postulate: that the state should refrain at least from influencing in any way the intrinsic value of money.
(Ludwig von Mises, 1912, p. 288; my translation)

With the inflationary bias of governments, inflation can only be absent in the long run if the hands of the rulers are bound by an adequate monetary regime or constitution. Without a separation of powers, for instance in an autocracy, there can however be no credible commitment to a stable monetary constitution, since the dictator can always change it. In such a political system, monetary stability depends only on the interests of the ruler.

But let us turn back to the evidence contained in the figures. During the 19th century and until 1914 all important countries were first on a silver, then on a gold standard (Bardo and Schwartz 1984). Only Great Britain was on the gold standard all the time from the end of the Napoleonic wars. This meant that at any time each citizen could demand the conversion of banknotes into silver or gold (and vice versa) at a fixed price, the silver or gold parity of the respective currency. This convertibility consequently gave the right to control the issue of money to the population. Since the treasury, the banks and later the central bank had always to keep sufficient silver and gold reserves to be able to convert the notes issued by them on demand, they could never create too much paper money. As a consequence the stock of money was limited by the available silver or gold reserves and the marginal costs of producing these metals. The hands of the government were completely bound. It is thus not surprising that no inflationary trend existed during the 19th century and until 1914.

The monetary constitution of the gold standard was abolished at the outbreak of World War 1 and, after a brief restoration in the 1920s, during the Great Depression. From then on, all major countries were on a discretionary paper money standard. This meant that either the government or the central bank and no longer the citizens determined the supply of money, which was no longer limited by the available reserves of precious metals. Consequently, the hands of government were much less or not at all bound. Not surprisingly, this has led to inflation since 1914 and 1930 until today (Figure 2.1).

Our hypothesis that only constraining the influence of politicians and governments by a monetary constitution leads to lower rates of inflation, is also supported by considering the evidence available since the end of World War 2 (Figure 2.2). Looking at the development of the cost of living index we observe that countries with central banks strongly independent of the government, like Switzerland, Germany and the United States, enjoyed a much lower increase of the price level than countries where this was not the case, like France, Britain and Italy. It has to be stated, however, that the rate of inflation was still higher than in the 19th century even in the countries with independent central banks. For even independent central banks are not as independent of the pressure of public opinion and politics as the more or less automatically functioning gold standard, where even central bankers had little discretion. A monetary constitution securing the independence of the central bank limits inflation, but not as much as the gold standard.

Finally, there is another feature contained in Figure 2.2 supporting the hypothesis. Until about 1970 the increase of cost of living indices is lower and much more similar for the six countries than afterwards. We have already mentioned above that a worldwide monetary regime of fixed exchange rates (the Bretton Woods system) existed during this period until 1971/73. This system bound the hands of the monetary authorities of the participating countries with the exception of the US Federal Reserve system, with gold convertibility of the dollar limited to central banks. For as long as the fixed exchange rates with the US dollar were not abolished or a de- or revaluation did not take place, central banks could follow an independent monetary policy only to a very limited degree dependent on their gold and dollar reserves. Let me add in passing that this monetary regime of tying one's money to a stable currency can be further strengthened by introducing a so-called Currency Board System (Hanke, Jonung and Schuler 1993), in which the central bank or currency board is only allowed to create money in exchange for a specific stable currency at a fixed exchange rate, like in many cases the US dollar (Hong Kong, Argentina) or in some the DM (Estonia, Bulgaria).

2.6 SOME OTHER CHARACTERISTICS OF MONETARY CONSTITUTIONS

Given the above results, the question arises, under which conditions is it probable or feasible that stable monetary regimes emerge (Bernholz 1986)? It is preferable, however, to postpone the analysis of this question until the characteristics of moderate and high inflations have been discussed. Instead, we propose to discuss in this section some other characteristics of monetary constitutions besides their role in providing price stability, which may be important if we wish to evaluate them.

Several empirical studies seem to show that from 1880/90–1914 the variability or rather the variance of variables like the growth rate of GDP, real interest rates and employment has been greater, in developed countries, than for the 1950 to 1990 period. From this evidence some scholars, among others monetarist Alan Meltzer (1986), have drawn the conclusion that a discretionary paper money regime with an independent central bank is preferable to the gold standard. Yet, whether one prefers the disadvantage of a higher rate of inflation or a smaller variance of those real variables is, of course, a value judgement not amenable to scientific treatment. But there are other problems involved. First, the period from 1950 to 1990 covers different monetary regimes, as we have seen. It is thus not convincing to put the figures for this period together in econometric tests. For instance, we know quite well that with flexible exchange rates not only a high variance of real exchange rates but also long swings of them around purchasing power parities are present, lasting from five to twelve years (Bernholz 1982). This is connected with a tendency towards undervaluation for countries with higher rates of inflation and towards overvaluation of the domestic currencies for countries with more restrictive monetary policies.

> *Thus, if the numerical value of the paper money falls,* [in terms of silver money, which implies that the exchange rate rises] . . . *the nominal prices* [in terms of the paper money] *of labour and merchandise do not rise in the same proportion, so that it follows that the paper buys more labour and merchandise compared to silver than it could buy before its fall; in other words, its real value remains more or less below its numerical value* [that is the price of silver and the exchange rate for foreign silver money]. *By contrast, if the numerical value of the paper money rises, . . ., the nominal prices of labour and of merchandise do not fall in the same proportion. . . . But . . . it is no less confirmed by experience that the two values always tend to approach each other or to regain their old relationship* [that is to move towards purchasing power parity]; *however, to reach it in fact it is absolutely necessary that the numerical value of the paper money no longer changes, or that it moves in the opposite direction that to which it has taken before; for otherwise it is impossible that the real value, which moves much more slowly, can ever rejoin the numerical value.* (Heinrich Friedrich von Storch, Professor of Economics in St. Petersburg, 1815/1997, pp. 226 f.; my translation)

As an example the undervaluation of the Turkish pound from 1980–94 is presented in Figure 2.5. Turkey experienced during this period a high inflation, which, however, never approached even from afar a hyperinflation.

Undervaluation (overvaluation) means that the purchasing power of the domestic currency is higher (lower) at home than its purchasing power abroad. An undervaluation stimulates exports and makes imports more expensive,

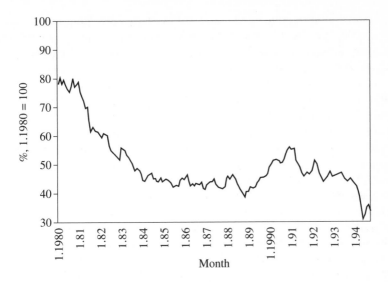

Note: Undervaluation is present if figures <100%

Source: International Monetary Fund: International Financial Statistics, Monthly Reports

Figure 2.5 Undervaluation of Turkish lira, 1980–94

whereas the opposite is true for an overvaluation. Also, the former implies an inflationary and the latter a disinflationary effect through the prices of imported goods. These qualitative characteristics of flexible exchange rates have been observed whenever they were present since at least the 18th century (Bernholz 1982; Bernholz, Gaertner and Heri 1985). Empirical evidence for many other historical cases will be presented in Chapters 4 and 5. Also, in a model one of the most important reasons for undervaluation will be derived (Section 5.5). These characteristics of flexible exchange rates have to be contrasted with the gold standard, the nature of which implies fixed exchange rates allowing only small fluctuations of rates between the upper and lower gold points.

With fixed exchange rates combined with a discretionary paper money standard things are again different. First, under such a monetary regime an overvaluation of the currency develops for more inflationary countries quite in contrast to a regime of flexible exchange rates. This leads to some difficulties for the export and the import-competing industries and finally to an exhaustion of currency reserves. A well-known example of such problems was the situation of Britain in the 1950s and 60s. On the other hand, the countries with less expansionary monetary policies experience an undervaluation. This led for countries like Switzerland and Germany under the Bretton Woods system to 'imported inflation' during the same period. Similar problems were experienced by the countries of the so-called European snake from 1973–79 and the European Monetary System from 1979–1994, where in both cases the countries involved had fixed exchange rates among participating currencies and where the DM took the role of the US dollar (Bernholz 1999).

It is not surprising that these relationships led sometimes to dubious and often belated political actions. With fixed exchange rates imported inflation led to belated revaluations, for instance in the cases of Germany and Switzerland. The pressures on the export and the import-competing industries and the threatening exhaustion of foreign exchange reserves gave rise to several belated and sometimes too drastic devaluations, especially of the UK pound but also of the French franc and the Italian lira.

With flexible exchange rates an overvalued currency often causes the central bank to intervene in the exchange markets, but, what is more dangerous, it also motivates government to introduce restrictions on the free convertibility of currencies and (or) protective measures against import goods. For instance, when the US dollar was highly overvalued in 1985, many bills to restrict imports were introduced in the US Congress. If an undervaluation develops, interventions in the opposite direction are often undertaken by the central bank, whereas the government sometimes introduces restrictions on the free flow of capital. No such political interventions occurred during the gold standard.

In closing, a warning seems to be appropriate. One may be inclined to conclude from the empirical facts and one's value system that the gold standard is preferable to a discretionary paper money regime. Though there is nothing wrong with this position, the introduction of such a monetary constitution by a small or even by a middle-sized country on its own is not advisable. For in this case the rate of inflation would be smaller than in other countries, with the consequence that the implied system of flexible exchange rates would lead to a strong overvaluation of the currency. And since the share of exports and imports in GDP is higher the smaller the country, rather adverse consequences would follow for the export and import-competing industries and consequently for employment. It follows that only large countries or currency blocs like the United States and the European Union could nowadays introduce the gold standard without great initial disadvantages.

2.7   CONCLUSIONS

From our presentation and analysis we can draw the following conclusions:

1.   The political system tends to favour an inflationary bias of currencies. All major inflations have been caused by princes or governments.

2. All hyperinflations in history have occurred during the 20th century, that is in the presence of discretionary paper money regimes, with the exception of the hyperinflation during the French Revolution, when the French monetary regime, too, was based on a paper money standard.
3. Monetary regimes binding the hands of rulers, politicians and governments are a necessary condition for keeping inflation at bay.
4. Metallic monetary regimes, especially the gold and silver standards, have shown the largest resistance to inflation, followed by independent central banks combined with discretionary paper money regimes. Dependent central banks in such regimes have a strong inflationary bias. The stability of regimes with independent central banks can also be reached by fixing the exchange rate to a currency with a metallic standard or an independent central bank. Such a relationship can be further strengthened by the introduction of a currency board.
5. Compared to a regime based on a gold standard, a discretionary monetary regime with an independent central bank seems to show a smaller variance of real variables like the growth rate of GDP, unemployment and real interest rates.
6. With flexible exchange rates there exist, however, a much greater variance and mid-term swings of exchange rates around purchasing power parities lasting several years, which influence the competitive position of export and import-competing industries and the price level.
7. Given flexible exchange rates, a higher inflation than in the main trading partners tends to bring about an undervaluation of the domestic currency. The opposite is true if fixed exchange rates are present.

In subsequent chapters we have to analyse these results in more detail, given different monetary regimes. Moreover, the question has to be answered, how and under which conditions stable monetary regimes can be introduced and maintained, in spite of the inflationary bias of political systems.

NOTE

1. A great part of Chapter 2 has been taken from Bernholz, Peter (2001), 'Monetary Constitution, Political-Economic Regime, and Long-Term Inflation', *Constitutional Political Economy*, 12, pp. 3–12.

REFERENCES

Bernholz, Peter (1982), 'Flexible Exchange Rates in Historical Perspectives', *Princeton Studies in International Finance*, 49, July. Princeton: International Finance Section, Dept. of Economics, Princeton University.

Bernholz, Peter (1986), 'The Implementation and Maintenance of a Monetary Constitution', *The Cato Journal*, 6(2), Fall, 477–511. Reprinted in James A. Dorn and Anna J. Schwartz (eds), *The Search for Stable Money*, Chicago and London: The University of Chicago Press (1987), pp. 83–117.

Bernholz, Peter (1999), 'The Bundesbank and the Process of European Monetary Integration', in Deutsche Bundesbank (ed.), *Fifty Years of the Deutsche Mark. Central Bank and the Currency in Germany since 1948*, Oxford and New York: Oxford University Press, pp. 731–89.

Bernholz, Peter, Gaertner, Manfred and Heri, Erwin (1985), 'Historical Experiences with Flexible Exchange Rates', *Journal of International Economics*, 19, 21–45.

Bordo, M.D. and Schwartz, A.J. (eds) (1984), *Retrospective on the Classical Gold Standard*, Chicago: University of Chicago Press.

Capie, F. (1986), 'Conditions Under Which Very Rapid Inflation Has Appeared', in *Carnegie-Rochester Conference Series on Public Policy*, 24, Amsterdam: North-Holland, pp. 115–68.

Frey, Bruno S. (1978), 'Politico-Economic Models and Cycles', *Journal of Public Economics*, 9, 203–20.

Hanke, Steve H., Jonung, Lars and Schuler, Kurt (1993), *Russian Currency and Finance: A Currency Board Approach to Reform*, London: Routledge.

Machicado, S. Flavio (1986?) *Estudio, Diagnostico, Debate: Las Finanzas Publicas y la Inversion*, La Paz: Ildis. Without date.

Meltzer, Allan H. (1986), 'Some Evidence on the Comparative Uncertainty Experienced Under Different Monetary Regimes', in Colin D. Campbell and William R. Dougan (eds), *Alternative Monetary Regimes,* Baltimore: The Johns Hopkins University Press, pp. 122–53.

Mises, Ludwig von (1912), *Theorie des Geldes und der Umlaufmittel*, Muenchen and Leipzig: Duncker und Humblot.

Muehlpeck, Vera, Sandgruber, Roman and Woitek, Hannelore (1979), 'Index der Verbraucherpreise 1800–1914', in Oesterreichisches Statistisches Zentralamt, *Geschichte und Ergebnisse der Zentralen Amtlichen Statistik in Oesterreich 1829–1979*, Wien.

Soetbeer, Adolf (1886), *Materialien zur Erlaeuterung und Beurteilung der Wirtschaftlichen Edelmetallverhaeltnisse und der Waehrungsfrage*, Berlin: Puttkammer and Muehlbrecht.

Spinelli, F. and Fratianni, M. (1991), *Storia Monetaria d'Italia*, Milano: A. Mondadori.

Statistisches Bundesamt (1981), *Statistischzes Jahrbuch fuer die Bundesrepublik Deutschland*, Wiesbaden.

Statistisches Bundesamt (2000), *Statistisches Jahrbuch 2000 fuer das Ausland*, Wiesbaden.

Storch, Heinrich Friedrich von (1997), *Cours d'Economie Politique*, Hildesheim, Zuerich, New York: Olms-Weidmann. Reprint of the edition of St. Petersburg (1815) by A. Pluchart & Co., Vol. 6.

Wagner, Adolph (1868), *Die Russische Papierwaehrung*, Riga.

Zielinski, Ludwik (1898), Der Rubel jetzt und vor 100 Jahren, *Zeitschrift fuer Nationaloekonomie und Statistik*, III. Folge, Vol. 16, 433–82, Jena: Gustav Fischer.

3. Inflation under metallic monetary regimes

3.1 INFLATION CAUSED BY AN ADDITIONAL SUPPLY OF THE MONETARY METAL

Inflation has probably been a characteristic of human history since money has been used as a means of payment. With money based on a metallic standard two possible reasons for a permanent or continuous rise in prices can be present. First, the supply of the metal on which a currency is based can increase. This can happen when new natural deposits, let us say of gold or silver, are detected; or else, when great treasures consisting mainly of gold and silver are taken as booty in a war and then put into circulation as money. Second, the metallic currency may be debased by lowering the content of silver or gold in coins by substituting copper or by reducing their weight without changing their nominal face value. Or, the face value of coins is increased without increasing the content of gold or silver in the same proportion.

In this section we will discuss the first of these alternatives, which has only led to rather limited inflations. We know that general but limited price increases occurred several times in antiquity because captured foreign treasures were put into circulation. So it seems that a doubling of prices took place after Alexander the Great had coined the treasures won after the defeat of Persia (Heichelheim 1930, pp. 9, 40f., 1955, p. 503). It appears that the price level rose less after the booty from Gaul and Egypt reached Rome; this had been won by the victories of Caesar and Augustus (Suetonius: *Caesar* 54, *Augustus* 41; Cassius Dio: Book 51, 21), respectively.

Another example of an increase of the price level over a long period is the so-called Great Price Revolution of the 16th century. This price increase was brought about by the great inflow of gold and especially silver (as already noted by the School of Salamanca, for instance by Azpilcueta de Navarro (1556), and twelve years later by Jean Bodin (1568); see also Grice-Hutchinson (1952) for the School of Salamanca), stemming in a smaller part from the booty the Spaniards made when they destroyed the Aztec and Inca empires, and in a greater part from the newly established silver mines in Mexico and Peru. This additional supply of the monetary metal led to an increase of the price level from 100 in 1603 in Old Castile and Leon to 180,

and to 256 in Andalusia (Figure 3.1) according to the indices constructed by
Earl Hamilton (1933). Even this is not a very impressive inflation, for it
amounts to an average annual rate of 1.16 and 1.86 per cent, respectively. The
record is similar for the following decades. The reason for the earlier inflation
in Andalusia has probably to be seen in the fact that the silver arriving with the
fleets from America went first to Seville and Cadiz, and that the additional
money supply moved only slowly northwards, given the limited transportation
facilities of the times. Moreover, sharp short-term fluctuations of commodity
prices occurred because of bad and good harvests, given the greater relative
importance of these goods for consumer budgets compared to modern times.

Several economic historians have doubted that the rises in the price level in
different European countries were caused by the inflow of silver from Latin
America, and have adduced many other explanations like cost-push, the raising of prices by newly introduced monopolies, wars and growth of the population. They are sceptical concerning the explanation using the quantity theory
of money mainly because they think that not enough specie reached the different European countries and (or) that specie flows were not timed well enough
to explain the inflation in several cases. It seems, however, that these

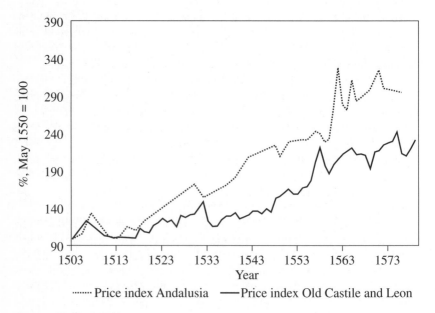

Source: Hamilton (1933)

*Figure 3.1   Development of commodity prices in Andalusia and Old
             Castile/Leon, 1503–1579*

approaches have been convincingly rejected at least with the analysis by Fisher (1989), who used the quantity theory of money together with the monetary approach to the balance of payments (see below Chapter 6) to test econometrically the relationships predicted by this theory for Spain, France, England, Germany and Austria. Let us mention, however, that this approach combines the theory that the quantity of money determines the price level in all countries which enjoy the same metallic standard with the law of one price for tradeable goods (except for transportation costs), and that the implied adaptation of prices in other countries to those of Spain leads to an additional demand for money, which then causes an inflow of specie, that is of metallic money.

Munro (1998), on the other hand, has adduced evidence that the inflow of gold and silver from America had been small until about 1540, whereas Central European silver production rose to rather high levels in the decades before. But this does not refute our hypothesis, since it can be maintained, whatever the origin of the additional silver supply. A substantive inflow of gold as a monetary metal occurred several times in the 19th century. We recall the Californian Gold Rush from 1848 and the Alaskan Gold Rush and the discovery of large gold deposits in South Africa in the 1890s. But it has already been shown that this additional supply did not exert a permanent influence on the price level (Figure 2.1), though there may exist a relationship with the upward movement of prices during the middle and that beginning at the end of the century. Also, economists of that period like Jevons (1884) were concerned that the supply of gold might be too great, and thus cause a rise of the price level, or, in the long run, too small to prevent a falling price level because of the growth of the real economy, which increased the demand for money as a means of payment. Probably this growth of money demand has indeed helped to prevent a long-term increase of the price level. This especially in view of the fact that the supply of what we nowadays call money has also risen because of the ever widening use of banknotes and chequing accounts as means of payment.

But there are three other factors limiting the inflationary impact of an additional supply of the monetary metal. First, the additional amount of gold or silver stemming for instance from the discovery of new deposits is small in comparison to the already existing stock of gold or silver. This fact is especially important since, second, if many countries are on the same metallic standard, the additional amount enters into the circulation of all these countries and increases the money supply not only in the country where the deposits have been exploited. And, if the price level rises, this implies that gold or silver becomes cheaper in terms of most other goods, especially labour. As a consequence, mining an ounce of gold or silver becomes more expensive compared to its value, so that the production will be reduced. In this sense there exists in a metallic monetary regime a self-regulating feedback mechanism.

3.2 THE DEBASEMENT OF METAL STANDARDS BY RULERS

Often it has crossed my fancy, that the city loves to deal
With the very best and noblest members of her commonweal,
Just as with our ancient coinage, and the newly minted gold,
Yea for these, our sterling pieces, all of pure Athenian mould,
All of perfect metal, all the fairest of the fair,
All of workmanship unequalled, proved and valued everywhere
Both amongst our own Hellenes and Barbarians far away,
These we use not: but the worthless pinchbeck coins of yesterday,
Vilest die and basest metal, now we always use instead.
Even so, our sterling townsmen, nobly born and nobly bred,
Men of worth and rank and mettle, men of honourable fame,
Trained in every liberal science, choral dance and manly game,
These we treat with scorn and insult, but the strangers newliest come,
Worthless sons of worthless fathers, pinchbeck townsmen, yellowy scum,
Whom in earlier times the city hardly would have stooped to use
Even for the scapegoat victims, these for every task we choose.
(Aristophanes, *The Frogs*, 718–34)

The analogy applied by Aristophanes in *The Frogs* is perhaps the first description of the debasement of a metallic currency, the Athenian silver drachma, as well as of the newly minted gold coin. It seems to follow from the quotation that the silver and gold coins were substituted by copper or bronze coins during the Peloponnesian War. This took place from 406 BC and the new coins must have had the same nominal value as the old. For only then can it be explained how the bad new coins drove the good silver and gold money out of circulation, as mentioned in the quotation. This fact is well known under the name of Gresham's Law and occurs in metallic standards if two kinds of money with a different *intrinsic* value of their metal content but with the same nominal value are in use. We will return to this law later.

Whereas the Greek city states mostly abstained from a debasement of their currencies, this happened more often in Hellenistic and Roman times. During the Punic Wars, Rome as well as Carthage debased its currencies. The same happened to Hellenistic states when Rome extended its power to the east (Heichelheim 1930, p. 45 ff.).

Afterwards when Hannibal was endangering Rome in the dictatorship of Fabius
Maximus one-ounce asses [of bronze, whereas formerly these coins contained two
asses] *were made and it was decided to exchange the* [silver] *denarius for sixteen*

of these [as compared to ten old asses before] . . . . *Thus the state profited by a half, but in paying soldiers the denarius was counted as 10 asses* (Pliny, *Natural History*, 33, 45).

Later, the debasement of the Roman silver currency, the denarius, became important under Septimius Severus and his successors and accelerated during the course of the third and fourth centuries AD. In the latter century the denarius had totally lost its silver content and had become a pure copper coin (Mickwitz, 1965/1932, pp. 81ff.). We are thus again confronted with the experience that good money is driven out by bad. But because of the lack of price quotations it is difficult to judge the magnitude of this inflation. Only for Egypt do we know more, because many papyri have been preserved in the desert climate. According to Bagnall (1985, pp. 61–5) the following development of the price level took place in Egypt (Figure 3.2) during the fourth century AD. Scholars agree that a pronounced inflation took place during the third and fourth (Bagnall 1985) centuries AD. *'Between the reigns of Emperors Claudius (AD 41–54) and Constantius (AD 337–361), the price of wheat on the open market in Egypt, expressed in drachmas, increased more than a million-fold. Dramatic inflation of prices is one of the central economic facts of the third and fourth centuries AD'* (Lendon 1990, p. 106).

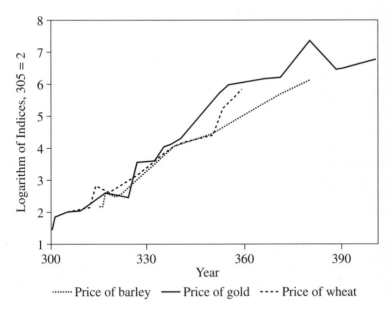

Source: Bagnall (1985)

Figure 3.2   Price indices for gold, wheat and barley, 301–400 AD

But this development is less dramatic than it sounds, for it amounts to an average annual rate of inflation of 4.4 per cent. And according to Wassink (1991, p. 482) the inflation began in fact only in 238 AD:

> *In that year the money in the treasury was insufficient to meet immediate expenditures such as the payment of the army. The army was of course the basis of the government's power. The total absence of any concept of state credit forced the Emperor to debasement of the currency. This debasement of 238 was unique because for the first time in Roman history it was done without a defensible monetary policy.*

From that time inflation slowly accelerated, since first the good money was driven out of circulation, so that the total money supply rose only scarcely in the beginning. After that it seems to have reached an annual average of 3.65 per cent between 250 and 293, to rise to 22.28 per cent from 293–301 (Wassink 1991, p. 466), that is until emperor Diocletian's abortive monetary reforms. This is certainly most impressive for an inflation, given a metallic monetary regime, but is dwarfed by comparison with what is possible under a discretionary paper money regime (compare Table 2.1). And if we take the more reliable figures concerning the development of the price of wheat (Bagnall 1985, p. 64) during the most inflationary period of the fourth century AD from 305–380, we get 'only' an average annual rate of inflation of 14.4 per cent.

There is still a controversy going on among scholars, whether debasement of the denarius and drachma and an increase of the money supply were responsible for this inflationary development or not. Lendon (1990) doubts the former hypothesis and explains inflation in the fourth century instead as follows:

> *So long as the coins circulated at a [nominal] value higher than that of the bullion they contained, their value rested upon public confidence, and there was always the danger of panic, whether set off by the death of the reigning emperor, retariffing the coins or any number of unrecoverable causes. Confidence once destroyed cannot readily be restored, and each blow to the coin's esteem would add to the public suspicion, driving the value of the coins ever down, and the prices of commodities ever higher.* (p. 126)

In my view this explanation contradicts the empirical evidence from other historical episodes, especially those with inconvertible paper monies. Though it is true that inflationary expectations and insecurity about future monetary policies rise when inflation is already present, and that this leads to an acceleration of inflation, no cases are known in which inflation arose only because of pessimistic expectations, especially not when metallic money was circulating. I thus consider the statement by Bagnall to be more convincing: *'One of the results of this study is the view, that the increases of prices are principally a result of changes in the metallic content of money and not an independent phenomenon'* (1985, p. 2).

Let us return to Figure 3.2. We know already that a currency tends to be undervalued when it is inflating (Section 2.4). This means that the price which has to be paid for a unit of a stable foreign currency, that is the exchange rate, has risen more than the domestic price level for goods. Now during the fourth century AD the Roman gold coin, the solidus, introduced through the unsuccessful monetary reforms undertaken by Diocletian, remained rather stable. As a consequence, the price of gold coins in denarii has to be thought of as an exchange rate between two currencies. But then the exchange rate would presumably have moved up more strongly during the whole period than the price level of goods. Now it seems that we encounter here, indeed, the first evidence for the validity of this hypothesis, for the index for the price of gold is mostly higher than that for wheat and barley, though the distances seem to be small, since we had to use logarithms on the vertical axis. It should be mentioned, however, that Professor Bagnall pointed out in a private communication that though this hypothesis is not contradicted by the facts, the data are too scarce to make the evidence conclusive.

At least beginning with the end of the Western Roman Empire, Western Europe moved towards a more primitive economy characterised by demonetisation and the return to barter. But slowly the economy recovered and turned back to money as a means of payment, beginning with the monetary reforms of Charlemagne and culminating with the minting of a new gold coin, the fiorino d'oro, by Florence in the 13th century. As a consequence princes and rulers soon began again to tamper with the value of their currencies. As Henri Pirenne (1951) explained, when looking at European developments during the Middle Ages:

> *The progress of monetary circulation provided princes with the possibility to use it to their own advantage. Possessing the right to mint coins, they believed themselves to be authorised to use this in the interest of their treasury to the detriment of the public. The more money became indispensable for economic life, the more it was changed by those who had the right to strike it. . . . At the end of the 12th century, the monetary disorder had reached a point that a reform imposed itself.* (pp. 256, 258)

Except for the last sentence this explanation is quite in tune with our analysis of political influences introducing an inflation bias into the economy (Section 2.4). Pirenne, however, gives no explanation why a reform should have imposed itself to end the monetary disorder. We shall return to this problem later, when we try to explain under which conditions stable monetary regimes have a chance to be introduced. At the moment we turn to give some examples

Table 3.1   Value of florin in different currencies

Country	ca 1300	ca 1400	ca 1500	Currency
Castile	5.8	66	375	Maravedi
	100	1137.9	6465.5	
Cologne	6.67	42	112	Schilling
	100	630	1680	
Flanders	13.125	33.5	80	Groot
	100	255.2	609.5	
Austria	2.22	5	11	Schilling
	100	225	495	
France	10	22	38.75	Sou
	100	220	387.5	
Hanse	8	10.5	31	Schilling (of Luebeck)
	100	131.25	387.5	
Rome	34	73	130	Soldo
	100	214.7	382.35	
Florence	46.5	77.92	140	Soldo
	100	167.56	301.1	
Bohemia	12	20	30	Groschen (of Prague)
	100	166.67	250	
Venice	74	93	124	Soldo
	100	125.68	167.57	
Aragon	11.5	12.71	16	Sueldo
	100	110.51	139.13	
England	2.67	3	4.58	Shilling
	100	112.5	171.88	

Source: Spufford (1986), Table 1

of the many debasements which took place under metallic monetary regimes up to the 17th century. Unfortunately, price data are not available for the mediaeval period. As a substitute we show the development of the exchange rates of some currencies for the florin of Florence (Table 3.1) which was kept stable with about the same gold content for three hundred years.

As we can see from the table, the debasement of the currency was most pronounced for the maravedi of Castile and the schilling of Cologne. Still, if we calculate the average annual increase of the exchange rate for these two currencies, we obtain only 2.11 and 1.42 per cent. Accordingly, the devaluation of the other currencies compared to the florin was scarcely noticeable measured by modern experiences. Moreover, we have to take into account a specific characteristic of monetary regimes during this period. The value of coins deteriorated because of wear and tear and monetary authorities did not exchange old coins at their face value for new ones. As a consequence, when they issued new coins with full metallic value, Gresham's Law worked: the bad old money drove out the good new coins. This led to a scarcity of circulating money, which the authorities sought to overcome by issuing the new coins with a metal content corresponding to that of the old coins. In this way a slight debasement of the currency took place with a positive fiscal side-effect, but not necessarily with fiscal considerations as its prime cause.

Let us end this section with another, more pronounced example of a debasement, namely that of the small coins of Castile in the 17th century, the vellon money, the maravedi, whereas the silver content of the internationally used silver coin was kept nearly constant (Hamilton 1947) (see Figure 3.3). Note that in Figure 3.3 the reciprocal of the silver content of the maravedi has been depicted besides the price of silver, since the latter series ends in 1680. Both give identical index figures except for two years. The reciprocal allows us to show the results of the stabilisation of the vellon money. It should be mentioned that the debasement of the vellon money had begun already at the

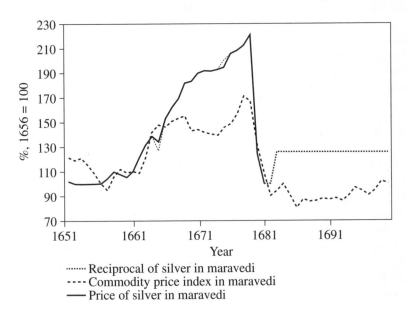

.... Reciprocal of silver in maravedi
---- Commodity price index in maravedi
—— Price of silver in maravedi

Source: Hamilton (1947)

Figure 3.3 Commodity price index and price of silver in maravedis in Spain, 1651–1700

beginning of the 17th century (Lozanne 1997, Motomura 1994). It was probably caused by the financial needs of the Spanish Empire, which was involved
in many wars during the period to maintain its realm, when at the same time
the inflow of silver from its American dominions began to decrease.

We note first that the average annual rate of inflation in terms of the
commodity price index was rather mild. It amounted only to 2.46 per cent for
the years from 1656 to 1678, when the index reached its peak. Moreover, one
can derive several important qualitative characteristics from the figure, which
hold quite generally, even for later paper money inflations. First, we see that
the price of silver in vellon went up more strongly than the price index for
commodities from 1661, when inflation accelerated. We know already that we
have to treat the price of silver, which determined the value of the stable
Spanish silver coins, as an exchange rate. Consequently, an undervaluation of
the maravedi occurred because of inflation. Second, when the vellon currency
was stabilised beginning in 1680, the price of silver fell much more strongly
than the commodity price index. The two lines in Figure 3.3 intersect, which
means that purchasing power parity was restored. Third, the exchange rate was
finally fixed by the reform at a somewhat undervalued level, that is the price
index shows a lower value than the exchange rate. Such a policy has expansionary consequences for the real economy for some time, namely until the
price level has moved up to the exchange rate and purchasing power parity is
restored. Since these are typical qualitative characteristics of inflation and
stabilisation, we will return to them later to analyse their economic and political causes and consequences.

3.3   REASONS FOR THE INTRODUCTION AND MAINTENANCE OF STABLE METALLIC MONETARY REGIMES

We have already quoted Henri Pirenne (1951): *'At the end of the 12th century,
the monetary disorder had reached a point that a reform imposed itself'* (p.
256). This is certainly a true statement, but first, it does not explain why monetary disorder should lead to reforms. And second, there may be other reasons
for establishing and maintaining a stable metallic monetary regime. To understand these relationships, let us look at the relevant developments before and
after the end of the 12th century.

We observe first that new stable currencies were indeed introduced beginning at the end of this century. In 1192, Doge Henry Dandolo of Venice issued
a new silver coin, the gros or matapan, which had the value of 12 old
Carolingian deniers (pennies). This new money was soon used internationally
and imitated in other European countries. A few decades later, in 1252,

Florence issued its first gold coins, the florins (fiorino d'oro), following the example of Emperor Frederick II in Sicily. In 1284 Venice issued a replica, the ducat or zechin, and other countries and princes soon imitated this practice. The florin was widely used in Western Europe as a unit of account and in international transactions, presumably because of its stability in terms of other currencies, which was maintained for more than 300 years. And other currencies were not as stable, as shown in Table 3.1.

What were the reasons for these developments? Venice and later Florence were centres of international commerce. Their merchants and rulers, because of the tax revenues resulting from a flourishing commerce, were strongly interested in an international currency accepted everywhere which reduced transaction costs and thus widened international trade. Note also that the rulers of these city states belonged themselves to the merchant class. Finally, it is interesting to note that the beginning of the introduction of these new stable currencies took place not only when the domestic monetary disorder had reached its peak, but when the Byzantine gold currency, the solidus and later the hyperpyron, which had been used as international currency during previous centuries (Botha 1987, Hendy 1985), had fallen into decline. As a consequence, Venice and later Florence had good reasons to introduce currencies which could serve as international means of payment. On top of this, there was another factor favouring the introduction and maintenance of stable currencies. Venice and Florence were small political entities, even if we take into account the offshore dominions of the former. As a consequence, if their money was used internationally, the gain for their treasuries from minting these coins at a nominal value slightly higher than the intrinsic value plus minting expenses, with the purpose of benefitting from the seignorage, was presumably higher than what they could have gained from debasement. For debased coins could be used as legal tender only in their restricted domains, whereas the stable currency was widely accepted also abroad.

But why did other kingdoms like France, and the German princes, also turn to introducing stable money afterwards? Probably because they saw the success of the Venetian and Florentine examples in ending monetary disorders, which also had negative consequences for the real economy, and because they wanted to reap themselves some of the seignorage by minting stable coins.

Our hypothesis seems to be supported, too, by later evidence. When Philip II of Spain found himself with deep fiscal problems in the second half of the 16th century because of the increasing debts of the crown, the Spanish silver coin, the piece of eight (real de a ocho), the precursor of the US dollar, which imitated it, had already been well established as the international means of payment. As a consequence, Philip preferred three open bankruptcies of the crown instead of escaping his financial troubles by debasing the silver currency, that is by foregoing the seignorage, and by losing the prestige connected with a currency accepted all over the world. And his successors, from Philip III, Philip IV and Carlos II, who found themselves in even worse fiscal plights, since the inflow of silver from the mines in America diminished, never debased the piece of eight, but preferred to debase the vellon currency (Motomura 1994), as we have seen above.

It remains, however, to explain why the vellon currency, the maravedi, was finally stabilised in 1680, after eighty years of debasement, and after earlier reform efforts had failed. It seems that besides the disorders created in the real economy by a rather small but variable inflation, the consequences of Gresham's Law may have been responsible for this decision. To quote Hamilton (1933, p. 212):

> ... the inordinate issues early in the reign of Philip IV greatly accelerated the hitherto gradual displacement of silver as the money of account. .... It is impossible to date exactly the definitive establishment of vellon as the chief circulating medium and sole accounting unit, but the change took place around 1622–1623 in most of the records I have utilised. It seems safe to say that throughout the second quarter of the seventeenth century prices and wages were uniformly quoted in terms of vellon. And in this period the alternation of sudden inflation and deflation wreaked havoc on the economic life of Castile.

Given these facts it is not surprising that several, however unsuccessful, reforms were tried, among them one by the then responsible Minister, the Duke of Olivarez, in the 1640s (Lozanne 1997). Two important relationships should be mentioned here. First, inflation will remain rather limited as long as bad money, here the vellon, is still driving out the good silver money. For this means that the total money supply is scarcely changing. We have already mentioned this fact for the Roman Empire of the third century. Second, if the international money has left the country, no reserves are any longer available for international payments. Castile had thus to rely on its exports and (or) the diminishing inflow of silver for its disbursements, including the payments for its international political and military engagements.

3.4   PRICE AND EXCHANGE CONTROLS

An inflation of the magnitude occurring during the last decade of the third and during the greater part of the fourth centuries in the Roman Empire was an event which took the rulers by surprise and which they could not understand, given the absence of any monetary theory to speak of. As a consequence, it is not surprising that Diocletian and his co-regents introduced maximum prices for 1200 products and services (including 130 grades of labour, and various freight rates) through an edict issued in 301 AD, after the currency reform of 296 had faltered (Wassink 1991, pp. 489–90): '*The Preamble to the Edict gives the reasons for the issuing of maximum prices. It shows that the emperors did not understand the origins of the inflation phenomenon. They believed that prices rose while the harvests were good because of the boundlessness of human greed'* (p. 490).

The death penalty was introduced for asking higher prices than set in the edict. But like all such measures taken later in history, the introduction of price controls proved to be a failure. Until 305, when Diocletian abdicated and the price decree was no longer in effect, numerous death penalties, the disappearance of goods from the market and disturbances in the labour market were the consequences (Michell 1947).

During the Spanish vellon inflation similar measures were introduced. But at this time monetary theory had already been developed by the School of Salamanca during the 16th century. Scholars like Juan de Mariana (1609) warned against the monetary debasement by Philip III with sound economic arguments. Also, the Castilian estates, the Cortes, demanded on several occasions that the issue of debased vellon should be ended, and even offered the king tax increases in exchange for solemn promises to end this practice, promises which were broken after a few years. Under the pressure of ailing government finances the Spanish kings and their advisors went on with their inflationary policies, preferring rather to take administrative measures against the currency substitution (the working of Gresham's Law) and inflation, events which they had caused with their own monetary policies. '*As early as 1625 Spanish economists commenced to complain that despite the treasures of the Indies vellon had driven gold and silver completely out of circulation . . .*' (Hamilton 1933, pp. 89–90).

At this time the official position taken was that foreigners smuggled counterfeited vellon coins into Spain, selling them for silver coins at a premium on the official parity with the maravedi, which reached about 50 per cent in 1626 (p. 81), and thus gaining huge profits from this operation. Following up on this position:

> *On October 14, 1624, a royal pragmatic* [of Philip IV, 1621–1665) *provided a penalty of death and the confiscation of goods for bringing vellon money into the kingdom . . . going near to a boat in which it was brought to the coast, exchanging it for merchandise or silver, transporting or hiding it, or in any way aiding in smuggling it. . . . acceptance of smuggled vellon in exchange for goods or in payment of debt was punished by perpetual exile and the loss of half of one's goods. . . . On February 2, 1627, jurisdiction in the trials of vellon smugglers was transferred to the courts of the inquisition, and on September 13, 1628, the ordinary death penalty was replaced by burning at the stake.* (pp. 80–1)

Other regulations concerned fixing of prices for many commodities and also of the exchange rate of silver in terms of vellon, at that time expressed as a premium on the legal parity. First fines and penalties were introduced to prevent any premium on silver. When this measure proved to be a failure, a maximal permitted premium was postulated and increased several times, combined with a further stiffening of penalties. In 1610 a maximum premium of 10 per cent, in 1636 of 25 per cent and in 1641 of 50 per cent was introduced. In 1642 another absolute prohibition of the premium was tried, followed again by a maximum premium of 40 per cent in 1647 and 50 per cent in 1651 (Hamilton 1933, pp. 98 ff.). By then the sanctions against infringement of the maximum not only included *'loss of goods and citizenship for the first offence,* [but] *nobles became subject to six years' imprisonment and plebeians to a like term in the galleys; for the second offence the penalty for the plebeian or noble was death'* (p. 99).

It goes without saying that all these fines and penalties did not prevent the further rise of prices and especially of the exchange rate of silver (Figure 3.2).

Another problem arising when debasement of the currency is intended, is how to remove the old heavier coins with a higher silver content from circulation and to bring them to the mints. When it became necessary in 1651 to reinforce the armies of Milan and Flanders and also to send others to other territories:

> ... *it was necessary to choose between additional taxes and inflation. The rise in prices and the increase in the premium on silver ... were feared less than the results of further imposts. On November 11, 1651 His Majesty ordered that all pieces of 2 maravedis be carried to the mints within thirty days for restamping to quadruple their tale* [their nominal face value]. *The possession of unstamped coins after the expiration of the period of grace was declared illegal, and their expenditure was subjected to a penalty of death and the loss of one's goods.* (p. 87)

But in spite of these stern sanctions only small quantities of coins were surrendered.

3.5 CONSEQUENCES OF INFLATION FOR THE REAL ECONOMY

Economic theory tells us that inflation should have no negative consequences if it were to take place without unexpected fluctuations and were correctly predicted (Parkin 1992). In historical reality this is, however, never the case, especially at the beginning of an inflation. By contrast, such an event is usually unexpected by the public and thus leads to an economic upswing, which ends, however, when people have adjusted their expectations to inflation. Moreover, empirical evidence abounds that the (unexpected) variance of the rate of inflation increases with its magnitude. What is more, unexpected reversals of monetary policy seem to be the rule, especially when inflation

accelerates, and if uninformed rulers try to react to consequences not foreseen by them. As a consequence, one can expect no damage from inflation
in the real economy only as long as it remains small and smooth. This suppo-
sition seems to be confirmed for two of the historical episodes we have
discussed, namely the developments during the Roman Empire from
Emperor Augustus to the beginning of the third century AD and during the
so-called Great Price Revolution of the 16th century. In the Roman case the
economy may even have been stimulated for some time by the additional
supply of money (Wassink 1991). Similarly, Hamilton (1933, p. 202)
mentions negative real consequences only for the period beginning with the
year 1581, and adds that:

> *In 1600 Francisco Soranzo, a Venetian envoy, reported that 'in all Spain are found*
> *a great scarcity and an inexpressible dearness of all things', and a memorial to the*
> *Crown adopted by the Cortes on November 18, 1600, complained that as conse-*
> *quences of exorbitant prices, nakedness and sickness stalked the land, that the*
> *number of beggars, thieves and prostitutes had increased, that only through hypothe-*
> *cation of property had the rich been able to live, and that the poor were dying of*
> *hunger.*

Developments became worse with the long-lasting vellon inflation. Though it
was itself an outflow of the fiscal problems of the Spanish monarchy in its
battle to maintain European supremacy and its over-extended worldwide
empire against the forces of France, England, the Netherlands and Sweden,
this 'solution' of the problems itself contributed to the decline of the Spanish
economy. As Hamilton (1933, p. 103) expressed it:

> *While many beneficial effects flowed from the constant, and therefore predictable*
> *and dependable, rise in prices in the sixteenth century, it was not so with the sudden*
> *inflation and deflation of the seventeenth. The numerous and wide fluctuations in*
> *prices upset calculations, stifled initiative, and impeded the vigorous conduct of*
> *business enterprise. Although in some respects a result of economic decadence,*
> *vellon inflation was one of the most powerful factors in the economic decline of*
> *Castile.*

Similar, but more devastating consequences followed from the debasement of
money and the ensuing inflation in the Roman Empire of the 3rd and 4th
centuries. It is difficult to escape the impression that the change of the fiscal
system to requisitions and taxes in kind, to payment of the army in kind, and
the spreading of barter from about the middle of the 3rd century were mainly
a consequence of monetary disorder, of contradictory changes in monetary
policy, the vanishing of good money because of the workings of Gresham's
Law, and of the denarius inflation following later (Wassink 1991, pp. 482ff.).
When the emperors had once embarked on this slippery road, they went on to

complete this obnoxious system (Jones 1966, pp. 35ff.). Since people were not willing to work and to deliver goods for a debased currency calculated with a higher nominal value than corresponded to its intrinsic or market value, they had to be forced to work for the taxes in kind.

> *An organised requisition in kind soon, and certainly under Diocletian, meant that it became illegal for peasants to leave their registered domicile. . . . [The] agricultural population became hereditary tied to the soil. This hereditary caste system extended gradually; Diocletian compelled the sons of soldiers to serve in the army, while the workers in the mints and the weaving and dyeing factories which Diocletian created were state slaves and their service also hereditary. Goldminers and washers too were later a hereditary caste. Other hereditary classes which probably already existed in Diocletian's days were the guilds of bakers, butchers, bargees, carters and so forth in Rome and the diocesan guilds of skippers . . . who carried corn and other public cargoes to Rome.* (Wassink 1991, p. 485f.)

All these measures together with the abortive price controls limited the domain of the monetary economy, removed incentives and motivation, and hindered innovations and the division of labour, which are preconditions for a productive economy. It is difficult to believe that the subsequent inflation of the 4th century did not worsen this sad state of the Roman economy, even after the maximal prices of Diocletian's edict had been removed.

3.6 CONCLUSIONS

We have drawn the following conclusions in this chapter:

1. Many debasements of metallic currencies occurred in history which led to inflations. They were brought about by reducing the weight of coins, by substituting a less valuable metal for a more valuable (like copper for silver) in the coins and (or) by increasing the nominal value of coins without increasing their weight and metal content in the same proportion. All of these debasements were caused by the political factors mentioned in Chapter 2, among which the financial strains brought about by war were prominent.

2. The debasements of currency had as a consequence that the good old coins were driven out of circulation by the new bad ones (Gresham's Law), if the exchange rate between the two kinds of coins was legally fixed. The old coins were either hoarded, melted down or exported to foreign countries to pay for imports. This meant that the total money supply only increased substantially after all good coins had been driven out of circulation, a fact which retarded the onset of inflation.

3. Some debasement of coins often became necessary because wear and tear had reduced the weight of the old coins. If this was the case, the intrinsic value of new coins had to be somewhat decreased to prevent the good new coins being driven out by the bad old coins.

4. Inflations were also sometimes caused when large additional supplies of the monetary metal were introduced into circulation.

5. Most of these inflations were rather moderate judged by modern experiences. They usually amounted on the average to not much more than two per cent annually.

6. The biggest average annual inflation reported seems to have occurred in the Roman Empire during the fourth century. If we can believe the figures calculated – and we have raised some doubts about them – this inflation reached an average annual figure of about 41 per cent during the period from 324–341.

7. Inflation usually led to an undervaluation of the inflating currency which ended with the stabilisation of this money.

8. Reforms introducing stable and valuable coins usually occurred when monetary disorder led to a negative development of the real economy and thus of the finances of the rulers.

9. These forces working for reform were greatly strengthened when no internationally acceptable money remained because of the working of Gresham's Law and when substantial seignorage could be gained by introducing new international currencies.

10. All administrative measures by rulers or governments to stem the inflation arising from the increase of the money supply or debasement proved to be in vain, even if their violation was threatened with the death penalty. This was true for all regulations imposing maximum values for prices or exchange rate, as well as those trying to prevent the working of Gresham's Law.

11. Negative or even slightly stimulating consequences of inflation were only present with very low and smooth, predictable rates, provided that the rulers did not follow an erratic monetary policy. In the absence of one or more of these conditions grave damage resulted in the real economy in both cases, the Roman developments of the 3rd and 4th centuries and the Castilian vellon inflation of the 17th century.

REFERENCES

Azpilcueta de Navarro, Martin (1556), *Comentario Resulotorio de Usuras y Cambios*, Salamanca.

Bagnall, Roger S. (1985), 'Currency and Inflation in Fourth Century Egypt', *BASP*, Suppl. 5, 54.

Bodin, Jean (1568), *La Response de Maistre Jean Bodin, Advocat en la Cour, au Paradoxe de Monsieur de Malestroit Touchant l'Encherissement de Toutes Choses et le Moyen d'y Remedier*, Paris.

Botha, D. J. Joubert (1987), 'Monetary Economics of the Byzantine Empire', *Working Paper*, Johannesburg: Dept. of Economics, University of the Witwatersrand.

Fisher, Douglas (1989), 'The Price Revolution: A Monetary Interpretation', *The Journal of Economic History*, XLIX, Dec., 883–902.

Grice-Hutchinson, Marjorie (1952), *The School of Salamanca: Readings in Spanish Monetary Theory, 1544–1605*, Oxford: Clarendon Press.

Hamilton, Earl J. (1933), *American Treasury and Price Revolution in Spain*, Cambridge, Mass.: Harvard University Press.

Hamilton, Earl J. (1947), *War and Prices in Spain, 1651–1680*, Cambridge, Mass.: Harvard University Press.

Heichelheim, Fritz (1930), 'Wirtschaftliche Schwankungen der Zeit von Alexander bis Augustus', in Arthur Spiethoff (ed.), *Beitraege zur Erforschung der wirtschaftlichen Wechsellagen. Aufschwung, Krise, Stockung*, Heft 3, Jena: Gustav Fischer.

Heichelheim, F. (1955), 'On Ancient Price Trends from the Early First Millennium BC to Heradius', *Finanzarchiv*, 15(3), 498–511.

Hendy, Michael F. (1985), *Studies in the Byzantine Economy*, New York: Cambridge University Press.

Jevons, William St. (1884), 'A Serious Fall in the Value of Gold Ascertained and its Social Consequences Set Forth', in *Investigations in Currency and Finance*, Chapter 2, 1863, reprint, London: Macmillan.

Jones, A.H.M. (1966), *The Decline of the Ancient World*, London and New York: Longman.

Lendon, Jon E. (1990), 'The Face on the Coins and Inflation in Roman Egypt', *Klio*, 72, 107–34.

Lozanne Roldan, Claudia de (1990), 'La Crisis Española de Siglo XVII y su Implicacion', in *Algunos Aspectos de las Finanzas Reales de Nueva España*, Mexico, D.F.: ITAM, Instituto Tecnologico Autonomo de Mexico.

Lozanne Roldan, Claudia de (1997), *Geldtheorie und Geldpolitik im fruehneuzeitlichen Spanien. Muenzabwertungen: Problembewusstsein und Stabilisierungsvorschlaege (1618–1642)*, Saarbruecken: Verlag fuer Entwicklungspolitik Saarbruecken.

Mariana, Juan de (1609), 'Tratado y Discurso Sobre Moneda de Vellon', Koeln. Original in Latin: *De Monetae Mutatione*.

Michell (1947), *The Edict of Diocletian: A Study of Price Fixing*, London and New York: Macmillan.

Mickwitz, Gunnar ([1932],1965), *Geld und Wert im Roemischen Reich des Vierten Jahrhunderts n. Chr.*, Amsterdam: Adolf M. Hackert.

Motomura, Akira (1994), 'The Best and Worst of Currencies: Seignorage and Currency Policy in Spain, 1597–1650', *The Journal of Economic History*, 54, March, 104–27.

Munro, John H. (1998), 'Precious Metals and the Origins of the Price Revolution Reconsidered', in Clara E. Nuñez (ed.), *Monetary History in Global Perspective, 1500–1808*, Sevilla: Universidad de Sevilla, 35–49.

Parkin, M. (1992), 'Inflation', in P. Neuman, M. Milgate and J. Gatwell (eds), *The New Palgrave Dictionary of Money and Finance*, London and New York: Macmillan, Vol. 2, 394–400.

Pirenne, Henri (1951), *Histoire Economique de l'Occident Médiéval*, Paris: Desclée de Brouwer.

Spufford, Peter (1986), *Handbook of Medieval Exchange*, London: Offices of The Royal Historical Society, University College.

Wassink, Alfred (1991), 'Inflation and Financial Policy Under the Roman Empire to the Price Edict of 301 AD', *Historia*, XL (4), 465–93.

4. Moderate paper money inflations

4.1 THE INTRODUCTION OF PAPER MONEY

Paper money was probably first introduced in Europe in Sweden during the 17th century in the form of banknotes (Deutsche Bundesbank 1971). Many banks (like the Bank of England, founded in 1694) and governments soon followed this example during the 18th century. Consequently, there existed during the following two centuries usually two kinds of paper money, namely banknotes and government-issued paper money notes. When they were first put into circulation, all these notes were convertible at a fixed exchange rate of one to one into copper (Sweden), silver or gold coins with full intrinsic value. But in the course of the following decades, more and more countries abolished convertibility, beginning with the paper money experiment undertaken by John Law in the beginning of the 18th century with the co-operation of the regent, the Duke of Orleans, when the French Crown was facing bankruptcy because of the massive spending by Louis XIV on wars and luxury expenditures. As a consequence a moderate inflation and a return to a pure metallic standard followed after a few years (Hamilton 1936/37, Luethy 1959). Sweden followed with inconvertibility of its banknotes, moderate inflation and stabilisation in the mid-century (see below). Finally at the end of the century most European countries, including England, were on a discretionary paper money standard, mainly but not only because of the wars related to the French Revolution and the imperialistic policy of Napoleon (Buesch 1800). After the Napoleonic wars most countries returned to convertibility, often, like Britain, at the old parity. Later developments during the 19th century have already been sketched (Chapter 2).

America saw suspensions of convertibility and paper money inflations during the first half of the 18th century. Many of the states of British North America followed this route, for instance Massachusetts (see below) and Rhode Island, which *'probably sinned most in her abuses of paper money'* (Brock 1975, p. 37). The North American development culminated with the Continental Currency of the emerging United States issued to finance the War of Independence against Britain. This inconvertible paper currency soon lost more and more of its value, and was finally fully driven out by better money. (For an explanation of this characteristic of high inflations, which occurs when flexible exchange rates are present, and which I have called Thier's Law, compare Section 5.3 below). Even today the expression 'not worth a Continental' is used in American language. The American inflation during the War of Independence is the only high inflation which we consider in this chapter, which is mostly devoted to moderate inflations.

The paper money inflations occurring in Europe and America were, however, not the earliest to take place in the world. It is well known that the Chinese were the first to invent paper and block printing. As a consequence it is not surprising that they also invented paper money before 1000 AD, and also that their rulers were the first to bring about paper money inflation by financing budget deficits. Just about all Chinese regimes after 1000 issued too much paper money which became inconvertible at a fixed parity into copper after some time and led to (moderate) inflation.

In the next two sections we turn first to some examples of early European and American paper money inflations, and afterwards analyse the inflation under the Chinese Ming dynasty.

4.2 PAPER MONEY INFLATION IN SWEDEN DURING THE 18TH CENTURY

The Swedish experience with paper money inflation is very instructive for several reasons. First, because this historical event has in many respects the characteristic of a monetary experiment, since Sweden's main trading partners all remained on silver or gold standards. Second, Sweden had a kind of republican regime in which two parties, the Hats and the Caps, vied for government power in elections. Third, the economic relationships characteristic of inflation combined with this political system and its inflationary bias to produce a typical pattern of events. Fourth, the holder of the first chair in economics at the University of Uppsala, P.N. Christiernin, correctly foresaw the reasons for and consequences of the inflation and also of the measures proposed to eliminate it. His advice, which is also typical, was not listened to by politicians, with dire consequences. Perhaps as a consequence he abolished the chair in economics for one in philosophy (for a full description see Eagley 1971).

One can easily understand that Sweden was the first country in Europe to introduce banknotes. For its metallic monetary regime was based on a copper standard, and copper is heavy compared to its value, so that greater payments in copper coins implied heavy transportation and transaction costs. After some earlier private and public experiments in paper notes the Swedish Riksbank began to issue daler banknotes. As early as 1745 banknotes were made irredeemable in silver by a directive of October 1745 (Eagley 1971, p. 7). Even then the quantity in circulation was kept within certain limits between 1745 and 1755, but began to increase rapidly when Sweden entered the Seven Years' War in 1756. It grew from 6.9 million dalers in 1745 to 13.7 in 1755, to 20.9 in 1756 and to 44.6 million in 1762 (Sveriges Riksbank 1931). Deficit financing on the part of the Government was the main reason for this development. Loans to the Crown increased to 56.4 per cent of total bank loans in 1766. In 1759, even the copper coins began to command a premium over the banknotes, that is their intrinsic value had become higher than their face value. As a consequence, the convertibility of banknotes into copper coins was suspended. Sweden was on a pure paper money standard (Eagley 1971, p. 8).

During all this time, that is from 1739 to 1765, the Hat party was in power, whereas the Cap party formed the opposition. During this period the Hat party tried to promote economic growth in Sweden and favoured especially the development of the textile industry by different inducements. This industry as well as the iron and other industries received direct financial support, low interest loans and were protected by high import tariffs (Eagley 1971, pp. 13ff.). The first of these measures contributed to the expansion of the note issue, which finally went out of control when Sweden entered the Seven Years' War in 1756. A first consequence of these policies until 1761 was a booming real economy. Afterwards, however, economic activity declined, perhaps as a negative consequence of lasting inflation (Eagley 1971, p. 12). The inflationary consequences followed with a lag (Figure 4.1).

As can be seen from the figure, exchange rate and price level began to rise strongly only in 1760, whereas the boom had already begun several years before. We observe that, as in most other historical inflations described, the exchange rate increased more quickly and strongly than the price level, that is an undervaluation of the Swedish currency developed. It is also important to note that the circulation of currency increased even earlier and more strongly than the exchange rate. This is also typical, at least for the beginning of moderate inflations. It means that the real stock of money rises during this period.

If we denote the circulating money by M, the exchange rate by w, the domestic price level by P and the foreign price level by P, we can state these relationships formally as follows:

1. Define *purchasing power parity* as $P(t) = cw(t)P^*(t)$, where $c > 1$ stands for transportation costs, customs duties and so on. t stands for time. P, P* and w are functions of time since they change over time. Now assume further that purchasing power parity held in 1755. Note that this assumption puts us on the safe side, since there may have been some undervaluation even before, because of monetary expansion.

2. Let us further assume that $P^*(t) = P^* = $ constant, that is that it was stable because foreign countries remained on metallic standards.

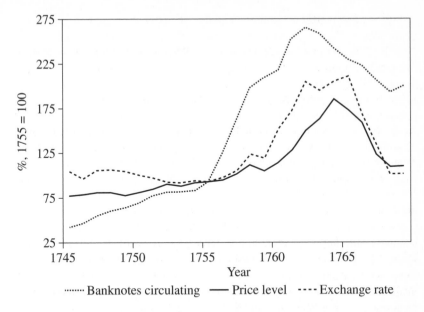

Sources: Data on banknotes circulating and exchange rate: Sveriges Riksbank (1931). Price index: Amark (1921, p. 106). Compare also Joerberg (1972, vol. 2, pp. 47 ff).

Figure 4.1   Paper money inflation in Sweden, 1745–1769

Taking logarithms for the equation we get: $\ln P(t) = \ln c + \ln w(t) + \ln P^*$. Differentiating this equation with respect to argument t it follows that

4.1 $(dP/dt)/P = (dw/dt)/w$,

since c and P^* are not dependent on t. The relationship of equation (4.1) is called the *relative purchasing power parity*. As we can see from Figure 4.1 this relationship was violated in the years following 1756. Instead we have

(4.2) $(dP/dt)/P < (dw/dt)/w$.

Equation (4.2) thus provides a definition of *relative* undervaluation, that is in our case relative to the situation in 1755.

3.   We define the *real stock of money* as $M(t)/P(t)$.

If again we take the real stock of money in 1755 as normalised to 100 per cent = 1, we see that the real stock of money is above normal in the following years:

(4.3) $M/P > 100$ per cent $= 1$.

The real stock of money increases during moderate inflations at least in the beginning.*

Let us now turn to the reactions of the political system to the economic developments sketched above. First, it is not surprising that the Hat party was re-elected and remained in power as long as the economy was booming because of monetary expansion and as long as the adverse consequences of inflation were not felt by the public. But this changed, for from 1760 inflation and especially devaluation of the currency accelerated, and after 1761 the boom of the economy also subsided. As a consequence voters became disappointed with the Hat party and the Cap party was elected into power in 1765. Given economic developments it is understandable that the Cap party had and soon instituted a deflationary programme. They were correctly convinced that the devaluation of the currency and inflation as well as their negative real effects were a consequence of the voluminous issue of banknotes. Thus *'Cap policy specified that the deflation would be accomplished through the reduction of banknotes in circulation, and set a target rate of reduction for the exchange rates'* (Eagley 1971, p. 36).

The volume of banknotes in circulation was reduced by 13.5 per cent between 1766 and 1768. Nowadays economists know quite well that such a policy will first lead to a decrease in output and employment, and only thereafter to a fall of the price level.

But even before these measures were taken, the Swedish economist Christiernin had already warned against taking them. For he not only made clear that devaluation and inflation were the consequence of the increase of the money supply through the issue of banknotes, but also that the high exchange rate worked like an export subsidy, and that a reduction of the banknotes in circulation would lead to a depression in the economy. Consequently Christiernin recommended a stabilisation at the present exchange rate (Eagley 1971). But the Cap party did not listen, voters felt the brunt of their negative policies, the Caps were defeated in the election of 1772 and the Hats returned to power. But already in the same year a *coup d'état* by Gustav III ended representative democracy, established an absolute monarchy and precluded further experiments in deflation. Banknotes were made convertible into silver at the prevailing market exchange rate in 1777 (Eagley 1971, p. 36). This currency reform meant that Sweden went over to a silver standard (Joerberg 1972, vol. II, pp. 127ff.) The era of the paper daler had come to an end like the political-economic play typical of representative government unbound by a monetary constitution.

Returning to Figure 4.1 we observe that the index of banknotes in circulation had already begun to fall before the Caps won a majority in the Swedish parliament, the Riksdag. This is probably due to the fact that Sweden concluded a separate peace treaty with Prussia in 1762. For the same year we also observe a reduction in the exchange rate for the Hamburg Mark Banco (a pure silver standard). But the exchange rate only began to decrease strongly and more quickly than the price level when the Caps succeeded in grasping power. In about 1768 purchasing power parity was restored after about thirteen years. Thereafter a small overvaluation even developed. This is a typical pattern when inflation is ended by monetary restraint, as we will see for other historical experiences.

4.3 PAPER MONEY INFLATION IN MASSACHUSETTS, 1703–1749

Massachusetts enjoyed, like other British colonies in North America, a relatively high level of self-government. Beginning in 1690, related to an expedition against French Quebec, the colony used this prerogative to issue bills of credit to finance its budget deficit, which soon circulated as paper money notes (Brock 1975, pp. 21f.). Because of an originally fixed exchange rate with English silver coins and an over-issue of the bills of credit partly caused by later wars, this bad money drove out the good silver money, and Benjamin Franklin later recounted that no coins were seen in Massachusetts. The price of silver in paper shillings began to rise and could not even be contained at a higher level after 1710 (Figure 4.2):

> *Before 1710 the sums outstanding in bills were small relative to the amount of silver in circulation. In 1709 there was perhaps as much silver in circulation as there were bills. . . . After 1710, however, the situation changed. Bills were emitted in larger quantities. Moreover, silver left the colony at a more rapid rate, for these were years during which the balance of trade with England was extremely unfavourable. . . . The result was, that as the demand for silver for making payments abroad grew, and as the supply of the metal within this colony dwindled . . . those that needed it to make remittances to Britain began to bid one against the other for it, and its price rose. The existence of a stock of silver in a colony served to retard the rise of the price of the metal. . . . As soon as the stock was exhausted, the rise became more rapid.* (Brock 1975, pp. 29f.)

As in other cases already considered, as long as Gresham's Law worked the money supply did not rise much and price level and exchange rate remained rather stable. But after the good money had been driven out, this changed and nothing could prevent a rise of exchange rate and prices. We differ, however, from Brock's interpretation concerning the balance of payments. As will be shown later, it always moves into a deficit when Gresham's Law is at work (Chapter 6).

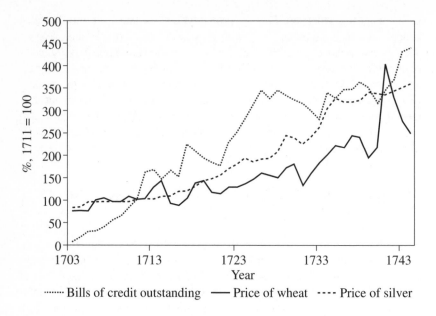

······ Bills of credit outstanding   —— Price of wheat   ---- Price of silver

Note: Prices of silver for 1740, 1742–43 and 1748 interpolated in Figure 4.2

Sources: For wheat and silver prices in paper shillings: Cole (1938), Tables 36 and 38, pp. 117 and 119. For bills of credit outstanding: Brock (1975), Table II (revised), Part B, pp. 591–3

Figure 4.2   Paper money inflation in Massachusetts, 1703–1744

We also observe that the amount of bills of credit, similar to the Swedish experience, rose more than the exchange rate for silver, which increased to a higher level than the price of wheat, except for 1741, when probably a bad harvest occurred. This means that the real stock of money increased, provided that these events were not caused by a growth of the real economy. This is, of course possible, but since inflation did not subside, it is probably not the only cause of the growth of the real stock of money. Also, the paper currency was undervalued, if we can assume that the general price level moved in tune with the price of wheat.

The expansion of the paper money supply went on and accelerated until 1749 (Figure 4.3). This led to a higher rate of inflation and of devaluation of the paper currency from 1744, when another war with France took place. Because of the high inflation we have had to take logarithms on the vertical axis of Figure 4.3. The real stock of money grew further and undervaluation was maintained except for 1748–49, when a small overvaluation developed. After the end of the war inflation ended in 1749–50 by a currency reform,

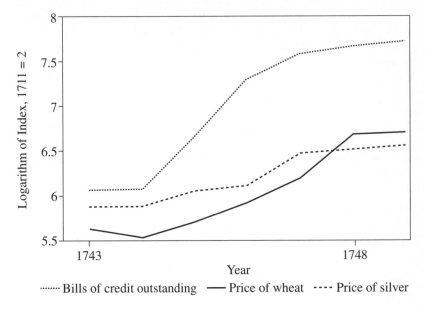

Note: Prices of silver for 1743 and 1748 interpolated in Figure 4.3

Sources: For wheat and silver prices in paper shillings: Cole (1938), Tables 36 and 38, pp. 117 and 119. For bills of credit outstanding: Brock (1975), Table II (revised), Part B, pp. 591–3

Figure 4.3   Paper money inflation in Massachusetts, 1744–1749

through which Massachusetts returned to a silver standard, and the bills of credit were redeemed at the rate of 7.5 to 1 of the new silver currency. As we will see later, it is not uncommon that undervaluation ends shortly before a currency reform, probably in expectation of the stabilisation connected with the latter.

4.4   INFLATION DURING THE AMERICAN WAR OF INDEPENDENCE

During the American War of Independence against Britain the war efforts of the emerging United States were to a large degree financed by issuing a new paper money, the Continental Currency. The new confederation was not able to introduce and to raise taxes, and its member states were not able or not willing to contribute more than limited financial assistance. Foreign credit was very limited and foreign subsidies, especially from the French ally, in no way sufficient. As a consequence a violent inflation soon set in, the highest which had until then occurred in history (Figures 4.4 and 4.5).

The *monthly* rate of inflation reached its maximum with 47.4 per cent in November 1779, which means that it approached closely the mark of 50 per cent that Cagan (1956) chose as a defining line for a hyperinflation and which was transgressed first during the French Revolution about 15 years later.

Again all measures taken by the Government to suppress the rise of prices and the devaluation of the Continental Currency were to no avail: *'Violent measures were continually resorted to, and stores closed, or pillaged: their owners fined or imprisoned. All things were done that an ill regulated patriot-ism could suggest. But in vain – every day the prospect grew more gloomy'* (Phillips 1972 [1865/66], p. 60).

In this case it is clear that the increase of the real stock of money at the beginning of the inflation was not caused by real growth of the economy, since

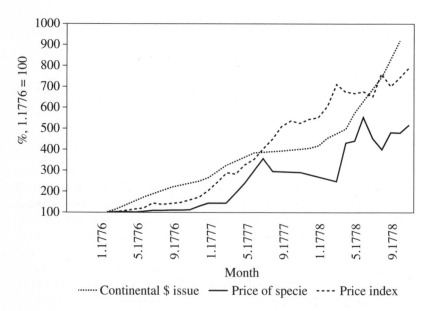

Note: The values of the total issue of Continental paper money and of the price index have been interpolated for a number of years.

Sources: For Continental paper money issued: Phillips (1976), vol. 2, p. 198. For the weighted arithmetic average price index of 15 commodities: Bezanson (1951), p. 344. For the price of specie in paper dollars: Bezanson (1951), pp. 26 and 65

Figure 4.4   American 'Continental' paper money inflation, 1.1776–10.1778

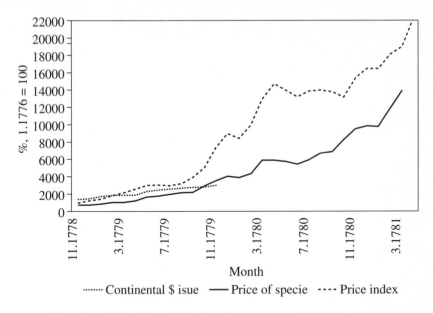

······· Continental $ isue ——— Price of specie ---- Price index

Note: The values of the total issue of Continental paper money and of the price index have been interpolated for a number of years

Sources: For Continental paper money issued: Phillips (1976), vol. 2, p. 198. For the weighted arithmetic average price index of 15 commodities: Bezanson (1951), p. 344. For the price of specie in paper dollars: Bezanson (1951), pp. 26 and 65

Figure 4.5   American 'Continental' paper money inflation, 11.1778–4.1781

the economy was hit hard by the war and by high inflation. On the other hand, note the later fall of the real stock of money when inflation accelerated, which occurred in 1777 to 1778, and again from 1779. This is a common trait of high and all hyperinflations. People try to spend their money as quickly as possible, since they expect that it will soon lose its value by future inflation. But since the paper money is not accepted in foreign countries, the nominal amount of it circulating cannot be reduced. As a consequence, prices rise more quickly than the supply of the paper money and the real stock of money decreases.

We see also from the figures that an over- instead of an undervaluation developed in this case. The price of specie (silver coins) is not rising as much as the price index. This is one of the few exceptions to the rule which has been formulated above that an inflation usually leads to an undervaluation of the respective currency. It seems that, in this as in other cases, the damage done by war to the production of goods and the impossibility of importing many foreign goods (because of the British blockade and occupation of the main harbours) were responsible for this exceptional development. For the latter made specie, that is currency which could be used for imports, less valuable. We will consider such exceptions again later.

In 1790 a currency reform was tried by introducing new bills which bore an interest of 5 per cent, which were promised to be redeemed together with the accrued interest in specie at the end of 1786. But people had lost confidence in the promises of the Continental Congress, even after the war had been won. As Josiah Quincy expressed it in a letter to Washington on 27 November, 1780:

> *Our new paper money issued by recommendation of Congress no sooner began to circulate, than two dollars of it were given for one hard one. To restore the credit of the paper, by making it a legal tender, by regulating acts, or by taxes, are political manoeuvres that have already proved abortive, . . . I am firmly of the opinion, . . ., that there never was a paper pound, a paper dollar, or a paper promise of any kind, that ever yet obtained a general currency but by force or fraud, generally by both.*
> (Letters to Washington, vol. III, p. 157, quoted from Phillip 1972, p. 171)

The new currency was rejected and substituted by specie and more stable state paper money. It died a natural death because of currency substitution, which took place as usual, given a now flexible exchange rate, the higher the rate of inflation and the longer it persisted:

> *The presence of specie had been for some time a common incident in the states; from the beginning of the year 1780 hard money, as it was called, had been plentiful. This was occasioned by large sums by various means coming from the English Army at New York, and spreading through the states; also, by large sums remitted by France to their army and navy here; also by large importations of hard money from the Havannah and other places abroad; so that hard money was never more easily collected than at that time.* (Webster's *Essays,* p. 75, quoted by Phillips 1972, p. 173)

As we will see later, during currency substitution at what are now flexible exchange rates, the opposite of Gresham's Law takes place, that is good money drives out the bad. Currency substitution usually becomes important only at rather high rates of inflation, but can then not be prevented by any government sanctions, and is a typical trait of every high inflation.

4.5   PAPER MONEY INFLATION DURING THE AMERICAN CIVIL WAR

When the American Civil War broke out, the Treasury of the Northern states saw itself obliged to have recourse to credit, but soon *'found it difficult to sell enough government securities to the public on the terms specified by Congress to meet the increased expenditures arising out of the war'* (Kindahl 1961, p. 31). As a consequence it sold bonds indirectly to the public with the help of a syndicate of banks. The banks had to transfer specie to the Government for the bonds they obtained and tried to sell. In December 1861, the price of Government bonds dropped sharply.

> *The banks were unwilling to sell the bonds at a lower price, and so did not replenish their [*specie*] reserves in that manner. A general fear of suspension [*of convertibility into gold*] led to a withdrawal of gold from the New York City bank by individuals and by the banks of the interior. The New York banks thereupon suspended specie payments on December 30. Soon after, the other banks in the country suspended specie payments also, and the government refused specie payments on its own Treasury demand notes, which had been in circulation since August, 1861.* (Kindahl 1961, p. 31)

Following these events the Government issued dollar notes, which were turned into legal tender. In this way the 'greenbacks', the dollars as we know them today, came into existence. Inflation and devaluation took off, and the smaller denomination silver coins soon disappeared from circulation, as had to be expected according to Gresham's Law. The further development is sketched in Figure 4.6. Note that the price of gold has to be considered as an exchange rate with Britain, which was on a gold standard. As in the other moderate inflations considered before, we observe again that the real stock of money increased, since it rose more strongly than the price level, which also lagged behind the exchange rate until 1864. In this year it became clear that the North would soon be victorious in the Civil War, and people could rightly expect an imminent end to additional issues of paper money to finance the war, an expectation which was fully justified in the course of the following years. It is thus not surprising that the exchange rate began to fall in 1864. An overvaluation developed, since the decrease of the price level was now slower than that of the exchange rate. In 1879 the price level finally about equalled the pre-war level reached by the exchange rate. Purchasing power had been re-established and gold convertibility was restored at the old parity (Kindahl 1961, Table 2, p. 36).

From Figure 4.6 we see however that the nominal money supply stayed at about 180 per cent, whereas the price level fell to 100 per cent in 1879, so that the real stock of money remained at 180 per cent. This fact can, however, be explained if economic growth is taken into account. According to figures calculated by Kuznets, Net National Product rose from 5822 million in 1869 to 7888 million current dollars in 1879 (Kindahl 1961, Table 3, p. 39). That is, it grew by 35.5 per cent. If we assume a similar growth for the eight years from 1861 to 1869, the index of the Net National Product would have grown to 171 per cent from 1861 to 1879, which would show that the real stock of money rose not much more than Net National Product.

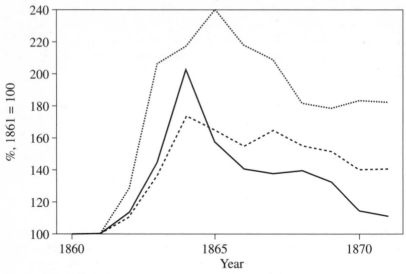

----- Circulating currency ——— Price of gold in 'greenbacks' ---- Cost of living

Sources: For currency in circulation and cost of living: *Historical Statistics of the U.S.*, Series X, Part 2, p. 993, and Series E, Part 1, p. 212, Department of Commerce, Bureau of the Census, Sept. 1975. For price of gold: Mitchell (1908), p. 4.

Figure 4.6   'Greenback' paper money inflation in the USA, 1861–1871

In concluding this section, it is worthwhile to mention two facts. First, California remained on the gold standard during the whole period, though it belonged to the Northern states. Second, inflation was much more pronounced in the Southern Confederate states of America, as should be expected. More interesting, an overvaluation developed there for the whole period, a fact which supports our hypothesis put forward in the last section, that interruption of foreign trade is responsible for an overvaluation during inflation, for the Southern harbours were successfully blockaded by the North during the Civil War.

4.6   CHINESE PAPER MONEY INFLATION UNDER THE MING REGIME[1]

It has already been mentioned that the Chinese were the first to invent paper, printing and thus before 1000 AD paper money. Their governments were the first to monopolise the issue of paper money and to create paper money inflation.

Chinese paper money probably first evolved from deposit certificates, the so-called *flying money*, which were introduced during the reign of Emperor Hsüan-tsung (806–820 AD) of the T'ang dynasty. But the deposit certificates themselves were in fact only like drafts used to 'send' money to other places and therefore not money in the proper sense (Chüan 1938, Liao 1941, Yang 1952). The first true paper money appeared as convertible private money before 1004 under the Northern Sung Dynasty. It was called *chiao-tzu* or *exchange medium* and was limited to Szechuan and thus not a national currency. Later on, the Government forbade the use of this private paper money after several runs on the issuing firms led to inconvertibility or bankruptcies.

But since a real need for paper money existed the chiao-tzu were issued again, but this time (1024) by a Government monopoly. This money later spread to other Chinese provinces. In the beginning the issue of this state paper money was strictly limited and official reserves were sufficient to maintain convertibility into the copper coins used as commodity money. But from 1072 the Government issued more and more paper money to finance its budget deficit. Inconvertibility and inflation were the consequence. The Chinese were thus the first in history to suffer from paper money inflation (Liao 1941, Yang 1952).

From then on, nearly every Chinese dynasty up to the Ming began by issuing some stable and convertible paper money and ended with pronounced inflation caused by circulating ever increasing amounts of paper notes to finance budget deficits (Tullock 1957, Liao 1941, Yang 1952; for an econometric study of developments under the Southern Sung along the lines of Cagan (1956) see Lui (1983)). The inflationary cycle ended in most cases when, with flexible exchange rates to copper and (or) silver (in the form of bullion), this good money had driven out the bad paper money, similar to the fate of the Continental Currency during the American War of Independence. This process of currency substitution was, however, not completed under the Northern and Southern Sung dynasties, since they were conquered before that by the Nu-chen Tartars establishing the Chin dynasty in Northern China in 1127 and the Mongols occupying South China in 1276, respectively (Gernet, 1972). It seems also that the Northern Sung succeeded with a currency reform in stabilising their money shortly before their downfall (Liao 1941, p. 186). Whether this would have been a permanent success must remain open to question.

During the last years of the Mongol (Yüan) dynasty, paper money inflation accelerated and it seems that the public repudiated the notes:

In the capital paper money was only calculated in units of ten ting (= 500 kuan), [2] *and for this one could not even get 50 liters (a tou) of millet. Moreover, the whole exchange of goods for the paper money stapled at government agencies and by private persons came to a total halt, so that people considered it to be worthless paper and the government household soon dried up.* (Yüan-shih, History of the Yüan, chapter 97, 3a seq.; quoted and translated from Franke (1949), p. 96)

From this quotation it seems that the paper money was driven out by barter and (or) good copper money. The latter interpretation is supported by the establishment of copper mints in 1351, though they were abolished again in 1354. But Franke adds (p. 100):

These very ephemeral issues of money [by the leaders of the uprisings against the Mongols] *would be unimportant if they all had not had one common characteristic: in all cases they speak of metallic and not of paper money. This amounts to a clear hint that a return to a metallic currency was more popular than a continuation of the badly reputed Mongolian paper money regime.*

As far as inflation is concerned, the available data are very rudimentary (Franke, pp. 144–55). Moreover, they often refer to prices officially fixed by the Government and not to market prices. Still *'we can observe for grain an increase of prices by a factor of 25 to 50 or more between 1261 and 1355, depending on the local supply situation'* (Franke, p. 148). Salt prices increased by a factor of 55 to 60 between 1261 and 1343 (p. 149). And whereas in 1309 the official price for one pound of salt was 0.25 kuan tshung-t'ung paper money, it rose to more than 1 kuan in 1343.

It seems, therefore, that only the Mongol (Yüan) dynasty (Franke 1949) and the Ming dynasty (see below) saw a complete currency substitution of their bad paper monies by metallic money. In the later Ming dynasty (until 1644) no paper money circulated. The same was true for most of the rule of the Mandchu (Tsing) dynasty which held sway until 1852.

In 1368 the Mongols had finally been defeated by Chinese revolutionary forces and power been consolidated by one of the military leaders, who made himself Emperor under the name of Hung-wu (1368–1398) and founded the Ming dynasty (1368–1643).

Given the bad experience of the population with paper money inflation and the repudiation of paper notes, it is perhaps not surprising that the Ming regime only ordered the minting of copper coins in 1368, whose face value corresponded to the value of the metal. But in 1375 the Ming Government also began to issue paper notes in denominations of 1 kuan = 1000 cash, 500, 300, 200 and 100 cash (Liao 1941, Li 1956; a reproduction of a 1 kuan note of the Ming can be seen in Deutsche Bundesbank 1971).

One string (kuan) in paper currency was worth 1000 copper cash, or 1 tael of silver; 4 strings were equal to one ounce[3] of gold. People were forbidden to use gold, silver or goods as the media of exchange, but the exchange of gold or silver for paper notes was allowed. In the collection of commercial taxes both copper and paper currencies were used; they were paid 30 per cent in copper cash and 70 per cent in paper notes. For amounts less than 100 cash, however, copper was used exclusively. (Li, p. 283)

From this it follows that gold and silver were convertible at fixed parities into paper notes, but this does not imply that paper notes were convertible at the fixed parities into gold and silver bars or into copper coins. Thus Li (p. 284) states that *'the paper currency . . . was not limited in amount by the currency regulations, and was not convertible.'* But though the first statement is obviously true, the second may not be quite correct for the beginning of paper note issue. For 70 per cent of commercial taxes could be paid in paper notes at the parity of 1 kuan paper money = 1 kuan string of copper coins = 1000 cash copper coins. Land taxes, too, could be partially paid in paper notes at the official parities with copper coins or silver (Li, 1941, p. 206). Thus the Government may well have thought that these parities could be maintained without a monetary authority being obliged to exchange paper notes into copper coins, silver or gold at the parities (Huang 1974, p. 69). Otherwise the fixing of parities would not make sense. We may in fact speak of a limited convertibility for tax purposes. On the other hand, it is obvious that such a limited convertibility could not be maintained when too many paper notes were issued to cover the budget deficit. Unfortunately nothing is reported by the authors mentioned above about the years immediately after 1375, since the next facts given refer to 1385 and 1390. It may well be that this shows that everything was 'normal' for a few years, in other words that the public accepted the paper money to build up their optimal portfolios of copper coins and paper notes and that no immediate inflationary pressure resulted. But of course we cannot know for certain.

There is, however, some other evidence which seems to support our hypothesis that the parity with copper money was maintained during the first years of paper money circulation. According to Li (1956, p. 284) *'There was a steady increase in the amount of paper notes issued, while the supplementary coins, being a good commodity with real value, were driven off the market.'*

It follows that Gresham's Law[4] that bad drives out good money was at work, which presupposes, as is well known, a fixed exchange rate (Bernholz and Gersbach 1992), here between paper and copper money. From this it can be concluded that a fixed parity must have been maintained in the early years of the Ming inflationary cycle. But this would suggest that tax-based convertibility was working during the first years of paper money. We have just mentioned that Gresham's Law was at work during this time, since the bad paper notes drove the good copper coins off the market. Li (1956, p. 289) also quotes from an Edict to the Board of Finance from 1394: *'Those who dare clandestinely use* [copper coins] *or bury them shall be convicted.'* The latter obviously means that these coins were withdrawn from circulation and hoarded by people.

Finally, Huang (1974, p. 76) states that *'Moreover a large proportion of the coins minted in the early Ming circulated overseas.'* Huang seems to attribute this fact mainly to Cheng Ho's naval expeditions of the 15th century and to the amounts of copper coins granted to foreign emissaries. But this must only have accounted for part of the outflow, because of the general validity of Gresham's Law and the outflow to be expected already during the early years of the inflation.

Given the huge size of the Chinese empire and the underdeveloped communication and transportation system compared to modern times, it had to be expected that the periods in which the exchange rates or parities were still fixed and when this was no longer the case would overlap during the Ming inflationary experience. For under such conditions, the Government would often not be able to enforce the parities of paper notes with copper coins, gold and silver in certain regions of the empire even with high fines and penalties. And in fact in 1394 the Government issued the following edict (quoted from Li 1956, p. 289):

> *Edict to the Board of Finance: Let the proper government agencies recall all* [copper] *cash into the government and exchange it with the same amount of paper currency; copper coins should henceforth be banned from circulation. All copper coins owned by soldiers, civilians and merchants must be delivered to the government within half a month. Those who dare clandestinely use or bury them shall be convicted.*

This probably shows that former efforts of the Government to prevent a premium on copper coins (compared to the parity) and (or) the quotation and appreciation of higher prices in paper notes than in copper coins had been in vain. Otherwise the complete banning of copper coins could not be understood.

Also, though the price data gathered by the authors mentioned above from the original sources are very scanty, they seem to show that inflation must already have begun around 1380 and that at least the silver and copper coin parities of paper notes must have broken down before 1390 (Table 4.1). In spite of the older prohibition (of 1375) to use (unminted) gold and silver as means of payment, they were, because of the inflation in terms of paper money and the recent edict banning copper coins, more and more substituted for paper notes in market transactions. Thus their use was again strictly forbidden in 1397 and this regulation was strengthened in 1403 (Liao 1941,

Table 4.1   Commodity, precious metal and copper prices in Ming China in terms of notes of paper money (kuan)

Year	Gold		Silver		Copper coins		Copper refined		Rice		Grain	
	1 Liang	Index	1 Liang	Index	1 Kuan	Index	1 Catty	Index	1 Tan	Index	1 Picul	Index
1375	1	100	1	100	1	100	0.16	100	1	100	1 (6)	100
1385			3 (3)	300							2.5	250
1386									2.5	250		
1390			5 (3)	500							4	400
1393					6.31	631						
1402 (1)	400 (2)	10 000	80 (2)	8 000	80 (2)	8 000	4 (2)	2 500	25 (2)	2 500	25 (2)	2 500
1404											30 (2)	3 000
1407	400	10 000	80	8 000								
1403/24	400	10 000	83.33	8 333					25 (4)	2 500		
1425											55 (7)	5 500
1426	8 000	200 000	2 000	200 000								
1432									15 (5)	1 500		
1436			1 000	100 000								
1440s			500	50 000								
1448					500	50 000						
1488			333 (2)	33 300								
1488/1505			750	75 000								

Notes:

(1) The figures for 1402 are from a table published by Torao (1903) and contained in Li (1956), who discusses it extensively. The date to which the table refers is not known. According to Li (p. 288), a date of about 1407 is probable. Comparing the figure for grain for 1404 with that in the table, it seems probable that the date should be earlier than 1404 given inflation. Thus we have inserted 1402.

(2) Officially fixed price, with market price probably much higher.

(3) Liao (1941, p. 205) writes: 'Not long afterwards (i.e., after 1375) paper money devalued to 3 to 5 kuan per liang silver.' We have ventured to translate this statement into two entries of 3 and 5 kuan, respectively, for 1385 and 1390, which seemed best to correspond to 6.31 kuan paper notes for 1 kuan copper coins in 1393, and to 2.5 kuan for one picul of grain in 1385.

(4) Average of 20–30.

(5) Officially fixed price for calculating salaries of Government employees. The market price was probably much higher.

(6) Assumed from the fact that the officially fixed price in 1390 was still 1 kuan, whereas the market price amounted to 4 kuan per picul grain.

(7) Average of 40–70.

Sources: Liao (1941), Li (1956) and Huang (1974)

p. 204). The edict of 1403 states:*'The use of gold or silver as the medium of exchange is prohibited. Those transgressing against this shall be adjudged guilty of a major crime. Anyone who provides information leading to their capture shall be rewarded with the gold or silver involved in the case'* (Li 1956, p. 289).

That the penalties were severe is shown by an order of 1404 that the death sentences of those convicted of the infraction of this law should be commuted to exiling them and their whole families to modern Jehol (Li, p. 285).

As can be seen from Table 4.1, inflation went on in spite of these drastic measures. Moreover, it even accelerated, since more and more paper notes were issued (Huang 1974, p. 70). As a consequence, gold, silver and barter were mainly used for transactions in the market about 1425 (Liao 1941, p. 205; Huang 1974, p. 70). In a vain effort to prevent this substitution of good money[5] and of commodities for paper notes, a Government order ruled as follows in 1428:

> *Those who refuse to use the paper notes shall be fined 1000 strings* [kuan] *for every string refused. The relatives, neighbours and neighbourhood heads who are cognisant of these matters but do not report them shall be fined 100 strings for every string so refused. Those who clandestinely carry on business behind closed doors, and those who raise commodity prices, shall be fined 10,000 strings; the relatives, neighbours and neighbourhood heads who conceal such information shall be fined 1000 strings.* (Li 1956, p. 289)

Besides such efforts the Government introduced in 1425 shop franchise fees levied on shopkeepers, which had to be paid in paper money. In 1429 the rates of these levies were increased five-fold and their scope widened. The idea was to decrease the amount of paper notes circulating. A report at the year-end of 1431 showed that 200 million kuan in paper notes had been collected. In 1433 the revenue increased to 288 million kuan. The deflationary effort seemed to be successful and the Emperor declared: *'Now both within and outside the capital paper money is circulating well'* and ordered a reduction of the tax rates to about one third. Further reductions reduced the rates until 1442 to 10 per cent of those of 1429 (Huang 1974, p. 71).

It should be mentioned that in 1404 a salt tax to be paid fully in paper had been introduced with the same purpose (Huang, p. 70; Liao 1941, p. 206). The land tax was also to be paid in paper notes from 1407 (Liao, p. 206). As Huang puts it (p. 71): *'Clearly a golden opportunity for currency reform presented itself at this point'* in 1433. But the Government did not seize the opportunity, issued again more and more paper notes to cover the budget deficit, and thus prepared the ground for the completion of the substitution of the bad paper money by silver bars and copper.

. . . by 1448 the use of copper coins had become prevalent, the rate of exchange being two copper cash for one string. Palace guards were therefore sent to inspect the markets in the capital; anyone found using copper cash in the transactions was fined ten times [the sum involved in the original transaction]. Actually, however, these restrictions were not effective. On the contrary, most business transactions were conducted with silver or copper currency. (Li 1956, p. 289)

Already in 1435/36 the Government had legalised the use of copper coins, a decree which was interpreted by the population as legalising the use of silver and gold payments, too (Huang 1976, p. 72; Li 1941, p. 205). Twelve years later this edict was however rescinded (Li, p. 205). In 1436 the court authorised the collection of land taxes in silver (Huang, p. 72).

After the last strong effort in 1448 to enforce the sole circulation of paper money had been abolished, the prohibitions on the use of silver and copper coins were rescinded in 1450 (Huang, p. 76). The commutation of taxes into silver or copper coins proceeded more slowly, though it was absolutely necessary to bring up Government revenues again. The household salt tax was commuted in 1468 to silver or copper cash. But only after 1488 did the commutation of taxes into silver become the usual practice (Li 1956, pp. 290f.). The Government went on to pay part of the salaries of its officials in paper money for about a hundred years after paper money had fallen into disuse, though taxes were seldom collected in paper notes. *'Such whittling away of official salaries in effect compelled the officials to engage in corrupt practices in order to maintain themselves'* (Li, p. 292).

One other characteristic of inflations mentioned above for other historical cases can also be documented for the Ming dynasty inflation. In fact, the evidence for an undervaluation of paper money in terms of copper coins, silver and gold is rather strong. From Table 4.1 we can see that at least from 1402 (that is from the table presented by Torao (1903), the date of which cannot be exactly determined, see Note (1) to Table 4.1) the prices of gold, silver and copper coins had moved well ahead of those of rice, grain and, importantly, of refined copper (bars). But the prices of the former have to be considered to be exchange rates, for gold and especially silver bars and copper coins were used as alternative means of payment and could also be used for payments in foreign countries. Quantitatively, the undervaluation was also quite pronounced (Figure 4.7).

Obviously, if one takes the 1402 exchange rate for copper kuan and transforms the prices of goods expressed in paper notes to the same expressed in silver or copper coins, one gets very low prices by long-term historical standards. This has been done by Li (1956) in the table republished (pp. 285–6) by him for 29 goods (of which only three are contained in our Table 4.1). He concludes (p. 286):

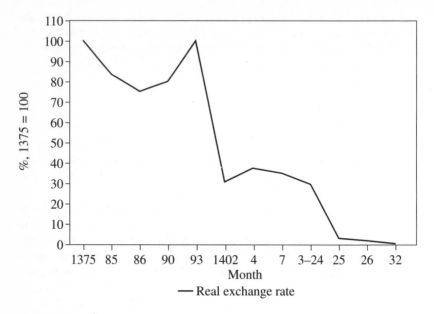

Note: Because of the scarcity of data, the indices for rice and grain, and those for gold, silver and copper have had to be combined into two indices. The real exchange rate was obtained by dividing the former index through the latter and multiplying by 100 to get an expression in per cent. * Formally, the real exchange rate is defined as: P/(wP*).

Sources: See Table 4.1

*Figure 4.7   Ming inflation in China, 1375–1432 (rice and grain
              price/indices)/(silver and copper coin price indices)*

> *According to the above table, one bolt of cotton cloth cost only 250 copper cash or
> 0.25 tael of silver; one tan of rice, only 312.5 copper cash or 0.3125 tael of silver;
> and one catty of beef, only 125 copper cash or 0.125 tael of silver. These figures
> would seem to be unreasonably low, even for the old days of lower costs of living.
> Since price fluctuations had become erratic, however, the people did not at all feel
> that the cost of living was low. Those who depended on wages for a living found that
> their wages did not increase as rapidly as the prices of things they had to buy with
> depreciated paper currency. Those whose income was based on the sale of products
> were also dissatisfied at receiving payment in depreciated currency.*

These remarks confirm the presence of undervaluation, though the author did
not quite understand the phenomenon. Note also that even in modern high
inflations, wages usually lag behind the increase of the price level.

Another remark by Li (pp. 287ff.) also refers to undervaluation. It shows at
the same time that officials tried to maintain the old official parities: '*The*

merchants calculated the prices in terms of hard currency and invariably felt that the commodity prices were too low; the officials calculated in terms of paper notes, and invariably felt that prices were too high. Hence commodity prices became a matter of contention between officials and merchants.'

4.7 CONCLUSIONS

1. During inflation an undervaluation of the paper money develops compared to gold, silver or copper specie or to more stable paper money. This seems however not to be true in cases in which the free exchange of goods and services with foreign countries is interrupted.
2. An increase of the money supply first stimulates economic activity, whereas price increases lag. On the other hand, if the rate of growth of the money is substantially diminished or even becomes negative, then depressive consequences are felt before the price level recedes. The exchange rate moves down more quickly and strongly than prices. An overvaluation of the currency tends to develop.
3. As has been shown for the case of Sweden, the developments just sketched lead to political reactions which may even strengthen or bring about sequences of events.
4. If a moderate inflation turns into a high inflation, economic activity is adversely affected.
5. Wage increases usually lag behind the rise of the price level.
6. Currency substitution plays an important role if inflation is progressing, and the fixed exchange rate can no longer be maintained in spite of the most severe sanctions against asking different rates. If inflation becomes high enough and lasts for some time, this will lead to an ever more far-reaching substitution of the unstable by stable money (Thiers' Law), that is by specie, or (and) as in the case of the American War of Independence, by more stable (state) paper money. Finally the bad money will be perfectly driven out of circulation, and the unstable money become worthless.

From the above we can construct the picture of a full inflationary cycle. First paper money with no intrinsic value is introduced. This money is initially fully convertible at a fixed rate, for instance one to one, into metallic currency whose intrinsic value corresponds to its face value. These paper notes are welcome to most people because they are not as heavy and are easier to store and to transport (first phase). But with more and more of the paper money issued, convertibility becomes difficult, since official reserves dwindle (second phase), and may no longer be expected. Then the bad money begins to drive out the good (third phase). Finally, when just about all the good money has vanished, the exchange rate can no longer be kept fixed, and the good money drives out the bad.

NOTES

1. Section 4.6 is based mainly on Bernholz, Peter (1997), 'Paper Money Inflation, Gresham's Law and Exchange Rates in Ming China', *Kredit und Kapital*, 30 (1), 35–51.The article was written when I was a guest of the International Centre for Economic Research, Australian National University, Canberra. I am grateful to the Centre for their support. I would like to thank Igor de Rachewiltz for his help in finding some of the literature used.
2. Originally, when in 1260 the chung-t'ung yüan pao-ch'ao paper money was introduced by the Government of Emperor Kublai Khan, one kuan was set equal to one kuan (string) of 1000 cash copper coins.
3. Li (1956) translates 'liang' for silver with 'tael', but for gold with 'ounce' (p. 283, footnote).
4. It seems that Sir Thomas Gresham did not formulate 'Gresham's Law' and that it had already been known before him. The term 'Gresham's Law' was probably coined by MacLeod. For evidence, see Jastrow (1923, 45–50) and for a formal description of Gresham's Law, Bernholz and Gersbach (1992).
5. Here we consider unminted gold and silver as a primitive form of money. This is justified, since they were used as means of payment and because the paper money was later, to a large extent, driven out rather by silver bars than by copper coins.

REFERENCES

Amark, Karl (1921), 'En Svensk Prishistorisk Studie', *Ekonomisk Tidskrift* Vol. 23, 1–24.

Bernholz, Peter and Gersbach, Hans (1992), 'Gresham's Law: Theory', in Peter Newman, Murray Milgate and John Eatwell (eds), *The New Palgrave Dictionary of Money and Finance*, Vol. 2, London: Macmillan, pp. 286–8.

Bezanson, Anne (1951), *Prices and Inflation During the American Revolution, Pennsylvania, 1770–1790*, Philadelphia: University of Pennsylvania Press.

Brock, Leslie V. (1975), *The Currency of the American Colonies 1700–1764*, New York: Arno Press.

Buesch, Johann Georg (1800), *Schriften ueber Staatswirtschaft und Handlung*, 3. Teil, Hamburg: B.G. Hoffmann.

Cagan, Philip (1956), 'The Monetary Dynamics of Hyperinflation', in Milton Friedman (ed.), *Studies in the Quantity Theory of Money*, Chicago: University of Chicago Press.

Ch'üan, Han-shêng (1938), 'The Inflation at the End of the Sung Dynasty and Its Effects on Prices', *Bulletin of the Institute of History and Philology*, Academica Sinica, 10, 193–222.

Cole, Arthur H. (1938), *Wholesale Commodity Prices in the United States 1700–1861*, Cambridge, Mass.: Harvard University Press.

Deutsche Bundesbank (1971), *Fruehzeit des Papiergeldes*, Frankfurt/Main.

Eagley, Robert V. (ed. and trans.) (1971), *The Swedish Bullionist Controversy. P.N. Christiernin's Lectures on the High Price of Foreign Exchange in Sweden (1761)*, Philadelphia: American Philosophical Society.

Franke, Herbert (1949), *Geld und Wirtschaft in China unter der Mongolen-Herrschaft*, Leipzig: Otto Harassowitz.

Gernet, Jacques (1972), *Le Monde Chinois*, Paris: Armand Colin.

Hamilton, Earl J. (1936/37), 'Prices and Wages at Paris Under John Law's System', *Journal of Economics*, LI, Reprint 1964, 42–70.

Huang, Ray (1974), *Taxation and Government Finance in Sixteenth-Century Ming China*, Cambridge: Cambridge University Press.

Jastrow, I. (1923), *Textbuch*, Vol. 4: *Geld und Kredit*, Berlin, 5th ed.

Joerberg, Lennart (1972), *A History of Prices in Sweden, 1732–1914*, Lund: CWK Gleerup.

Kindahl, J.K. (1961), 'Economic Factors in Specie Resumption: The U.S., 1865–1869', *Journal of Political Economy*, 59, 30–48.

Li, Chien-Nung (1956), 'Price Control and Paper Money in Ming', in Zen Sun E-Tu and John de Francis (eds), *Chinese Social History. Translations of Selected Studies*, Washington, DC: American Council of Learned Societies.

Liao, Bao-Seing (1941), 'Die Geschichte des Chinesischen Geldes', *Sinica*, 16, 162–216.

Luethy, Herbert (1959), *La Banque Protestante en France de la Révocation de l'Edict de Nantes a la Révolution*, Ecole Politique des Hautes Etudes, Centre de Recherches Historiques, Affaires et Gens d'Affaires, XIX, Paris: SEVPEN.

Lui, Francis T. (1983), 'Cagan's Hypothesis and the First Nationwide Inflation of Paper Money in World History', *Journal of Political Economy*, 91(6), 1067–74.

Milgate, Murray and Eatwell, John (eds), *The New Palgrave Dictionary of Money and Finance*, London: The Macmillan Press, pp. 286–8.

Mitchell, Wesley C. (1908), *Gold, Prices and Wages under the Greenback Standard*, Berkeley: University of California Press.

Phillips, Henry Jr. ([1865/66], 1972), *Continental Paper Money. An Historical Research*, Clifton: Augustus M. Kelley.

Sveriges Riksbank (1931), *Sveriges Riksbank, 1668–1924*, Stockholm.

Tanzi, V. (1977), 'Inflation, Lags in Collection and the Real Value of Tax Revenues', *IMF Staff Papers*, 24, 154–67.

Torao, Asai (1903), *History of Chinese Laws and Institutions*.

Tullock, Gordon (1952), 'Paper Money – A Cycle in Cathay', *The Economic History Review*, Second Series, 9, 393–407.

Yang, Lien-shêng (1952), *Money and Credit in China: A Short History*, Cambridge, Mass.: Harvard University Press.

5. Characteristics of hyperinflations

INTRODUCTION

In the last chapter we analysed the characteristics of a number of moderate inflations under paper money standards. In all these cases it was advantageous that the main trading partners enjoyed metallic monetary regimes, so that the situation was closer to an experiment than in the time after 1914/1930 when all countries had moved to discretionary monetary regimes. We will later discuss a few such cases of moderate inflations, when we turn to examine the conditions under which successfully stabilising monetary reforms can be expected. In the present chapter, however, we will analyse only hyperinflations, for the following reasons. First, whereas it is still possible to enumerate all paper money inflations which occurred before 1914, when most countries were still on a metallic standard, this is no longer true for all such cases since that date. But the number of hyperinflations which have occurred can still be counted (see Table 2.1). Second, and more important, hyperinflations make it easier to find out the characteristics of high inflations because of their extreme nature.

> *I have lost all feeling for numbers* [during the last phase of the German hyperinflation]. *Yesterday* [8 October 1923] *we paid for the cinema together with the fare for the tram 104 million* [marks]. ... *today is again a last 'cheap day' for stamps (today still 2 million for a long distance letter, tomorrow 5)* (p. 752). *The dollar jumps daily by billions – on Saturday by 17* [20 October] *–, prices follow, a loaf of bread costs now 1.5 billion* (p. 753).
>
> *Yesterday* [Tuesday, 6 November 1923] *we experienced our wildest day concerning money. On Monday morning I had received about 870 billion – who still counts figures below 100? –* [as part of my salary], *received yesterday the same amount and the notice that I would get double the sum today. I had given the order to sell 3 pre-emptive rights for stocks in Mittelsprit. ... I received of this 4 billion 3.4 after*

the fees and a percentage for speedy payment had been deducted.

Somewhat more than 4 billion had thus to be spent at once. The dollar had been kept artificially at 420 million, abroad the mark stood two to three times lower. At noon a new rate is quoted, to which all shops adapt immediately. I went home, dragged Eva along with me, and we hurried through the shops, searching for goods and comparing prices.

... And always one stands in line [16 November] *for several hours at the cashier's office* [to get part of the salary]. *When the money has finally arrived, it has to be spent breathlessly before finally the next gold mark rate* [the price of a mark of 1914 calculated by using the dollar exchange rate] *is quoted* (p. 758). (Victor Klemperer, Professor of Romance Languages at Dresden University, 1996; my translation, as of all passages quoted subsequently)

Before turning to the qualitative characteristics of hyperinflations let us recall that, though they are all extreme, they differ much in their speed. The worst, Hungary II and Serbia, showed maximal monthly rates of inflation which surpass any understanding (Table 2.1). To comprehend them, weekly or even daily rates of inflation have to be calculated and the latter rose during the worst weeks to more than 300 per cent. The third largest hyperinflation occurred in Germany, where the highest monthly figure reported was 29 526 per cent. By contrast the smallest hyperinflations in Belarus, Kazakhstan and Yugoslavia showed 'only' maximal monthly rates between 50 and 60 per cent.

In the last chapter we studied the development of inflation during the American War of Independence as a case nearly approaching hyperinflation. In this chapter we begin by analysing whether the French hyperinflation during the Revolution, which was the first hyperinflation in history, shows similar characteristics. This inflation, moreover, is the only hyperinflation in history during a time when most other countries were still on a silver or gold standard (Britain suspended convertibility only in 1797).

After this discussion of the first hyperinflation in history a different approach will be taken, when we begin to compare several hyperinflations in the following sections, to see whether they all show similar characteristics. This approach recommends itself to find out general traits, and because it would be boring to study in detail all single cases and then to compare them.

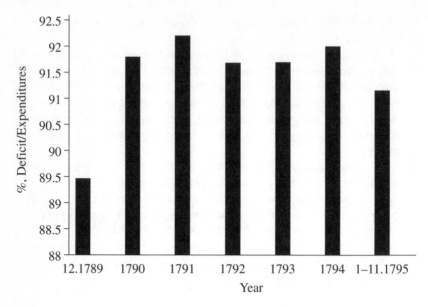

Source: Harris (1930), p. 51

Figure 5.1   French hyperinflation, 1789–1795, deficit as % of expenditures

5.1   SOME CHARACTERISTICS OF THE FRENCH HYPERINFLATION

During the French Revolution beginning in 1789 it soon became impossible to cover the financial requirements of the state, including the revolutionary wars, from ordinary revenues, especially since the Assemblée Nationale had lowered the taxes which were perceived by the population as repressive. To finance the budget deficit (Figure 5.1) the new authorities soon issued the *assignats*, which were constructed to be guaranteed by land, since their holders could later use them to acquire former Church property which had been nationalised. These *assignats* could first only be transferred through a formal endorsement, like drafts. They still mentioned the King and were denominated in *livres* which had until then only been a money of account, that is they had never circulated as currency before.

Soon more and more *assignats* were issued, turned into bearer papers, the royal name on them was removed and their denomination changed to francs (1 franc = 1 livre). Devaluation of the currency and inflation began (Figures 5.2 and 5.3).

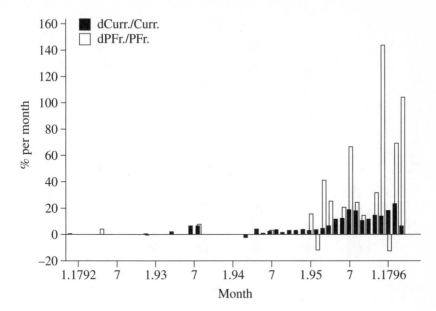

Sources: Falkner (1924), Harris (1930)

Figure 5.2   *French hyperinflation, 12.1791–3.1796: monthly rates of inflation and of growth of currency in circulation*

As shown in Figure 5.2 inflation began slowly but then speeded up considerably. Until 1791 inflationary tendencies were weak. The reason for this has to be sought in the working of Gresham's Law. For the French money supply probably did not increase much until the bad money, the *assignats*, had driven out the good money, mostly silver coins. Only then could inflation begin in earnest and even the most severe penalties and fines could not prevent an increase of the premium on silver, and thus a rise of the exchange rate. Even a law decreed by the Convention Nationale in August 1793, that

> *Each Frenchman convicted of having refused the payment of* assignat *money, or to have it taken or given at a discount, will be fined 3000 livres and be imprisoned for six months the first time. In case of reversion the fine will be doubled and he will be condemned to 20 years in prison in chains.* (Jastrow 1923, p. 67, my translation)

could not halt this process. Similarly, another law decreed in May 1794 proved ineffective, which was directed *'against all those who are found guilty of having bought or sold specie, to have paid, fixed or proposed different prices for payment in specie and* assignats, *or to have asked in which money payment*

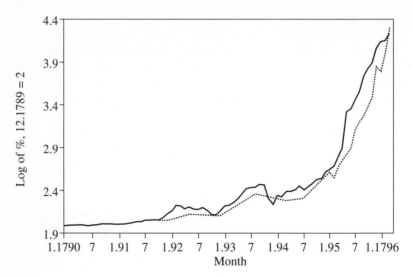

Sources: For German prices: Jacobs and Richter (1935); for French prices and paper money (currency): Falkner (1924), Harris (1930); for exchange rates: Bailleul (1797)

Figure 5.3   *French hyperinflation: development of exchange rate (upper line) on exchange rate for Basle currency and of price level relative to German price level*

should be received before concluding or finishing a transaction' (Jastrow 1923, p. 70, my translation).

Let us check next whether the undervaluation of the currency occurred in the French case, too. As can be seen from Figure 5.3, this was indeed the case. From 1792 the exchange rate moved ahead of the price level. The differences seem to be smaller in the figure than they were in reality, since logarithms have had to be taken. Only at the very end of the hyperinflation did the price level surpass the exchange rate. It is also important to note that this time we have not, as in the cases discussed before, assumed the foreign price level as given. For because of the revolutionary wars in which several European countries, among them Austria and Prussia, were involved, it could not be assumed that their price level would remain rather stable. Consequently in Figure 5.3 the French has been divided by the German price level to get the values for P/P*.

Next, the development of the real stock of currency circulating has to be analysed (Figure 5.4). As can be seen, it first increased in 1793 above normal and afterwards decreased all the time, until it had reached an insignificant level. As we will see, this is typical for all hyperinflations, and is also related to currency substitution, which sets in when inflation accelerates. Since this process threatened French monetary sovereignty, the authorities tried to mend the situation by a currency reform in 1796, which replaced the *assignat* with the *mandat* at a rate of 30:1. But this effort did not succeed, and the bad paper money was totally driven out of circulation by good specie: *'In all the markets nothing was to be seen but gold and silver, and the wages of the lower classes were paid in no other medium. One would have imagined that there was no paper in France. The* mandats *were in the hands of speculators only . . . '*. (Thiers, 1840, p. 111)

5.2 HYPERINFLATIONS ARE CAUSED BY GOVERNMENT BUDGET DEFICITS

In this section it will be demonstrated by looking at 12 hyperinflations that they have all been caused by the financing of huge public budget deficits

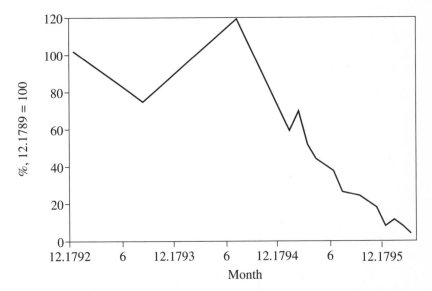

Notes: Falkner estimates the normal amount of currency in circulation on the eve of the Revolution (specie) at 2–2.5 billion *livres*. We have thus inserted 2.25 billion as 100 per cent for Dec. 1789. To calculate currency in circulation for the later months, we have assumed that the *assignats* first drove out the good money, as has to be expected from Gresham's Law. Total circulation is thus set to have remained at 100 per cent until the paper money in circulation surpassed the above amount. After that the amount of paper money (*assignats*) has been taken as currency in circulation.

Sources: For French prices see Figure 5.2. For currency in circulation: Falkner (1924)

Figure 5.4   French hyperinflation: real stock of money (currency in circulation/price level)

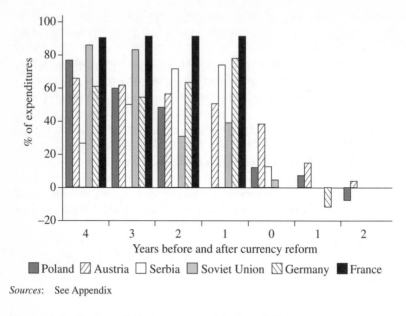

Sources: See Appendix

Figure 5.5   Six hyperinflations: annual budget deficits

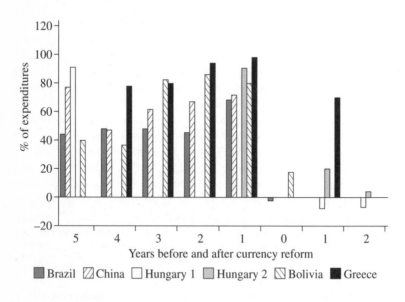

Sources: See Appendix

Figure 5.6   Six hyperinflations: annual budget deficits

through money creation. To demonstrate this we present the evidence for twelve of the twenty-nine cases of hyperinflation (Table 2.1) in Figures 5.5 and 5.6.

To make the different cases comparable the years in which the deficits occurred have been normalised with respect to the year in which a currency reform was attempted. The reforms were successful, except in the French and the Greek cases. The former has already been described. The latter, which took place at the end of 1944, did not succeed, as already suggested by the big budget deficit of the year following the reform. Another, this time successful reform, was then undertaken in 1946. The figures demonstrate clearly that deficits amounting to 40 per cent or more of expenditures cannot be maintained. They lead to high and hyperinflations, reforms stabilising the value of money or in total currency substitution leading to the same result.

It is also interesting to see what budget deficits of this size mean, if they are expressed as a percentage of GNP or GDP. An idea about this has already been given concerning the budget deficits during the Bolivian hyperinflation in the 1980s (Figure 2.4). A similar picture emerges for the German hyperinflation of the 1920s (Figure 5.7). The examples of both Germany and Bolivia suggest that at least deficits of about 30 per cent or more of gross domestic product are not maintainable since they imply hyperinflations.

It has still to be shown that all hyperinflations (Table 2.1) have been connected with huge public budget deficits. In the following table this information has been summarised as far as the data are available (Table 5.1). As can be seen from the column referring to budget deficits, our hypothesis that in all cases of hyperinflation deficits amounting to more than 20 per cent of public expenditures are present, is confirmed for all cases except for Belarus, Turkmenistan, Poland 2 and Yugoslavia. Whereas the first three show deficits of between 5.87 and 12.04 per cent of expenditures, the budget figures for Yugoslavia even present a surplus (Table 8.5(b)). As will be argued below (Section 8.5), especially the case of Yugoslavia, but also those of the other countries is incredible. As a consequence we maintain the position that the huge budget deficits strongly suggest that the hyperinflations were caused by issuing money to finance them. There is, however, one other possible explanation, namely that the budget deficits were caused by inflation. And in fact, there is empirical evidence that budget deficits are increased because of high inflation (the so-called Tanzi (1977) effect, which had, however, already been stated by Bresciani-Turroni (1937, p. 66 ff.). Since government expenditures lag its tax and other revenues, the purchasing power of these revenues is diminished until they are spent, and this the more the higher the rate of inflation. As a consequence the real budget deficit grows, if the amount of real expenditures is maintained.

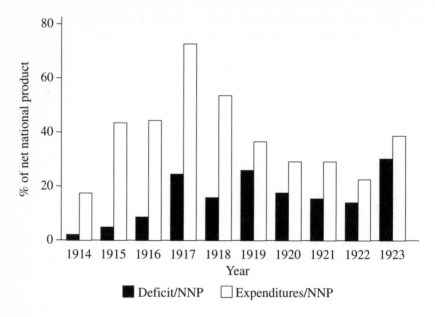

Sources: Budget figures for 1914–1919: Roesler (1957), pp. 195ff.; for 1920–1923: Statistisches Reichsamt (1924/1925), Deutschlands Wirtschaft, Waehrung und Finanzen (1923); for 1913 net national product: Hoffmann and Mueller (1959); for percentages of net national product of later years compared to 1913: Witt (1974), p. 424.

Figure 5.7   German hyperinflation, 1914–1923: expenditure and deficit of Reich as % of net national product (NNP)

It is possible to discriminate between these two explanations by analysing whether high budget deficits occurred long before high inflation occurred. This is clearly the case for the hyperinflations shown in Figures 5.1 and 5.5 to 5.7, as can be seen by comparing the respective years with those of the highest monthly inflations contained in Table 2.1. As a consequence, we draw the conclusion that the creation of money to finance a public budget deficit has been the reason for hyperinflations. To put this hypothesis into perspective, several comments are however necessary. First, one might believe that the budget deficits might also have been financed in the capital markets, so that money creation for this purpose was absent or rather limited. It is certainly true that part of the deficit was financed in this way in some of the cases. But in quite a number of them, like that of France, China, Georgia, Greece, Nicaragua, Serbia, the Ukraine, Zaire and Hungary 2 at the end of the Second World War, this option did not exist at all. And even in the remaining cases it is clear from the historical evidence that deficits of this magnitude could only be financed to a minor extent in the capital markets.

Table 5.1   Budget deficit, real stock of money and real exchange rate during hyperinflations

Country	Year(s)	Budget deficit/ expenditures	Real stock of money	Real exchange rate
Argentina	1989/90	+	+	+
Armenia	1993/94	+	+	+
Austria	1921/22	+	+	+
Azerbaijan	1991/94	+	+	+
Belarus	1999	−(+)	+	+
Bolivia	1984/86	+	+	+
Brazil	1989/90	+	+	+
Bulgaria	1979	+	+	−(OR)
China	1947/49	+	+	−(+)
Congo (Zaire)	1991/93	+	+	+
France	1789/96	+	+	+
Germany	1920/23	+	+	+
Georgia	1993/94	+	+	+
Greece	1942/45	+	+	+
Hungary 1	1923/24	+	+	+
Hungary 2	1945/46	+	+	+
Kazakhstan	1994	+	+	+
Kyrgyzstan	1992	+	+	+
Nicaragua	1986/89	+	+	(+/−)
Peru	1989	+	+	(+ BMR,−OR)
Poland 1	1921/24	+	+	+
Poland 2	1989/90	−(+)	+	+
Serbia	1992/94	+	+	+
Soviet Union	1922/24	+	+	−(+)
Taiwan	1945/49	+	+	−(+)
Tajikistan	1995	+	+	+
Turkmenistan	1995/96	−(+)	+	+
Ukraine	1993/94	+	+	+
Yugoslavia	1990	−(+)	+	+

Notes: A '+' means that the hypothesis concerning a budget deficit greater than 20 per cent of expenditures, that the real stock of money has declined way below normal, and that the real exchange rate shows an undervalutation, respectively, has been confirmed for the case. A '−' shows that the hypothesis has not been confirmed, and a '+' together with a '−' that the evidence is not clear.

BMR and OR mean that the black market and the official exchange rate have been used in calculating the real exchange rate: P/wP*.

Sources: See Appendix

Second, because of this conclusion, our hypothesis implies that hyperinflations have always been a monetary phenomenon. But this statement does not imply that the expansion of the money supply was the final reason for inflation. For such final reasons necessarily have to do with political or political-economic factors, since budget deficits occur because of real economic developments and especially political decisions. We will return to this point later.

5.3 REAL STOCK OF MONEY AND CURRENCY SUBSTITUTION

In this section we will analyse whether and how far the decrease of the real stock of the national currency is a general characteristic of hyperinflations. In doing so several hyperinflations will be bundled together (Figures 5.8 and 5.9). For this purpose the years before and after the occurrence of a successful or (in two cases, France and China) failed currency reform (denoted by the

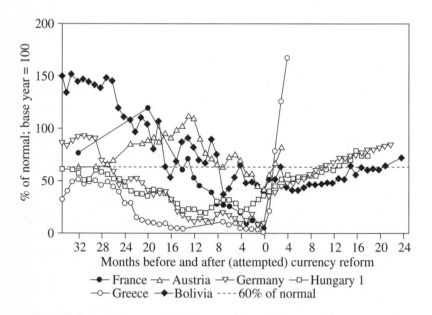

Sources: See Appendix

Figure 5.8   Real money stock during hyperinflation: six countries, 1790–1987

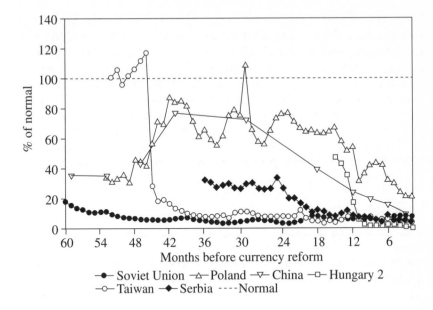

Sources: See Appendix

Figure 5.9 *Real money stock during hyperinflation: six countries,*
1917–1994

year 0) attempting to end the high inflation have been put on the horizontal
axis.

At the moment we are only considering the years before the currency
reform. The events after the reform will be discussed when such reforms are
analysed (Chapter 8). As can be seen from the figures, the real stock of the
national money fell below 'normal', that is 100 per cent, in all twelve cases,
and in most of them to very low or even negligible levels. Moreover, as can be
seen from Table 5.1, the hypothesis of a decreasing real stock of money during
hyperinflation is confirmed for all cases for which information is available. By
the 'normal' real stock of money we refer to its size in the year before the inflation began or when it had been very moderate.

An explanation of this fact has already been given. People and organisations want to rid themselves of the money before it has lost much of its
purchasing power. Since the economy as a whole, however, is swamped by
ever increasing amounts of it, and since foreigners prefer not to be paid with
it, prices rise more quickly than the money supply. In this way the real stock
of money, M/P, is reduced.

> *As a first sign of the distrust on the part of the population the coins vanished* [in Austria]*, for a piece of copper or nickel had at least some substantive value compared to printed paper. It is true that the state drove the printing press to maximal performance, to create as much of this artificial money as possible, following the recipe of Mephistopheles* [in Goethe's *Faust*]*. But it was unable to follow the speed of the inflation; as a consequence each city, each township and finally each village began to create for its own purpose 'emergency money', which was rejected in the next village, and later thrown away because it was recognised as having no value.* (Stefan Zweig 1944, p. 334)

But how then are the market transactions performed, given the small real amount of the national money still circulating and a volume of transactions which have certainly not fallen to the same degree, or may even have been growing or remained constant for some time? The economic literature has usually given two explanations: an increase of the velocity with which money circulates and a return to barter. It seems to be true that both have played a certain role.

> *From this time they* [the Austrian peasants] *tried to get only industrial products and asked for real goods for their own produce. Goods for goods; after humans had already fortunately returned with the trenches* [during World War 1] *to the times of cave-dwelling, they now abolished the thousands of years old convention of money and returned to primitive exchange by barter. A grotesque exchange began throughout the whole country. The people from the cities carried out to the peasants everything they could spare; Chinese vases and carpets, sabres and shotguns, photographic equipment and books, lamps and decorations.* (Stefan Zweig 1944, p. 333)

But one more important factor has been mostly neglected, namely the currency substitution taking place (but see Rostowski 1992, Sturzenegger 1994), to which we have already referred above and which we have called Thiers' Law.

Given a high inflation good money drives out bad money, given flexible exchange rates. This means that more and more transactions are performed in specie, as has been shown for the French hyperinflation, or in stable foreign currencies.

A typical chain of events is the following. First specie or foreign currency is used as a unit of account, then as a store of value and finally as a means of payment. Unfortunately, data for the amount of specie or foreign currency circulating are scarcely available. For the government is, of course, interested in preventing the use of such money and to force the national currency on people, to be able to finance its budget deficit with the inflation tax. As a consequence tough regulations and foreign exchange controls with heavy fines and penalties for violating them are enacted. It follows that the circulation of foreign money is illegal, so that no statistics exist for the amount circulating. But some rough estimates and qualitative descriptions of the situation are available. For instance, the League of Nations (1946, p. 48) wrote, when reporting on the high inflations of the 1920s: *'Thus in advanced inflation, "Gresham's Law" was reversed: good money tended to drive out bad, and not the other way round; the reason being the irreducible need for a serviceable medium of exchange in any modern economy . . .'*

Thiers' Law has been observed in many other historical cases of advanced inflations. Especially interesting are those in which, as in the French hyperinflation, governments were not able to substitute by a successful reform a stable money for the national currency. For in these cases stable money returned not only without, but against the determined efforts of governments to keep it out of circulation to preserve the national currency. In the end the returning stable money absolutely drove out the bad money, so that one can speak of a 'naturally emerging' or an unplanned currency reform. The government finally only legalized the stable money, since it was forced to decree that its taxes must be paid in stable money after the inflation tax had been eroded. In Table 5.2 we have described all such cases known to us, of which, however, only the French inflation of 1789–1796 has been a hyperinflation.

Now, if Thiers' Law holds, given the cases of Table 5.2, that is of countries getting rid of advanced inflation by a 'natural' return to stable and the repudiation of unstable money, we should also expect a gradual substitution of bad by good money in cases in which advanced inflation is later ended by a successful currency reform, that is by a change of the monetary regime. This can, indeed, be documented for several hyperinflations, like the Polish and German ones in the 1920s (League of Nations 1946, p. 48; Holtfrerich, 1980, pp. 301 seq.) and the Greek and Chinese in the 1940s (Delivanis and Cleveland, 1950, pp. 96–101; Shun-Hsin, 1963, p. 27).

As already mentioned, the amount of stable money circulating is usually not known to statistical bureaux. Moreover, the government may not even

Table 5.2 Advanced inflations ending in total natural substitutions of bad through good money

Country	Period	Earlier currency reforms that failed[1]	Kind of good money	Source
Ming China	1375–1448		Silver bullion, copper coins (limited)	Bernholz (1997)
USA	1776–1781	March 1780: new dollar bills 1 : 20	Specie and state paper money	Phillipps (1972, 170 seq.) Bezanson (1951, 325 seq.)
France	1789–1797	February 1796: mandats territoriaux 1 : 30	Gold and silver specie	Thiers (1840)
Peru	1875–1887	September 1880:[2] incas 1 : 8	Silver coins	Garland (1908, 58 seq.)
Mexico	1913–1917	June 1916: infalsificable currency 10 : 1	Gold and silver specie	Banyai (1976, 73 seq.) Kemmerer (1940, 114–15)

Notes:
[1] By a currency reform, we understand a change of the monetary regime with the intention of establishing a new stable money. The mere removal of zeros or introduction of newly denominated paper notes are not considered to be a currency reform.
[2] From the report given by Garland it is doubtful whether a currency reform was seriously intended.

want to publish this information as far as it is available. Thus no time series exist for these data, so that an econometric estimation of the relative real amounts of bad and good money in the hands of the public as a function, for example, of the rate of inflation, is usually not possible (but see the case of the Soviet Union discussed below). There exist, however, some estimates for the real amount of stable money in Germany in 1923, that is shortly before the monetary reform of 15 November 1923. Young (1925, vol. 1, p. 402) mentions that '*According to the 1924 report of the second committee of experts the value of foreign bank notes held in Germany at the end of 1923 amounted to about 1,200,000,000 gold marks.*'

And Beusch (1928, p. 8) reports that '*the substitution of the domestic currency by foreign media of payment progressed everywhere ... In August (1923) this sum was estimated to amount to 2–3 billion gold marks. If this is correct, then the value of foreign currencies in German economic transactions was nearly ten times as large as that of the circulating paper mark notes'* (my translation).

In addition to this amount, 1.1 billion gold marks of value-stable 'emergency money' were circulating together with value-stable issues denominated in rye, coal and other units. All this adds up to more than 4 billion gold marks in value-stable money, compared to 6 billion in 1914 and to a real value of 80–800 million gold marks of the inflating paper marks circulating after June 1923 (Lansburgh, 1929, pp. 43 seq.; Holtfrerich, 1980, pp. 209 seq.). It follows that Thiers' Law was fully at work in Germany in the early 1920s as in other advanced inflations. It is thus not surprising that Holtfrerich (1980, p. 310) concludes:

> ... that the stabilisation of currency was necessary in Germany rather because of a crisis of the state than of the economy. The economy had widely changed to a foreign currency standard, with which it could have lived ... The crisis originated since the Reich would and could not tolerate the use of foreign currency for domestic transactions wanted by the economy because of reasons of national self-preservation and especially as long as the inflation was needed as a source of revenues. (my translation)

Currency substitution has also played a dominant role in all hyperinflations in the second half of the 20th century. For instance in Zaire (Congo):

> Currency substitution presumably continued to develop at a rapid pace during this period: by end-1993, the stock of new zaires in circulation was worth only US $ 46 million at the parallel market exchange rate, down from US $ 158 million at end-1992 and more than US $ 300 million at end-1989. Rough estimates suggest that the circulation of foreign banknotes – primarily US dollars, but also CFA francs in the provinces next to BEAC member countries and Zambian Kwachas in southern Zaire – probably rose to the equivalent of US $ 300–400 million in Zaire. (Beaugrand 1997, p. 5).

It has been stressed that data on currency substitution are missing for hyperinflations since governments are interested and take every effort to prevent such a development. As a consequence it is not possible to analyse this process quantitatively. We know, however, of a few remarkable exceptions, one of them in the Soviet Union. At the end of 1922 the Soviet Government introduced during the hyperinflation, besides the circulating rouble notes, more stable chervonetz notes which were not issued by the Treasury but by the newly founded State Bank (for more details see Bernholz 1996). We can leave unanswered the question of whether the introduction of this new money was an effort to increase the dwindling proceeds of the inflation tax, or a result of the decision taken in 1921 to return for a while from 'War Communism', to a certain extent, to capitalism with free markets in the 'New Economic Policy', when civil war and foreign intervention had ended. The latter interpretation gains weight by the fact that the introduction of the chervonetz was followed sixteen months later by the stabilisation of the rouble in February/March 1924.

The introduction of the chervonetz was undertaken by empowering the State Bank, founded in 1921, by decree of 11 October 1922, to issue banknotes denominated from 1 to 50 chervonetz, with one chervonetz supposed to be equal to 10 pre-war gold roubles. A coverage of the new banknotes to the amount of 25 per cent in precious metals and stable foreign exchange was prescribed. Some 75 per cent of the banknote circulation had to be balanced by short-term assets and loans, which could be easily called back (Griziotti Kretschmann 1928). It is important to realise that the Treasury continued to issue the rapidly inflating rouble notes, since it was not able at that time to cover expenditures by ordinary taxes and non-inflationary borrowing. Note also that the exchange rate between the two currencies was, on the whole, freely determined in the market, and that the smallest denomination of the chervonetz was so great that it prevented full currency substitution. Finally, there remained a relatively small inflation also in terms of the chervonetz currency.

In Figure 5.10 the dependence of the degree of currency substitution on the difference of the rates of inflation in the rouble and chervonetz currencies is depicted. Moreover two other sets of values have been drawn: one based on a logarithmic and one on a logistic regression function. The latter has been used to account for the fact that the share of the real stock of rouble notes in total real note circulation cannot exceed 100 per cent. As one observes, this is not the case for values estimated with the logarithmic function.

As can be seen from the figure, the share of the strongly inflationary rouble currency as a percentage of total real note circulation decreases strongly with the difference of the rates of inflation. And the values calculated from the logistic and logarithmic regression functions show that this relationship is highly significant (see below).

It should also be observed that the rate of rouble inflation has to increase because of the currency substitution through the chervonetz. For in this case the real value of the circulating rouble notes shrinks, which must lead, given a constant or even increasing issue of roubles to finance the budget deficit, to a higher rate of inflation in terms of the rouble currency, whereas the opposite holds in terms of the chervonetz currency.

Estimation of regression functions: Let us now estimate the dependence of the share of rouble notes in total note circulation on the difference of the rates of inflation in the rouble and the chervonetz currencies. In doing so we can determine to what degree currency substitution depends on inflation. Define M and M* as the amounts of rouble and chervonetz note circulation, w as the exchange rate of the chervonetz expressed in roubles, and π and π^* as the rates of inflation in rouble and chervonetz currency, respectively. Defining m = (M/w)/(M* + M/w), so that m is the share of rouble notes in total note

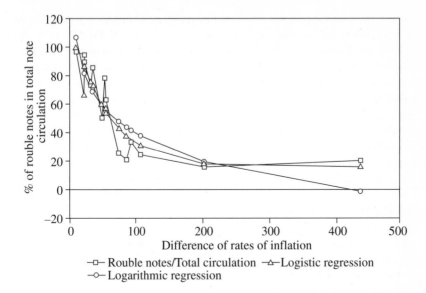

Notes: Rouble notes/Total note circulation: share of real rouble note circulation in total real note circulation; logistic regression and logarithmic regression: Values of shares calculated from the logistic and logarithmic regression functions.

Sources: For cost of living indices in 1923 roubles and in chervonetz from November 1922 until October 1923: Griziotti Kretschmann (1928); for November 1923 to February 1924: Griziotti Kretschmann (1924). For other data: Katzenellenbaum (1925)

Figure 5.10   *Soviet hyperinflation, 1923–1924: substitution of rouble by chervonetz (regressed by logarithmic and logistic functions)*

circulation, expressed in values of chervonetz, we estimate the following logarithmic and logistic regression functions:

$$\ln m(t) = 7.0718 - 0.5101\ln[1 + \pi(t) - \pi^*(t)] - 0.3254\ln[1 + \pi(t-1) - \pi^*(t-1)]$$
$$\quad\;\; (28.24)\;\; (-4.707) \qquad\qquad\qquad (-2.6393)$$

$$R^2 = 0.8759 \qquad DW = 1.3119 \tag{5.1}$$

$$\ln(100/m - 1) = -7.5437 + 1.3524\ln[\pi(t) - \pi^*(t)] + 0.4951\ln[\pi(t-1) - \pi^*(t-1)]$$
$$\qquad\qquad\quad (-8.2368)\;(3.5729) \qquad\qquad (1.1549)$$

$$R^2 = 0.746 \qquad DW = 0.96 \tag{5.2}$$

(t-values in brackets)

The results show that the share of the highly inflationary rouble notes in total note circulation is the lower the higher the difference of the rates of inflation. Both regression results are highly significant, though the logarithmic function leads to a better fit. We have now to take into account that currency substitution itself increases inflation in terms of the substituted currency, that is that reverse causality may also be present. For if people want to get rid of a currency the prices of goods denominated in it are driven up. As a consequence, $1 + \pi - \pi^*$ should be negatively dependent on m. Estimating the respective equation including a lag, the following results are obtained:

$$\ln[1 + \pi(t) - \pi^*(t)] = 8.261 - 1.3621\ln m(t) + 0.2185\ln m(t-1)$$
$$(19.303) \ (-1.9132) \qquad (0.2888)$$
$$R^2 = 0.7864 \qquad DW = 2.5122 \tag{5.3}$$

$$\ln[1 + \pi(t) - \pi^*(t)] = 8.3128 - 1.1473\ln m(t-1)$$
$$(21.116) \ (-6.8717)$$
$$R^2 = 0.7974 \qquad DW \ 2.5109 \tag{5.4}$$

Excluding the unlagged influence, that is (5.4) leads to a better result than (5.3). This makes sense since the $\pi(t)$'s and $\pi^*(t)$'s refer to the month before the date for which the m(t)'s are reported. We thus prefer the latter equation.

It follows that an increase in the difference of the rates of inflation in the two currencies decreases m(t) at the beginning of the next month, which itself then causes a rise of inflation. This interpretation of the above regression equations is in tune with the results of a Granger causality test. According to this test, $\ln[1 + \pi(t) - \pi^*(t)]$ is Granger caused by $\ln m(t-1)$, whereas $\ln m(t)$ is Granger caused by $\ln[1 + \pi(t-1) - \pi^*(t-1)]$ (with a probability of 82 per cent).[1]

5.4 UNDERVALUATION AND CURRENCY SUBSTITUTION

There were no marks to be had in Strasbourg ... so we changed some French money in the railway station at Kehl. For 10 francs I received 670 marks. Ten francs amounted to about 90 cents in Canadian money. That 90 cents lasted Mrs. Hemingway and me for a heavy day of spending and at the end of the day we had 120 marks left! (Ernest Hemingway 1922/23, p. 66)

... and thus hordes [of Bavarians] *went over* [to Salzburg] *with wives and children to indulge in the luxury of guzzling as much beer as their bellies could hold ... But the happy Bavarians did not know that a terrible revenge was approaching. For when the Austrian Crown stabilised and the mark plummeted downward in astronomical proportion, the Austrians went over* [to Bavaria] *from the same railway*

station in their turn. The same performance began a second time, but in the opposite direction. (Stefan Zweig 1944, pp. 336 f.)

It has already been shown for several historical cases, including the French hyperinflation, that inflation usually leads to an undervaluation of the respective currency. Here undervaluation is defined relative to the exchange rate and the quotient of the price levels in the two currencies considered, both set equal to 100 per cent, in a base year before the inflation began or when it had been very moderate for several years. The relationship that undervaluation is caused by inflation has been called by Paldam (1994, p. 138) Bernholz' Law, and can also be observed during most hyperinflations (Figure 5.11). In the following figures the months before the currency reform have been put on the horizontal axis. In all six cases sketched in Figure 5.11 real exchange rates show a pronounced undervaluation during the course of hyperinflation, but with some

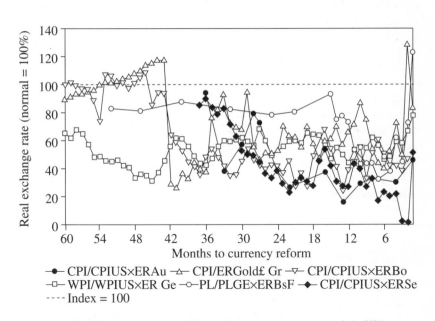

−●− CPI/CPIUS×ERAu −△− CPI/ERGold£ Gr −▽− CPI/CPIUS×ERBo
−□− WPI/WPIUS×ER Ge −○−PL/PLGE×ERBsF −◆− CPI/CPIUS×ERSe
---- Index = 100

Note: CPI, CPIUS refers to the cost of living in the respective country and the USA, respectively, WPI and WPIUS to the wholesale price indices; ERO designates the official and ERB the black market exchange rate.

Sources: See Appendix

Figure 5.11   French, Austrian, German, Greek, Bolivian and Serbian hyperinflations: real exchange rates 60 months before attempted currency reform

tendency to recover towards purchasing power parity or even to become over-valued when the currency reform is approaching. We have already mentioned that this latter tendency is probably caused by the expectation of a stabilisation of the currency. Though the undervaluation observed for these six cases seems to confirm the hypothesis, there are other cases which seem to contradict it (Table 5.2). Out of the 29 cases for which we have evidence available, six show a minus sign, though in four cases somewhat mitigated by plus signs. To interpret these signs and to further check the hypotheses, we have to consider the evidence for them more closely. Let us turn first to the Soviet Union and China (Figure 5.12), where the most pronounced overvaluation occurred. These countries seem to show that an important reason for this atypical development is, as in the case of the American War of Independence, their isolation from the outside world. The Soviet Union fought a bitter civil war with the Whites supported by Allied Forces which landed in the north and south of European Russia and in Vladivostok. Similarly, Chinese harbours were all controlled by Japanese forces during World War II, who also occupied Manchuria, Vietnam and Burma. Foreign exchange was thus not very valuable, since it could not be

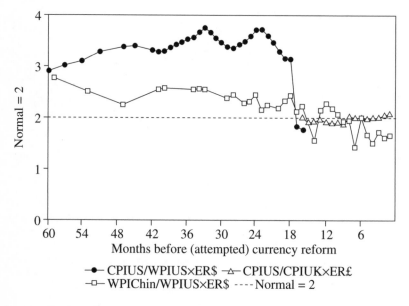

Sources: See Appendix

Figure 5.12   Real exchange rate during hyperinflation: Soviet Union 4.19–3.24 and China 5.44–4.49 (introduction of chervonetz in SU 11.1922)

> **Because of the customs regulations, which are very strict on persons returning from Germany, the French cannot come over to Kehl and buy all the cheap goods they would like to. But they can come over and eat. It is a sight every afternoon to see the mob that storms the German pastry shops and tea places. The Germans make very good pastries, ... that, at the present tumbling mark rate, the French of Strasbourg can buy for less amount a piece than the smallest French coin, the one sou piece. This miracle of exchange makes a swineish spectacle where the youth of the town of Strasbourg crowd into the German pastry shop to eat themselves sick and gorge on fluffy, cream-filled slices of German cake at five marks the slice. The contents of the pastry shop are swept clear in half an hour. ... As the last of the afternoon tea-ers and pastry eaters went Strasbourg-wards across the bridge the first of the exchange pirates coming over to raid Kehl for cheap dinners began to arrive.**
> (Ernest Hemingway, 1922/23 pp. 68 f.)

used to import foreign goods. This interpretation seems to be supported by the fact that the two currencies moved towards an undervaluation when the civil war and the allied occupation had been ended in the Soviet Union, and when Japan had been defeated, so that the isolation of China ended (see the last 14 to 16 months before the attempted currency reform) (Figure 5.12).

Foreign exchange controls could be another factor preventing the tendency towards undervaluation at least for some time. If this is true, one or both of the following events should be observed. First, whereas official exchange rates might show an overvaluation, black market exchange rates would move towards an undervaluation. Second, an overvaluation cannot be maintained permanently if the country is not isolated. For exports are hindered and imports are favoured by an overvaluation, and the pressure to use black instead of official markets increases with the difference between official and black market rates. The official market shrinks, which forces the authorities to devalue the official rate after some time. Both events can in fact be observed (Figures 5.13 to 5.15).

In Figure 5.13 the case of Peru is considered. The real exchange rate calculated with the black market rate is always below that calculated with the official rate, and shows an undervaluation for most but not all months. Unfortunately the black market rate is only available for part of the period. But when inflation was already high, though still far removed from hyperinflation,

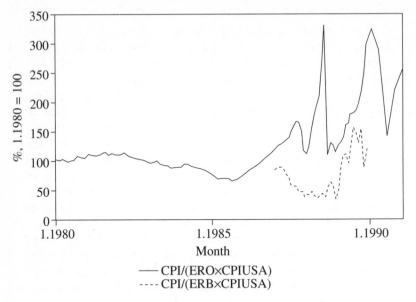

Notes: ERO official, ERB black market exchange rate for $. CPI, CPIUSA consumer price indices for Peru and USA, respectively. For CPI quarterly values since 2.1990.

Sources: IMF: International Financial Statistics, Monthly Reports. Quimica Suiza SA from World Bank: Most data 1987–1989.

Figure 5.13   Official and black market real exchange rate in Peru, 1980–1991

even the official rate showed an undervaluation. This changed, however, when inflation accelerated and reached 134 per cent per month in August 1990, to drop strongly afterwards again.

From this time a seesaw pattern can be observed. The authorities tried to maintain the nominal exchange rate in the face of high inflation, which led to a strong overvaluation. This brought about the negative consequences mentioned above. As a consequence the nominal official rate had to be adapted, so that the official real exchange rate moved back toward purchasing power parity, though it did not quite reach it. This pattern is repeated twice. A quite similar development is present in the case of Nicaragua (Figure 5.14), with the exception that the black market real exchange rate follows the same seesaw pattern, though it is also lower than the official real exchange rate most of the time.

The Bulgarian hyperinflation was very short and only figures for the official exchange rate are available. The real official exchange rate was overvalued all

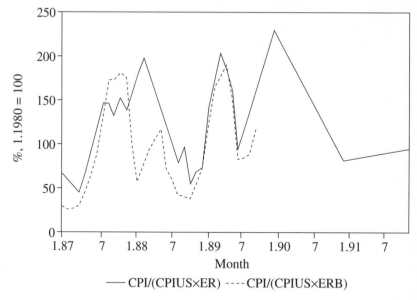

Sources: Black/free market exchange rate: Pick's (World) Currency Yearbook. Official and parallel market exchange rates: Banco Central de Nicaragua; kindly transmitted by William Tyler by intervention of Guy Pfeffermann. CPI, CPIUS: IMF: International Financial Statistics.

Figure 5.14   Hyperinflation in Nicaragua: real exchange rate, 12.1986–11.1991

the time, but showed also, though to a somewhat milder extent, the seesaw pattern.

The remaining historical case of a hyperinflation for which there exists some evidence contradicting the hypothesis that hyperinflation leads to an undervaluation of the currency is the Taiwanese hyperinflation (Figure 5.15). In the figure three real exchange rates have been drawn. The official and the black market real exchange rates with the US dollar, and the real exchange rate of the taipi with the faipi, the Chinese currency used in mainland China. As we can see, there was a strong overvaluation of the official exchange rate until 1947, probably again a consequence of the economic isolation which lasted for some time after the end of the war with Japan. Afterwards both exchange rates turn towards becoming undervalued. This is also true for the black market exchange rate. After the successful currency reform of July 1949 the official exchange rate with the dollar is overvalued again, whereas the other rates rather approach purchasing power parity. The official real exchange rate, moreover, again shows the seesaw pattern. This can be explained by the fact

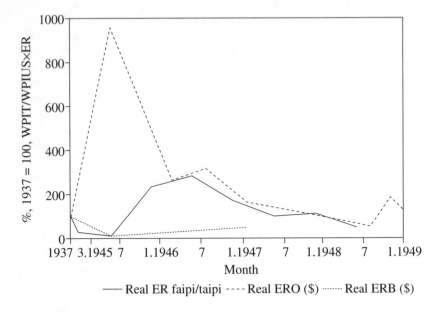

Sources: For money stock and wholesale price index for Taipei and a few exchange rates: Fu-Chi Liu (1970). For taipi–fapi exchange rates 1946–1949: Shun-Hsin Chou (1963). For conversion rates and new exchange rates for US $ from June 1949 to 1952: American International Investment Corporation (1977). For $ exchange rates of fapi and gold yuan, 1937–May 1949: Chang Kia-Ngau (1958). For exchange rates: Tzong-Shian Yu: Private communication by fax of October 3, 1991, from Chung-Hua Institute for Economic Research, Taipei, Taiwan, No. 75, Chang Hsin St.: 'The data you need have never appeared in any statistics or any book. However, thanks to the help of the Central Bank of China, I got them.'

Figure 5.15   Real exchange rate with US dollar: Taiwan 1937;
            3.1945–1.1949

that some inflation remained (see Chapter 8) in the following years and that the Government tried to maintain the nominal official exchange rate.

Taking everything together, it seems that the exceptions to the rule that a higher rate of inflation than in the main trading partners tends to bring about an undervaluation of the currency, can be explained by the economic isolation of the countries or (and) the effort of the governments to maintain by regulations, fines and penalties an overvalued nominal exchange rate.

What are the reasons for the undervaluation of the respective currencies during high inflations? A simple explanation can be given as follows (for a mathematical formulation see the next section). The value of a currency for its holder is given by its use as a medium of exchange when he uses it for his next purchase, compared to the higher transaction and information costs of barter, and the similar value it has for the next holders. The latter has, however, to be discounted, since it accrues only in later periods. The value of a one-time use can be measured by the opportunity cost the holder of money foregoes in the form of interest during the time of holding the money. For instead of keeping the money for a period he could have bought, immediately after receiving the money, an interest-bearing asset. As a consequence the total value of a unit of money is equal to the sum of the discounted amounts of interest which could instead have been earned on it for the expected lifetime of the money. But with inflation this calculation changes. For then all future uses of money have to be discounted with the rate of inflation, too, since this money can buy accordingly less in future transactions. As a consequence, when individuals compare the holding of two currencies, that with the higher rate of inflation is valued less than corresponding to purchasing power parity, since not only its present but also all its future uses are discounted with the rate of inflation.

> *. . . a famous British economist remembers how, as a boy, he spent a protracted period in the best hotels of German spas: his father had decided that this was infinitely cheaper than living in England. Mrs. E. Gluecksman tells of a week spent in a German sanatorium on the strength of a gift of £1. Mrs. Albury claims that a weekend in Germany could be had for threepence, Mr. Rosenthal got bed and breakfast for 50 French centimes.* (Guttman and Meehan, 1975, p. 71)

This simple explanation of undervaluation has, however, to be corrected in three respects. First, the difference in the prices of tradeable goods abroad and at home which is caused by the undervaluation leads to an increase of exports and a fall of imports, thus counteracting the undervaluation of the domestic currency by a rising supply of and a decreasing demand for foreign exchange. Second, as shown, the government increases the costs of holding more stable money by introducing regulations against using it sanctioned by heavy fines and penalties. Third, if just about all people in a certain country or region use a certain currency, it is advantageous to use the same kind of money, since it is easier to find a partner in purchasing or selling than for another currency which is scarcely known and used. As a consequence of these positive externalities of holding a certain currency, a rather high rate of inflation is necessary to substitute a money which is in the beginning used by nearly everybody.

The costs imposed by these positive externalities and by the government combine to limit the degree of undervaluation and to retard currency substitution. The latter becomes substantial only at rather high rates of inflation. From the empirical evidence it seems that differences in the rates of inflation of two currencies of 10–20 per cent per annum are not sufficient to engender more than a negligible currency substitution.

5.5   *UNDERVALUATION AS A CONSEQUENCE OF CURRENCY SUBSTITUTION: A SIMPLE MODEL

The present value of a unit of a currency is given by the discounted value of its use at the next payment to which it is applied and the discounted value it has for the next holder acquiring it at this time. The first, still undiscounted of these two values is given by the interest rate as the opportunity cost of holding money for one period. Assuming that each money holder holds the currency unit for at least one period, before spending it, we thus get for the value of one unit of money:

$$v(t,r) = r/q + v(t + 1)/q,$$

where $t = 0, 1, 2, \ldots, n - 1$ denotes time, r the real interest rate and $q = 1 + r$. Here r/q is the opportunity cost of holding one unit of money during the next period. It follows by repeatedly inserting the value for v that

$$v(0,r) = r/q + r/q^2 + r/q^3 + \ldots + r/q^n + v(n)/q^n. \tag{1}$$

Using the formula for a geometric sum, it follows from (1) that

$$v(0,r) = v(r) = 1 - 1/q^n + v(n)r/q^n, \quad \text{where } t = 0 \text{ denotes the present.} \tag{2}$$

Setting the last term for a sufficiently great n equal to zero, we get for

$$r: = 0.04 \qquad q: = 1 + r \qquad n: = 194$$

$$v(r) = 1 - \frac{1}{q^n} \tag{3}$$

$$v(r) = 1$$

For $n = 100$ we calculate that $v(r) = 0.98$ at an interest rate of 0.04. This means that for a sufficiently long time horizon of money holders, a sufficiently high interest rate and stable money, the present value of a currency unit is one, as it should be.

Next let us turn to a currency for which inflation is expected. Consider the opportunity cost of holding a unit of money, r. Then the expected value of using one unit of the currency at the end of the period is reduced by inflation. If the rate of inflation during this period amounts for instance to $\pi = 200$ per cent $= 2$, then the value of using the unit of money is reduced to $r/(1 + \pi) = r/(1+2) = r/3$, since its purchasing power has fallen to a third. During the next period it again loses two thirds of its value, so that the value of using it at the end of the third period amounts to $r/(1 + \pi)^2$ and so on. To get the total present expected value of a currency unit with a constant expected rate of inflation, we have to discount and to add these values similar to (1) and (2). Consequently, by setting $s = 1 + \pi$, it follows

$$V(0, r, \pi) = r/(qs) + r/(qs)^2 + r/(qs)^3 + \ldots + r/(qs)^n + V(n)/(qs)^n \quad (4)$$

Using the formula for a geometric sum, we derive

$$V(0, r, \pi) = V(r, \pi) = r(1 - 1/(qs)^n)/(qs - 1) + V(n, r, \pi)/(qs)^n \quad (5)$$

Setting again the last term equal to zero for sufficiently great n, we get for

$$r: = 0.04 \qquad q: = 1 + r \qquad \pi: = 0.1 \qquad s: = 1 + \pi \qquad n: = 100$$

$$V(r, \pi): = r \cdot \left[\frac{1 - \dfrac{1}{(q \cdot s)^n}}{(q \cdot s - 1)} \right] \quad (6)$$

$$V(r, \pi) = 0.278$$

The exchange rate w is defined as the ratio of the values of the two currencies, since a rational individual will only hold both currencies at an exchange rate reflecting their values. Normalising the exchange rate without any inflation to one, it follows for the exchange rate with inflation:

$$w(r, \pi): = \frac{V(r, \pi)}{v(r)} \quad (7)$$

$$w(r, \pi) = 0.278$$

This proves that a substantial undervaluation results from this approach for a period inflation of 10 per cent. Similar results follow for other inflation figures. As explained in the preceding section, relying only on this model would overestimate the degree of undervaluation in reality, since transaction costs, government fines and penalties and the positive externalities resulting from the dominant use of a currency (compare for a model Uribe 1997) have not been taken into account.

Moreover, for internationally traded goods there exists competitive pressure to bring into line the prices of goods in different countries, except for transportation and other transaction costs, customs duties and different indirect taxes.

5.6 OTHER CHARACTERISTICS OF HYPERINFLATIONS

Inflations have a tendency to accelerate once they have surpassed a certain level. *'Once inflation takes off, it accelerates at a fairly constant pace till it is stopped'* (Paldam 1994, p. 139). This is probably caused by the following facts, which have already been described above. First, the public tries to get rid of the depreciating money when they expect further inflation. But since the government creates additional money to finance its budget deficit, this can only succeed for the real stock of money if the price level is increasing more strongly than the money supply (these two facts are taken into account in the model described in Chapter 6). Moreover, the real budget deficit will even grow for some time because of Tanzi's Law. And finally, currency substitution sets in and lowers the base, namely the real stock of the inflating money, on which the inflation tax is imposed.

If inflation could be correctly foreseen this would probably not lead to some of the negative consequences for the real economy that are mentioned below. But the variability of inflation as measured by the standard deviation of inflation from its average rises with inflation. As Paldam (1994, pp. 139–49) demonstrates for 28 inflations, the standard deviation rises with inflation for rates higher than 5 per cent per year. This means that inflation becomes the less predictable the higher its rate.

5.6.1 Consequences of High Inflation for Capital Markets

Given that rates of inflation are the less predictable the higher average inflation, this usually has severe consequences for capital markets. Any credit given or bond bought should carry a nominal interest rate which takes account of the loss of value of the capital because of inflation, that is, roughly speaking, the nominal interest rate paid should equal the real interest rate plus the rate of inflation (this relationship is called the Fisher equation). But this is impossible, given the unpredictability of the latter. As a consequence, if the nominal interest rate agreed on in the contract is lower than the value which really occurs later, the creditor will lose money, and perhaps even part of his capital.

Our first purchase was from a fruit stand beside the main street of Kehl [in Germany, in September 1922] *where an old woman was selling apples, peaches and plums. We picked out five very good looking apples and gave the old woman a 50 mark note. She gave us back 38 marks in exchange. A very nice looking, white bearded old gentleman saw us buy the apples and raised his hat. 'Pardon me, sir,' he said, rather timidly in German, 'how much were the apples?'*

I counted the change and told him 12 marks.

He smiled and shook his head. 'I can't pay it. It is too much.'

He went up the street . . . I wish I had offered him some. Twelve marks, on that day, amounted to a little under two cents. The old man, whose life's savings were probably, as most of the non-profiteer classes are, invested in German pre-war and war bonds, could not afford a 12-mark expenditure. (Ernest Hemingway, 1922/23, pp. 67 f.)

In the opposite case the debtor will be worse off. These dangers are the greater, the longer the duration of the credit or bond. It is thus not surprising that credit and capital markets shrink during high inflation, and that usually only short-term credit is extended. For instance, during the high and hyperinflation in Argentina during the 1980s credit markets with a duration longer than 14 days vanished.

A way out of this predicament seems to be the indexing of the interest rate, so that the increase of the price index is added to the real rate of interest when the loan or bond becomes due. But this solution is also not without problems. First, it always takes some time until the value of the index has been calculated, and during this time a further devaluation takes place. With accelerating hyperinflation this lag becomes so important that only indexing to the exchange rate remains as a way out of this problem. Second, the question arises which index should be taken as adequate for debts: the cost of living index important for savers, or a wholesale price index more important for producers, or a price index for building houses for construction firms which are borrowing? Third, to calculate several indices is not without cost. Finally, governments mostly try to forbid indexing as long as possible, especially to the exchange rate, since they want to prevent the implied acceleration of inflation and encouragement of currency substitution. These and other difficulties have led to the result that indexing has not played an important role for capital markets in most inflations. A notable exception was Brazil during the 1980s and early 1990s. In this case even overnight credits with an amount corresponding to at least $3000 were indexed. But it is revealing that more than a dozen indices were used for different purposes.

The shrinking volume and time dimension of the loan and capital markets is of great importance to the real economy. In a decentralised market economy the final savers are households, whereas the final debtors are production firms (Figure 5.16). Perhaps the most important function of financial institutions

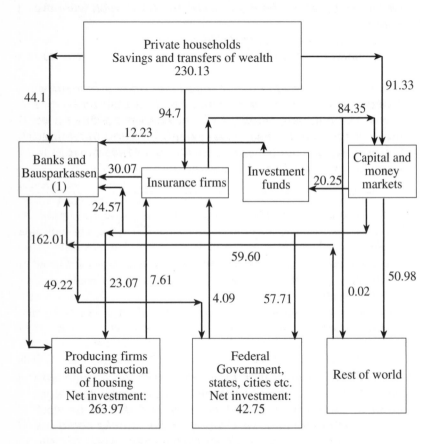

Note:　(1) Bausparkassen are Savings Banks specialising in receiving deposits from and later to extend credit to people intending to build their own house or flat.

Source:　Deutsche Bundesbank, Monatsberichte 1998

Figure 5.16　Development of wealth and how it was financed in Germany, 1997 (in billion DM)

like banks, investment funds and insurance firms and of capital markets in a decentralised market economy is, therefore, the coordination of consumption and savings by households with investment and production decisions by firms.

In this way factors of production are moved from producing consumer goods to that of investment goods. Production firms produce machinery, buildings, roads and invest in research to be able later to supply directly or indirectly more, better and new consumer goods. Since they have to pay for their inputs before the respective outputs can be sold, they have to go into debt to finance these roundabout production processes. As a consequence, high and erratic inflation has a devastating effect on the inter-temporally efficient allocation of resources.

5.6.2 The Development of Prices

Until now we have only considered the price level as a measure of inflation. But prices develop in bouts and unevenly during high inflations, which is another source of the rising inefficiency of the economy. To change prices is costly, and the problem of getting correct information is even more important. The extent of expected inflation has to be estimated apart from changes in the relative prices of the goods bought and sold by the firm.

When inflation begins, manufacturers and traders experience the fact that they can sell their goods for higher prices than had been expected. They interpret this first usually as an increase in demand for the goods they are selling, expect higher profits and try to expand their business. But when inflation goes on and accelerates certain groups of producers, and especially those whose manufacturing process takes much time, discover that their method of calculating the prices of their products by adding to manufacturing costs a usual margin of profits implies losses in real terms. For during the time necessary for the production process the prices of raw materials, machinery and labour have risen because of inflation.

> *But although the profits in paper marks were huge and lavishly spent, . . ., only the clever and smart operators could avoid the dwindling of these paper marks as the mark depreciated more and more rapidly. Often stocks could not be replenished with the proceeds from sales, working capital shrank, . . ., and they* [the business owner] *discovered that they had lived on their capital and so become much poorer. Small shopkeepers in particular were affected by this, and, . . ., many went to the wall.* (Guttman and Meehan, 1975, p. 85)

Given this situation, the calculation of prices is changed. Now not the costs at the time of the purchase of inputs, but at the time when the products are sold, are used as a basis for determining the prices of the goods sold. But this kind of calculation is extremely difficult, given the high variability of inflation. Also, as pointed out before, it takes time until price indices are available, and certain price indices may be inadequate to reflect the development of the prices of the input and output goods needed and produced by the firm. As a consequence, the use of indices, in spite of being used by ever more firms in their calculations, will lead to a distortion of relative prices, and still not allow a correct calculation.

But there exists a sector of the economy where the situation is different, namely all firms importing goods. For them the exchange rate provides a reliable measure to calculate their selling prices. With rising inflation this method of calculating prices spreads to producers, wholesale firms and retailers who buy or sell imported goods. Afterwards it is imitated for valuable durable goods and in the end used generally everywhere, especially when inflation has accelerated to a degree such that the lag in calculating indices becomes a severe problem. As a consequence, it is not surprising that during high inflation stable money or foreign exchange is used for calculating prices even before currency substitution sets in.

When we flew to Buenos Aires in September 1983 to study the high inflation [which had not yet turned into a hyperinflation], *I took mainly dollar notes with me, since I knew that they would get the best exchange rate in the parallel (black) market. At the airport I exchanged just the amount needed for the taxi to the hotel at the official rate. In the hotel we found that the prices were quoted in dollars. I then asked what the room prices would be if I paid with dollar notes instead of pesos. The man at the reception then offered a much lower price. The next day we went to the travel agency, whose address had been given to me on the plane as a place where I could exchange dollars in the parallel market. Here we exchanged an amount at an even more favourable rate.* (Peter Bernholz, personal experience of the author)

Since the dollar rose from 65 to 130 billion yesterday [29 October 1923], *I will have to pay a doubled price for my gas bill and several other things compared to yesterday. This will amount for gas to a difference of 150 billion.* (Victor Klemperer, 1996, p. 757)

Another characteristic which results from the costs of changing prices is a seesaw pattern of real prices, that is for nominal prices corrected for inflation. For prices can only be changed from time to time, though the respective interval is the shorter the higher the rate of inflation. But at each change the coming inflation has to be taken into account, so that nominal prices have to be set at a higher level than would correspond to the present market equilibrium. This means that real prices are also higher, but fall below this equilibrium level until the next rise of prices occurs. As a consequence, prices are sometimes above and sometimes below the value clearing the market, which implies an additional loss of efficiency.

It is not surprising that the same pattern can be observed for wages (Figure 5.17). For in the beginning of inflation labour unions and employers bargain over wages from time to time and try to factor the expected rate of inflation into their deliberations. With rising rates of inflation, however, this procedure becomes too clumsy and they agree on indexing wages. Finally, because of the problems already mentioned, they may even use the exchange rate for indexing wages.

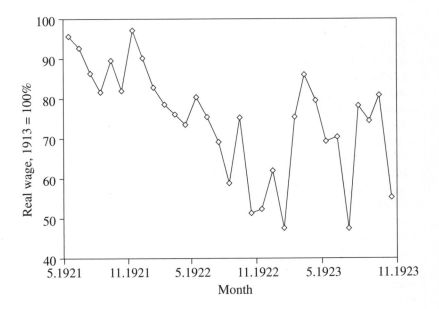

Source: Bresciani-Turroni (1937), p. 450

Figure 5.17 Real wage of a coalminer (hewer) during German hyperinflation

> **Unemployed men took one or two rucksacks** [during the Austrian hyperinflation] **and went from peasant to peasant. They even took the train to favourable locations to get foodstuffs illegally which they sold afterwards in the town at three- or fourfold the prices they had paid themselves. First the peasants were happy about the great amount of paper money which rained into their houses for their eggs and butter. . . . However, when they came to town with their full briefcases to buy goods, they discovered to their chagrin that, whereas they had only asked for a fivefold price for their produce, the prices for scythe, hammer and cauldron, which they wanted to buy, had risen by a factor of 50.** (Stefan Zweig, 1944, p. 333)

Let us turn now to the development of relative prices, which usually shows many distortions during high inflations. Especially the prices of services supplied by firms owned by the state or by cities, or prices regulated by them, remain far below the development of the general price level during the course of inflation. As an example we look again at the well-researched German hyperinflation which ended with a successful currency reform in November 1923 (Table 5.3). It goes without saying that rents for housing were regulated by the Government and that railway fares were set by the Reichsbahn, which was owned by the state.

Table 5.3   Development of several price indices and prices during German hyperinflation, 1913–1923 (1913/14 = 1)

Date	Price index Cost of living	Price index Food	Price index Clothing	Price index Accommodation	Price index of railway fares	Price index of shares
October 1923	3657 billion	4301 billion	6160 billion	54 billion	1.77 billion	171.3 billion

Sources: For price of railway fares and index of share prices: Bresciani-Turroni (1937), pp. 36, 71 and 452 ff. For other data: Holtfrerich (1980), p. 31. The original data are from Statistisches Reichsamt (1924/1925).

> **Ticket prices for trams in Budapest were adapted daily during the Hungarian hyperinflation** [the greatest in history]**, whereas those for railway tickets were changed only each fourth day. As a consequence, when I travelled one day to Rumania, taking the streetcar in Budapest to the railway station was very many times as expensive as my journey by train to the Rumanian border.** (Gyoergy Ligeti, modern composer, personal communication, 28 May, 2001)

Interestingly enough, share prices, usually considered to be a safe haven against inflation, also show a strong tendency to lag behind the general price level. This fact has been observed also for other inflations. In his empirical study of the movement of prices at the stock exchange, Donner (1934, p. 73) found that

The post-war inflation, however, led to a break in the development [the upward trend of stock market indices]. *Calculated in gold* [that is based on the pre-war value of money] *stock prices oscillated in France* [where a moderate inflation took place; see Section 7.2] *around 30 per cent below the level of 1913 in 1925/30, in Germany by 66 per cent. In Austria the total value of all joint stock companies amounted at the stock exchange only to 42 per cent of the value in 1913 (including additional issues of shares since then).*

An important reason for this development seems to have been the fact that '*the sum of dividends distributed was much lower than that paid in 1913, and the fall of dividends, owing to the policy followed by the companies, was even greater than the fall of net profits which the accounts showed*' (Bresciani-Turroni 1937, p. 262). Similar to shares, houses, even expensive ones, situated in the best quarters, were sold and bought at '*silly prices during the inflation*' (Bresciani-Turroni 1937, pp. 284, 299). This is also not surprising given the low rents allowed by government regulation.

> **I remain undisturbed concerning the fluctuations of share prices at the stock exchange** [on 16 November 1923]**. Generally speaking most values have turned to become worthless compared to the dollar.** (Victor Klemperer, 1996, p. 758)

Table 5.4   *Development of expenditures for several goods during Austrian*
              hyperinflation (first half of 1914 = 1)

Date	Housing (furnished room)	Tram fares	Newspaper	Bread (not controlled)	Suit (medium quality)	Contribution to sickness insurance
September 1923	8750	13 333	9583	12 609	12 167	8000

Sources: Calculated from Bordes (1924), pp. 240 ff. Original data from *Der Oesterreichische, Volkswirt*, 6 October 1923, p. 17.

A similar picture concerning the diverging development of the prices for different goods and of the lagging rents for housing relates to the Austrian hyperinflation (Table 5.4), which ended in autumn 1922 with a successful currency reform. Unfortunately the development of prices can only be compared for September 1923, one year after the reform had taken place. But it seems that we can be confident that the divergent development of prices during the inflation had not been corrected during this year.

Prices jumped at discretion [during Austrian hyperinflation]*; a box of matches cost twentyfold in a shop which had raised the price in time, compared to that in another one, in which a decent man still sold it at the price of yesterday. As a reward for this attitude his shop was emptied of all goods within an hour. For the fact was told by one to the other, and everybody ran to buy everything on sale, whether he needed it or not. . . . The most grotesque developments happened to rents, where the Government forbade any rise for the protec-tion of renters (who were the broad majority) and to the damage of landlords. Soon a middle-sized flat was less expensive than a lunch in Austria.* (Stefan Zweig, 1944, p. 335; my translation)

Let us turn now to wages. Here it has been found for both the Austrian and the German hyperinflations that whereas the wages of unskilled workers did not lag much behind the general development of inflation, this was much more the case for the wages of skilled workers and even more so for those of more high-ranking employees (for lagging German real wages see also Burdekin and

Table 5.5   *Development of the indices of different real weekly wages during the German hyperinflation, 1913–1923 (1913 = 100)*

Date	Unskilled railway workers	Skilled railway workers	Printers	Lower level civil servants	Middle level civil servants	Higher level civil servants
November 1923	62	46.4	54	69.9	49.5	38

Note: For public officials: 1923

Sources: Holtfrerich (1980, pp. 230–3). Original source: Statistisches Reichsamt (1925, pp. 41, 45).

Burkett 1995). According to Bordes (1924, p. 103), Sir William Ackworth declared in a report on the Austrian railways:

> *Detailed comparison between payments to the employees of the State railways in 1913 and in the month of July 1923, shows that, reckoned in gold, the average of the salaries and wages paid today amounts to only 64 per cent of those paid before the War. But while in the four lower groups, comprising more than one-third of the whole staff, the wages average 90 per cent of the pre-War scale, and in the middle groups range from 80 per cent to 60 per cent, in the seven groups at the top they range down from 33 per cent of the pre-War salary to less than 25 per cent, and in the case of the most responsible officials down to salaries less than 20 per cent, in extreme cases less than 10 per cent of the pre-War standard.*

This result is confirmed by the development of minimum wages for different categories of skilled and unskilled work in Austria (Bordes 1924, p. 103, table). A similar picture emerges for the development of wages during the German hyperinflation (Table 5.5).

5.7   ECONOMIC ACTIVITY AND UNEMPLOYMENT

From our earlier analysis and the empirical evidence we have to expect that in the beginning of inflation economic activity will rise, and that as a consequence employment will increase and unemployment fall. Later on, the inefficiencies and diverging developments of different prices and wages, and of the price level compared to the exchange rate, should lead to more and more problems and to misdirected efforts and investments, which should finally slow down economic activity.

Paldam (1994, pp. 142f.) has calculated the relationship between average rates of inflation and growth rates for 28 countries experiencing high inflation. He concludes that:

There are no signs of the popular idea that more inflation generates more growth. Below 10 per cent inflation there are no signs of any connection. However, the curve showing the average of the points does turn down [implying lower growth rates] *as inflation gets higher. The weak connection shown tallies well with the weakness of the theories predicting a connection.*
(See Driffill *et al.* (1990) for a survey)

If we look at the development of industrial production and of real national income during the German hyperinflation, the following picture emerges (Figure 5.18). As we can see, German industrial production and real national product decreased during the War and into 1919, when a moderate inflation took place. Afterwards both rose until 1922, to decline in 1923 when inflation sped up. The first month of hyperinflation, that is of an increase of the wholesale price index of more than 50 per cent, occurred in January 1920, but after this month a stabilisation took place. The monthly rate became

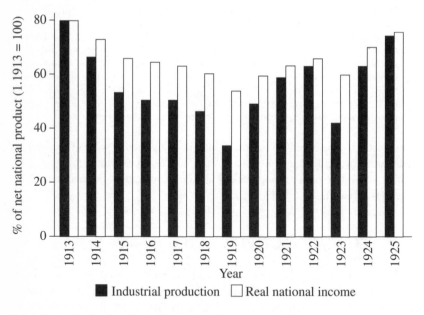

Note: For real national product the figures by Hoffmann *et al.* (1965) and Witt (1974) have been taken.

Source: Holtfrerich (1980), pp. 179, 221, Tables 32 and 40. For the original sources see these tables.

Figure 5.18   Development of industrial production and of real national product, Germany 1913–1925

negative in many months and never exceeded 6 per cent per month until June 1921. From July of this year it tended to rise again and the next bout of hyperinflation happened in August 1922 with a rate of 89 per cent. In most of the following months inflation accelerated to reach a monthly figure of 29 525.7 per cent in October 1923, shortly before the currency reform. This last dramatic development certainly had a negative influence on industrial production and on real national income, which again began to rise after the stabilisation. We conclude that the relationship is perhaps somewhat different from, but not in obvious contradiction of, the results reached by Paldam. The differences may result from the consequences of the War until 1919, and a recovery afterwards into 1922 when inflation was reduced in 1920 and not too high afterwards.

A similar picture emerges for the Austrian and German hyperinflations, when we analyse the development of unemployment (Figure 5.19). In both cases unemployment increased strongly when hyperinflation accelerated towards the end in 1922 in Austria and 1923 in Germany.

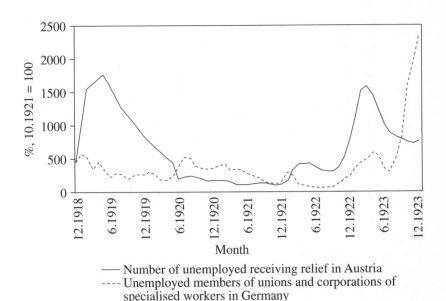

—— Number of unemployed receiving relief in Austria
---- Unemployed members of unions and corporations of
      specialised workers in Germany

Sources: Calculated from the tables of Bordes (1924, p. 11) and Holtfrerich (1980, p. 195). The original source of the latter is *Reichsarbeitsblatt* (1913/14 ff.).

Figure 5.19   *Development of unemployment during Austrian and German hyperinflations*

> ***Thousands of unemployed stood around and clenched their fists against the marketeers and foreigners in their luxury cars, who bought whole streets of houses like a box of matches.*** (Stefan Zweig, 1944, p. 358)

The remarkable rise of unemployment which Austria experienced in contrast to Germany was certainly a consequence of the dismemberment of the Austrian-Hungarian monarchy by the victorious Western Allies. But afterwards it decreased as in Germany before the acceleration of inflation took place. For a later discussion we have also to note the strong increase in unemployment following the currency reforms in the autumn of 1922 and in November 1923, respectively.

Finally a short remark on the consequences of hyperinflation on income distribution. Holtfrerich (1980, p. 268), after a careful examination of the available statistical evidence, concludes:

Wage and salary earners can, from this point of view, be seen as the group who have drawn in the long run the greatest benefit from the redistribution resulting from the inflation. And whereas entrepreneurs could just about hold their position, . . ., those who received unearned incomes were the great losers in this process. This follows also from the fact that the share of employed in the population was at 51.3 per cent much higher than before the war (1907: 45.5). For this means that during and after the inflation an additional part of the population, who had before relied on other sources of income, like wealth, were now forced to work for their living. (My translation)

5.8   THE POLITICAL ECONOMY OF HIGH INFLATION

Inflation is always a monetary phenomenon, quite in contrast to a one time rise of the price level because of bad harvests in former times or an increase of the price of oil by the Organisation of Oil Exporting Countries (OPEC) since the 1970s. But as mentioned before, in accepting this fact, it has still to be explained why the money supply rises more than the productive potential or the real gross national product of a country. In Section 2.4 we have already looked into reasons for the inflationary bias of governments. But apart from mentioning the fact that no hyperinflation has ever occurred without a huge budget deficit financed by money creation, our analysis has been confined to moderate inflations. Moderate inflations need not to be caused by financing through money creation all or a part of a budget deficit of the state, its subdivisions or of the losses of business firms owned or subsidised by the government.

As has been argued in Section 2.4, the party (parties) in power may introduce an expansionary policy to stimulate the economy and to lower unemployment exactly in time to increase their chances of winning the next election. Similarly, if aggressive unions enforce higher wage levels (Burdekin and Burkett 1996) or if OPEC lowers its production to increase the price level of oil, economic activity would decline and unemployment rise (compare for example Laidler and Parkin 1975). Given such a supply shock, the government may be tempted to increase the money supply to counter some of these negative consequences. Though it cannot reach this goal in the end, at least the situation may be better at election time, since the rise of the price level follows only later. However, when workers and their unions as well as entrepreneurs and consumers have adapted to the resulting inflation, only a further unexpected increase of the money supply can postpone the adverse consequences of the original shock.

Another cause for a moderate inflation may be an expansionary policy of the reserve currency country in an open economy with a fixed exchange rate to the reserve currency. Given such a system, the rate of inflation is finally determined by the monetary policies of this country (Section 2.2). Even if a country follows a less expansionary monetary policy than the reserve country, so that its price level tends to rise less, its exports will rise and its imports fall. A balance of payments surplus develops and the central bank has to buy the excess supply of foreign exchange with its own money, which enters monetary circulation. The money supply increases even more because the banks need to hold only part of the central bank money they receive as reserves and can extend their credit to customers. As a consequence the price level begins to rise, whereas at the same time the prices of goods imported from the reserve currency country have already begun to increase. This process is only halted when the rate of inflation has reached the level of that prevailing in the latter country, at least as far as tradeable goods are concerned. This is the so-called *imported inflation*, from which for instance countries like Switzerland and Germany were suffering during the Bretton Woods system, when the reserve currency (the dollar) country, the USA, was following a more expansionary monetary policy.

As mentioned, in all of these cases there *need not* but can be a financing of a budget deficit by creating money. In fact, this was certainly not the case during the period of imported inflation in Germany and Switzerland in the 1960s and early 1970s. But even if a budget deficit arises, this can be easily financed in developed countries with deep capital markets by borrowing in these markets. As already stressed, things look quite different for high inflations. We have thus to ask ourselves, which political forces are powerful enough to increase a budget deficit to such a level that money creation seems to be necessary to finance it, and this in such a magnitude that high and hyper-inflation result? Historically, three different chains of causation seem to have led to such developments.

The first possibility has already been mentioned. In this case the budget deficit and its financing by money creation are a consequence of wars, civil wars, revolutions (Capie 1986), or the break-up of states, like that of the Austrian-Hungarian monarchy after World War 1 or of the former Soviet Union in the early 1990s. In such cases governments are no longer able or do not dare to extract or to introduce the taxes which would be necessary to cover the often dramatically increased expenditures.

A second possibility is a strong push, for instance if a new populist government speedily increases minimum wages or all wages by a high percentage, and similarly public spending. In most such cases, moreover, controls setting maximum prices are introduced by governments.

> *What happens is remarkably similar in all six cases covered by Dornbusch and Edwards (1991), and other cases that come to mind: (1) The push generates a* **golden period** *of strong economic upswing, without inflation. The golden period typically lasts almost a year. (2) The resulting* **collapse** *is normally* **very strong**. *At the end of the year things start to turn sour. The shelves in the shops become empty. Inflation explodes. Real production starts to fall. The government loses popularity and credibility rapidly.* (Paldam 1994, pp. 148 f.).

It should be obvious that such policies could and can only be introduced in already weak or weakening political systems, in which parties or rulers are in desperate need to use extreme measures to gain or maintain popularity or power, in which knowledge of existing economic realities is very weak or non-existent, or in which utopian ideologies are believed and win the upper hand.

Third, there are countries also characterised by a weak political system which finance a substantial part of their budget with the help of foreign transfers. At the time when such transfers end, the government sees itself unable to reduce expenditures and (or) to increase taxes. It first turns to borrowing to cover the budget deficit. As soon as this possibility is exhausted, the deficit is covered by issuing money. This was the path followed by Bolivia in the first half of the 1980s.

In considering these three categories one should not, however, forget two facts. First, with a purely metallic monetary standard, inflation could never reach the same magnitude as experienced in the high inflations of the 20th century. Examples are the debasement of the currency in the declining Roman empire of the third and fourth centuries and the struggling Spanish empire in the 17th century. Second, as already stressed, even the weak political systems of the 19th century never engendered high or hyperinflations during the period of the silver or gold standards of that century. Though they often turned to inconvertible paper money, the example of the 'more civilised' countries always caused them to try to return to the 'sound' standard of convertible gold or silver currencies, and thus prevented them engaging in highly inflationary monetary policies. Only the hyperinflation of the French Revolution, the high inflation of the American War of Independence and that in the desperate Confederate States of the American Civil War proved to be exceptions to this rule. In the latter case the rate of inflation climbed to its highest monthly level of 40 per cent in March 1864. In some other months rates of up to 20 per cent were reached.

5.9 SOCIAL AND POLITICAL CONSEQUENCES OF HYPERINFLATION

Nothing else has made the German people as embittered, as hateful, as ripe for Hitler as the inflation. For the war, as murderous as it had been, had at least seen hours of triumph, ringing of bells, fanfares of victory. . . . but as a conse-quence of the inflation [Germany] felt only drawn into the dirt, cheated and humiliated. A whole generation did not forgive the German Republic these years and preferred to call back its own butchers. But all this lay in a distant future. From the outside it seemed that this desolate phantasmagory had ended like the dance of a will o' the wisp [with the currency reform; see below]. (Stefan Zweig, 1944, p. 361)

It has already been pointed out in Section 5.6 that hyperinflations had an immense influence on the distribution of income and wealth. According to Holtfrerich workers profited in the long run from the German inflation. But this was not true for the employees of the Government and for those people who belonged to the classes enjoying higher salaries before the War. Moreover, as we have seen, all people holding their wealth mostly in nominal financial assets lost most of their fortunes. On the other hand, all those prof-ited who had debts at the beginning of the inflation or were able to incur them during its course. And as we have mentioned, these debtors were mostly firms and their owners, whereas the nominal assets were held by private households. As a consequence, the middle classes were those hurt most by high inflations. As Paldam (1994, p. 150) puts it:

Those who had nominal fortunes lost everything. Those who had real capital got it for free. The regime/government was seen as having allowed an arbitrary redistri-bution to take place. In the next decade politics took a dramatic turn in all four [Central European countries which suffered from hyperinflation in the 1920s]. Germany acquired one of the worst regimes known. Austria soon lost its democracy, and such tendency as there was for a democratic development in Poland and Hungary ceased. A strong argument can be made that to uphold democracies, it is essential that the large groups in the centre support it. Inflations hit the savings of the middle class and therefore alienate the centre from the 'system' – and then they have to find somebody else to support.

Since the gold mark has been used, it has become clear how much suffering is hidden behind the frenzy of zeros. One billion equal to one mark, and a mark has scarcely the purchasing power of 0.4 to 0.5 pre-war marks, and often only of 0.3 marks [22 November 1923] (p. 759). **... Otherwise, I have had a bad time since the introduction of the gold- and Rentenmark** [in the German currency reform the new Rentenmark, equal to one billion old marks, was introduced; see Chapter 8]. **I have not to run as often to the cashier's office, the pressure of having to buy has ended for the time being. But an extreme poverty has revealed itself. Most insufficient payments, most insufficient reserves. Around 100 marks at home, 100 in shares and my salary for fourteen days: some 60 marks** [November 28] (p. 761).

Since the time when the gold mark was introduced, I am paid terribly poorly. The last time I received 16 dollars, that is about 67 marks for one week. Prices have fallen, but they have by far not reached pre-war levels. My holdings at the stock exchange are valued at scarcely 100 marks. My cash reserves at home have about the same value, and that is all. My life insurance is lost. 150 paper millions are equal to 0.015 Pfennigs [10 December 1923]. (Victor Klemperer, 1996, p. 763)

Though there is a lot of truth in these statements, it seems that they are somewhat exaggerated. The number of votes cast for the Nazi and Communist parties in Germany fell strongly after the successful stabilisation of the mark in November 1923. Support increased again to high levels only with the rising unemployment of the depression of the early 1930s. Hitler's grasp of government power would scarcely have happened without the depression. So it is highly probable that the German hyperinflation, though it had a socially and politically negative influence, was not a sufficient condition of Hitler's rise to power. Similar observations are probably true for Austria, Hungary and Poland.

On the other hand, democratic regimes succeeded in ending the Latin American hyperinflations in Argentina, Bolivia, Brazil and Nicaragua. In all these countries, democratic regimes are ruling today. In Chile, where inflation was high but did not reach the dimension of hyperinflation, the so-called 'Chicago boys' successfully ended the inflation under the dictatorship of Pinochet. This led to a successful real development of the economy which probably furthered the later democratisation of the country. In Taiwan, the less successful currency reform ending hyperinflation allowed, together with other reforms, an impressive economic development and finally a move towards democracy.

It is true that such positive developments did not happen in all cases after successful currency reforms. And hyperinflations led to losses in real economic activity which made it much more difficult to establish institutions favouring real economic growth. For instance, the poor Bolivian economy is still stagnating in spite of the successful currency reform of 1985. And the real economic problems of the so-called transformation countries of the former Eastern Bloc have certainly been exacerbated in most cases by high inflations.

Taking everything together we can conclude that hyperinflations are certainly a traumatic experience leading to dangerous damage to the social fabric. But this does not imply that a path to stagnation and political decline is a *necessary* consequence, at least not if a successful currency reform has succeeded in ending monetary instability.

One unexpected positive experience during high inflations is sometimes, as also often happens during other crises, a return to fundamental human values, like nature and the arts. This could at least be observed during the Austrian and German hyperinflations of the 1920s.

> *Just because of the unexpected event that money, which had formerly been the most stable object, lost its value day by day, men estimated more highly the real values of life – work, love, friendship, art and nature. The whole people lived more intensively than before in the midst of the catastrophe. Boys and girls hiked in the mountains and came back burned by the sun; restaurants with dancing music operated until late into the night; new firms and shops were founded; I myself believe I have never lived and worked more intensively than during these years. . . . We have never loved the arts more in Austria than during those chaotic years just because we felt that only the eternal within us remained as the really stable in view of the betrayal on the part of money.* (Stefan Zweig, 1944, p. 339)

5.10   CONCLUSIONS

In this chapter the main characteristics of hyperinflation have been studied. The following results were obtained from the evidence:

1. Hyperinflations are always caused by public budget deficits which are largely financed by money creation. If inflation accelerates these budget deficits tend to increase (Tanzi's Law).
2. Because of currency substitution (Thier's Law), increased velocity of money and some return to barter, the real stock of the inflating money diminishes very strongly. This proved to be true for all empirical cases examined. If inflation is sufficiently high and persists long enough, the bad inflating money can even be fully driven out of circulation. No statistical data are available for this process in most cases, but it was possible to estimate a regression equation for the Soviet hyperinflation of the 1920s.
3. Currency substitution implies an undervaluation of the inflating currency, which could be documented for most cases of historical hyperinflations. The exceptions could be explained either by the economic isolation of the respective country or foreign exchange controls. In the latter case a seesaw pattern of the development of real exchange rates can be observed.
4. Inflations have a tendency to accelerate and to show a variability (variance) which is the higher the higher the average rate of inflation.
5. Capital markets are usually reduced in scope and especially concerning the duration of contracts. As a consequence the inter-temporal coordination of saving and investment, consumption and production suffers because of high inflation.
6. The high variability of the rate of inflation makes the prediction of future inflation rates impossible. As a consequence the adaptation of wage contracts and of prices has to use *ex post* indexing and in the end an indexing to the exchange rate. Since adaptation cannot be undertaken continuously, the loss of value until the next adaptation has to be taken into account in setting wages and prices. This implies the development of typical seesaw patterns for both.
7. The development of different prices and wages diverges strongly during hyperinflations. Especially administered prices and prices of goods and services provided by government-owned firms lag strongly behind the general development. Whereas wages and salaries of the lower occupational categories nearly follow the course of inflation, the real wages and salaries of the higher categories are often strongly reduced.
8. High inflations do not promote growth of GDP and lower unemployment, except perhaps in the beginning. At the height of hyperinflation growth is negative and unemployment increases.

NOTE

1. For a detailed analysis see Bernholz (1996).

REFERENCES

American International Investment Corporation (1977), *World Currency Charts*, 8th edition, April, San Francisco.

Bailleul, Antoine (1797), *Tableau Complet de la Valeur des Assignats, des Rescriptions et des Mandats.* 11th ed., Paris: Journal du Commerce.

Banyai, R.A. (1976), *Money and Finance in Mexico During the Constitutionalist Revolution 1913–1917*, Taipei: Tai Wan Enterprises.

Beaugrand, Philippe (1997), *Zaire's Hyperinflation, 1990–96*, IMF Working Paper, 97/50, April, International Monetary Fund.

Bernholz, Peter (1996), 'Currency Substitution during Hyperinflation in the Soviet Union, 1922–1924', *The Journal of European Economic History*, 25 (3), 297–323.

Bernholz, Peter (1997), 'Paper Money Inflation, Gresham's Law and Exchange Rates in Ming China', *Kredit und Kapital*, 30 (1), 35–51.

Beusch, P. (1928), *Waehrungszerfall und Waehrungsstabilisierung*, Berlin: Springer.

Bezanson, A. (1951), *Prices and Inflation During the American Revolution, Pennsylvania, 1770–1790*, Philadelphia: University of Pennsylvania Press.

Bordes, Jan Walras de (1924), *The Austrian Crown: Its Depreciation and Stabilization*, Westminster: P. S. King & Son.

Bresciani-Turroni, C. (1937), *The Economics of Inflation*, London: Allen and Unwin. First edition, in Italian, 1931.

Burdekin, Richard C.K. and Burkett, Paul (1995), 'Money, Credit and Wages in Hyperinflation: Post-World War I Germany', in Pierre Siklos (ed.), *Great Inflations of the 20th Century: Theories, Policies and Evidence*, Aldershot, Hants: Edward Elgar.

Burdekin, Richard C.K. and Burkett, Paul (1996), *Distributional Conflict and Inflation, Theoretical and Historical Experience*, New York: St. Martin's Press, London: Macmillan.

Capie, F. (1986), 'Conditions in Which Very Rapid Inflation Has Appeared', in Karl Brunner and Allan H. Meltzer (eds), *Carnegie-Rochester Conference Series on Public Policy*, 24, pp. 115–68.

Chang Kia-Ngau (1958), *The Inflationary Spiral: The Experience in China 1939–1950*, New York: John Wiley & Sons.

Delivanis, D. and Cleveland, W. (1950), *Greek Monetary Development 1939–1948*, Bloomington, Indiana: Indiana University Press.

Deutschlands Wirtschaft, Waehrung und Finanzen (1923), Im Auftrag der Reichsregierung den von der Reparationskommission eingesetzten Sachverstaendigenausschuessen uebergeben, Berlin.

Donner, Otto (1934), 'Die Kursbildung am Aktienmarkt: Grundlagen zur Konjunkturbeobachtung an den Effektenmaerkten', in Institut fuer Konjunkturforschung (ed.), *Vierteljahrshefte zur Konjunkturforschung*, Sonderheft 36, Berlin: Hanseatische Verlagsanstalt Hamburg.

Dornbusch, Rudiger and Edwards, Sebastian (eds) (1989), *The Macroeconomics of Populism in Latin America*, Chicago: University of Chicago Press.

Driffill, J. L., Mizon, G. E. and Ulph, A. (1990), 'Costs of Inflation', in B.M. Friedman and F.H. Hahn (eds), *Handbook of Monetary Economics,* Vol. II, Amsterdam: North-Holland.

Falkner, S.A. (1924), *Das Papiergeld der Franzoesischen Revolution 1789–1797*, Schriften des Vereins fuer Socialpolitik, Munich and Leipzig: Duncker und Humblot.

Fergusson, Adam (1975), *When Money Dies*, London: William Kimber.

Fu-Chi Liu (1970), *Studies in Monetary Development of Taiwan*, Taipei, Taiwan: Nankang.

Garland, A. (1908), *Estudio Sobre los Medios Circulantes Usados en el Peru*, Lima: Imprenta la Industria.

Griziotti Kretschmann, Jenny (1924), 'Les Salaires et la Reforme en Russie des Soviets', *Revue International du Travail*, X (1), Juillet, 850–75.

Griziotti Kretschmann, Jenny (1928), 'La Riforma Monetaria Bolscevica', *Giornale degli Economista e Rivista Statistica*, LXVIII, August, 693–713.

Guttman, William and Meehan, Patricia (1975), *The Great Inflation, Germany 1919–1923*, Farnborough: Saxon House.

Harris, Seymour E. (1930), *The Assignats*, Cambridge, Mass.: Harvard University Press.

Hemingway, Ernest (1922/23), Dispatches in *Toronto Daily Star*, reprinted in William White (ed.) (1968), *By-Line*, Ernest Hemingway, Selected Articles and Dispatches of Four Decades, London: Collins.

Hoffmann, Walther G., Grumbach, F. and Hesse, H. (1965), *Das Wachstum der Deutschen Wirtschaft seit der Mitte des 19. Jahrhunderts*, Berlin and New York: Walter de Gruyter.

Hoffman, Walther G. and Mueller, J.H. (1959), *Das Deutsche Volkseinkommen 1851–1957*, Tuebingen: Mohr (Siebeck).

Holtfrerich, C.-L. (1980), *Die Deutsche Inflation*, Berlin and New York: Walter de Gruyter.

International Monetary Fund, *International Financial Statistics*, several issues.

Jacobs, Alfred and Richter, Hans (1935), 'Die Grosshandelspreise in Deutschland von 1792–1934', in Ernst Wagemann (ed.), *Sonderhefte des Instituts fuer Konjunkturforschung*, 37, Hamburg: Hanseatische Verlagsanstalt.

Jastrow, J. (1923), *Textbuch, 4, Geld und Kredit*, 5th edition, Berlin.

Katzenellenbaum, S.S. (1925), *Russian Currency and Banking, 1914–1924*, London: P. S. King & Son.

Kemmerer, E. W. (1940), *Inflation and Revolution*, Princeton, NJ: Princeton University Press.

Klemperer, Victor (1996), *Leben sammeln, nicht fragen wozu und warum, Tagebuecher [Memories]*, 1918–1924, 2 vols, Berlin: Aufbau Verlag.

Laidler, David and Parkin, Michael (1975), 'Inflation: A Survey', *Economic Journal*, 85, December, 741–809.

Lansburgh, A. (1929), 'Banken (Notenbanken)', in L. Elster and A. Weber (eds), *Handwoerterbuch der Staatswissenschaften*, Ergänzungsband, Jena: Gustav Fischer, 35 seq.

League of Nations (1946), *The Course and Control of Inflation: A Review of Monetary Experience in Europe after World War I*, Economic, Financial and Transit Department, Geneva: League of Nations.

Paldam, Martin (1994), 'The Political Economy of Stopping High Inflation', *European Journal of Political Economy*, 10, 135–68.

Phillipps, H. Jr (1972), *Continental Paper Money*, Clifton: Augustus M. Kelley. First edition 1865.

Roesler, Konrad (1967), *Die Finanzpolitik des Deutschen Reiches im Ersten Weltkrieg*, Berlin: Duncker und Humblot.

Rostowski, J. (1992), 'The Benefits of Currency Substitution During High Inflations and Stabilization', *Revista de Analisis Economico*, 7, 91–107.

Shun-Hsin Chou (1963), *The Chinese Inflation, 1937–1949*, New York and London: Columbia University Press.

Statistisches Reichsamt (1924/25), *Statistisches Jahrbuch fuer das Deutsche Reich*, 44. Berlin: Verlag fuer Wirtschaft und Politik.

Statistisches Reichsamt (1924/1925), *Zahlen zur Geldentwertung in Deutschland, 1914–1923*, Berlin: Verlag fur Wirtschaft und Politik.

Sturzenegger, Federico (1994), 'Hyperinflation With Currency Substitution: Introducing An Indexed Currency', *Journal of Money, Credit and Banking*, 26, August, Part I, 377–95.

Tanzi, Vico (1977), 'Inflation, the Balance in Tax Collection, and the Real Value of Tax Revenue', *IMF Staff Papers*, 24, 154–57.

Thiers, L.A. (1840), *History of the French Revolution*, translated by F. Shoberl, 3 vols, Philadelphia: Carey and Hart. First edition in French 1825.

Uribe, M. (1997), 'Hysteresis in a Simple Model of Currency Substitution', *Journal of Monetary Economics*, 40, 185–202.

Witt, Peter-Christian (1979), 'Finanzpolitik und Sozialer Wandel in Krieg und Inflation 1918–1924', in Hans Mommsen *et al.* (eds), *Industrielles System und Politische Entwicklung in der Weimarer Republik*, Duesseldorf: Droste Verlag, 395–426.

Young, J.P. (1925), *European Currency and Exchange Investigation*, Commission of Gold and Silver Inquiry, United States Senate, Serial 9, vol. 1, Washington, DC: Government Printing Office.

Zweig, Stefan (1944), *Die Welt von Gestern*, Stockholm: Bermann-Fischer.

6. Currency competition, inflation, Gresham's Law and exchange rate[1]

6.1 INTRODUCTION

In this chapter several characteristics of inflation, among them the working of Gresham's and Thier's Laws, which have been analysed before, will be considered together in a model trying to explain a complete cycle of inflation beginning with the introduction and ending with the demise of an inflating money in high or hyperinflation (Table 5.2). We have already studied two complete cycles, namely the events during the American Revolution and of the Ming paper money (Chapter 4). The idea of a complete cycle was first introduced by Subercaseaux (1912). In his highly interesting *El Moneda Papel* (pp. 279, 281) he calls the substitution of the inflating by stable money at the end of the cycle the *'abnormal way of re-establishing the metallic money (the demonetisation of paper money)'*. This is in contrast to the normal way of returning to a stable currency by changing the monetary regime through a currency reform. Four relevant stylised periods of inflation will be described in our simple model, which is related to the 'monetary approach' to the balance of payments and the exchange rate (see for example Frenkel and Johnson, 1976), to the theory of currency substitution (see for example Connolly, 1978 and Girton and Roper, 1981) and of competing monies (Starbatty, 1982).

The four periods contain characteristics corresponding to stylised facts which have been observed in many historical cases of inflation, and most of which have been described above. In period one, a new kind of money is introduced at a fixed parity with the old to finance a budget deficit. We call this money paper money. Since this kind of money is superior in some, but inferior in other respects to the old, it is readily accepted by the public and substitutes part of the old money, which will be called gold money. For instance, for higher denominations paper notes are more conveniently carried and transferred than coins. But only the gold money can be used for foreign payments, since it is also circulating abroad as currency.

In period two, after an optimal composition (portfolio) of the two monies has been reached by the public, the government goes on issuing the new, now bad money to finance the same constant real budget deficit. With a fixed parity or exchange rate between the two types of money, the additional new money surpasses the amount wanted by the public for its optimal portfolio and thus flows to the monetary authorities, who have to exchange it for the old one and thus lose official reserves. In both of these periods the balance of payments shows a deficit.

In period three, after official reserves have been exhausted, whereas the budget deficit remains, the government tries to maintain the parity (fixed exchange rate) between old and new money by making it legal tender and by trying to enforce its use with fines and penalties. As a consequence the bad money drives the good money out of the portfolios of the public. Gresham's Law works and the balance of payments is in deficit.

In period four, after the good money has left the country and with an ongoing budget deficit still financed by money creation, even the severest penalties cannot maintain a fixed exchange rate. The price level and the exchange rate begin to rise at an increasing rate. The balance of payments turns into a surplus. Thiers' Law holds the good drives out the bad money. Finally, it should be mentioned that periods three and four are usually interwoven in reality, since the fines and penalties imposed by the government may not be sufficient to prevent an increase of the exchange rate, a premium or agio (that is the premium in per cent paid for the gold or silver money compared to the value of the paper money) of the good money in a black market.

In many historical cases one or the other period of this stylised description has been wholly or partly absent. For instance, there may have been just one kind of money, namely paper money, circulating domestically in the beginning, with a fixed exchange rate to foreign money, and it is this paper money which is then inflated. In this case period one of the cycle is missing. Or the budget deficit is brought under control before period four can happen. Or the new type of money (for example banknotes or state-issued paper money) is not made legal tender and no fines and penalties for not using it are introduced, so that period three is absent. But the historical evidence shows that all periods have been observed, and that there are historical cases, such as those in Table 5.2, in which all periods have been experienced one after the other.

In setting up the model it will be assumed, as already mentioned, that domestic agents hold both a stable and an inflating kind of money and that only the former is also demanded in the rest of the world. This rest of the world is supposed to be large compared to the inflating small country. The increase of the money supply in this country will be supposed to arise from the financing of a constant real budget deficit, which is exogenous to the model.[2] To make the model not too complicated it will also be assumed that purchasing power parity holds in period four, too, contrary to the empirical data presented in Chapter 5.

As mentioned, the old money will be called gold and the new money paper money. This is, however, just a way to simplify speaking. The money which is 'value stable' over all periods can also be, for instance, foreign banknotes. And the inflating money can even consist of metal with a lower intrinsic value (given the parity) than the 'value stable' money. In the latter case, however, the highest possible rate of inflation is technically more limited than with paper money.

Before presenting the model and deriving results in Sections 6.3 to 6.7 we will present in Section 6.2 some additional empirical evidence for the stylised facts assumed or deduced for periods one to three. In Section 6.8 the results will be summarised.

6.2   EMPIRICAL EVIDENCE FOR PERIODS ONE TO THREE

First consider some empirical evidence for period one, which cannot usually be observed today, and for periods two and three. We turn first to Austria, which was on a silver standard when paper money, the 'Bankozettel', was brought into circulation in 1771. At first, the issue of this money was moderate and it remained convertible at 1 : 1 parity until 1797. It was highly esteemed by the public and commanded at times a premium of one to two per cent (Wagner, 1861, pp. 582–3). In 1788, 1794 and 1796 new amounts of paper money were issued, drove the metallic money out of circulation and led to an abolition of convertibility in 1797 and enforced circulation of the Bankozettel (Wagner, 1861, pp. 588–91). Thus the events of periods two and three took place.

It has already been mentioned that an early experiment in paper money was undertaken by John Law in 1716–1720. In the beginning the banknotes were convertible at a fixed parity and did not cause inflation until March 1719 (Hamilton, 1936/37; Luethy, 1959). According to Storch (1823, vol. 3, p. 401) the banknotes even gained *'one per cent or more against the (metallic) money in which they were payable'*. Things changed rapidly when Law began, from June 1719, to issue more and more banknotes to float the securities of the newly created Company of the Indies and, from September 1719, to buy back the interest-bearing public debt, which he had contracted to refund (Hamilton, 1936/37, pp. 54–5; Luethy, 1959, p. 318). Convertibility was suspended, inflation began, specie left the country and the use of gold and silver was forbidden. In January 1720, it was forbidden to keep more than 500 livres in specie or in any form of gold and silver. Violation of this order led to confiscation and an additional fine of 10 000 livres. Deposits with banks, notaries and governmental agencies had to be exchanged into banknotes. Moreover, in 1719 and also in 1720 Law tampered several times with the nominal value of gold and silver money, presumably to discourage its use (Hamilton, 1936–37, pp. 60, 64; Luethy, 1959, pp. 320–3).

It seems obvious from the latter part of this story that in reality periods two and three of our development of the model cannot be fully separated. But this would even be predicted by the model, if fines and (or) penalties were not raised sufficiently to fully prevent an increase in the exchange rate. The good money would, under such conditions, still be undervalued compared to the bad money and leave the country. But inflation would now begin with the rise of the exchange rate though, until specie had been driven fully out of circulation, at a lower rate than the growth of the paper money.

The events described above can be found in many other historical episodes. Let us just recall three of them. In the early 1700s Sweden was on a copper standard. But copper was costly to handle and to transport. As a consequence, so-called transfer notes were introduced, began soon to circulate as money and to be substituted for copper. In the 1730s, the notes carried up to two per cent premium compared to the copper plates. From the beginning of the 1740s more notes were issued, the paper money began to show a discount and the metal holdings of the Riksbank were gradually exhausted (Joerberg, 1972, vol. 1, pp. 78–9). Thus we can observe not only the events of period one but also of period two of our model. In 1745 convertibility was suspended and paper money made legal tender (Eagley, 1971; Bernholz, 1982).

We need only briefly refer to the experience of the United States during the Civil War. The issue of the new paper money, the 'greenbacks', did not initially endanger convertibility. But in 1862 the parity could no longer be maintained, because of excessive issues. Gold went to a premium, paper money was made legal tender and the free gold market suppressed for some time (Mitchell, 1908).

Finally we turn to Peru in the 1870s. Before 1875 notes had been issued by several banks which were convertible into silver. In this year, however, the Treasury showed a large deficit since the revenues stemming from guano sales were only just sufficient to pay the interest on the foreign debt incurred a few years before to finance the construction of railways. The deficit was covered by credits from the private banks, which issued additional notes of about the same amount. As a consequence they lost a great part of their gold reserves, which left the country. In December the Government allowed the banks to suspend convertibility of the notes issued by them for four months. But further issues of paper money to finance budget deficits prevented a return to convertibility and led to an increase of the exchange rate and to inflation (Garland, 1908, pp. 35–42).

The penalties introduced during period three have sometimes been much harsher than even those imposed by Law. As noted already in Chapter 5,

during the French Revolution the Convention Nationale decreed in a law of
August 1793 that:

> *Each Frenchman convicted of having refused the payment of assignat money, or to*
> *have it taken or given at a discount, will be fined 3000 livres and be imprisoned*
> *for six months the first time. In case of reversion the fine will be doubled and he*
> *will be condemned to 20 years in prison in chains.* (Jastrow, 1923, p. 67, my trans-
> lation)

In May 1794 harsh penalties were decreed

> *... against all those who are found guilty of having bought or sold specie, of having*
> *paid, fixed or proposed different prices for payment in specie and assignats, or of*
> *having asked in which money payment should be received before concluding or*
> *finishing a transaction.* (Jastrow, 1923, p. 70, my translation)

Measures against limiting the use of good money are by no means confined to
early times. Austria centralised the buying and selling of foreign exchange at
the Devisenzentrale in July 1922. Any violation of the rigid exchange controls
was punished with severe penalties and informers were rewarded (Bordes,
1924). Germany, too, introduced tougher and tougher exchange controls
during the great inflation (see Beusch, 1928, pp. 89–101, for a list of many
laws and executive orders from 1922). For instance, from December 1922
foreign exchange could only be purchased with the permission of the Internal
Revenue, though there were exceptions for firms having a confirmation from
their (public) chambers of commerce.

In the great Chinese inflation during and after World War II, selling and
buying of gold and silver were prohibited and severe penalties imposed from
1939–1943 and in 1947/48 (Shun-Hsin Chou, 1963, pp. 224–7).

6.3   *THE MODEL

We consider a small country and the rest of the world, which both use gold
(coins) as money. The total constant stock of money is called $\bar{G}$, the variable
stocks held by the rest of the world G^*, by the monetary authorities of the
small (domestic) country G^B, and by its public G. Thus

$$G^B + G + G^* = \bar{G} \tag{6.1}$$

Beginning at time $t = 0$, the small country has to finance a constant real
budget deficit of amount A, so that with price level P we get for the nominal
deficit D in terms of paper money

$$D = PA \tag{6.2}$$

The deficit is financed by issuing paper money. The change in the nominal amount of this money is given by the balance sheet identity of the monetary authorities (for example the central bank):

$$\dot{M} = w\dot{G}^B + D \tag{6.3}$$

where w denotes the exchange rate (or the parity) between the two kinds of money. The dotted variables denote their derivatives respective to time. Equation (6.3) implies that no money is issued by buying from the public assets other than gold.

Let us turn now to the domestic real demand for money. Here we differentiate between the real demand for both types of money and the real demand for each of them. It is assumed that total real demand depends positively on real national income Y, and negatively on the foreign nominal interest rate, r^*. The latter corresponds to the real rate of interest, since no inflation or deflation occurs abroad, where only gold money is used. In addition to these usual assumptions it is postulated that total real money demand depends negatively on a parameter s, which symbolises certain advantages of holding paper money compared to gold (such as smaller weight), and also transfer and penalty costs which may be imposed by the government on holding gold money. Taken together the total real money demand of the domestic public may be assumed to be:

$$L = aY^b (1 + r^*)^{-c} (1 + s)^{-d} \tag{6.4}$$

where a, b, c and d are positive constants. Subsequently, Y, r^* and except for period three, s are assumed constant.

The real demand for paper money, L^M, is supposed to be a constant fraction of total real money demand if s, r^* and r, the domestic nominal interest rate, are given. It decreases, however, with $r - r^*$ and increases with s. The real demand function for paper money thus looks as follows:

$$L^M = gL(1 + r - r^*)^{-h} (1 + s)^k \tag{6.5}$$

with g, h and k being positive constants.

The interpretation of (6.5) is straightforward. With given advantages of holding paper money, $s = const.$, and $r = r^*$, that is without paper money inflation (see (6.10)–(6.13)), the public wants to hold a fixed share, $g(1 + s)^k$, of total real money holdings in paper money, and the complementary share, $1 - g(1 + s)^k$, in gold money. This can be called the optimal portfolio of the two kinds of money *given* monetary stability. Note that the composition of the optimal portfolio depends on the size of s. On the other hand, if r rises, then it becomes relatively more costly to hold paper money, so that the composition of the optimal portfolio changes in favour of gold money. Note also that because of assumption (6.11) below, $r - r^*$ corresponds to the expected rate of change of the exchange rate.

From this discussion, it follows that the coefficient of L in (6.5), which we may call C, cannot be greater than one. For not more than the total real money demand can be demanded in terms of paper money. Consequently

$$C \equiv g(1 + r - r^*)^{-h} (1 + s)^k \leq 1 \tag{6.5a}$$

We also postulate that $0 \leq d < k$, for the influence of a change of s on total real money demand should be smaller than on the real demand for paper money. Finally, we assume that the real demand of the domestic public for gold money is equal to total real money demand minus the real stock of paper money, M/P, owned by the public:

$$L^G = L - \frac{M}{P} \tag{6.6}$$

For $s = s_0$, that is, for the initial value of s at time $t = 0$, we assume the strict inequality in (6.5a) to hold. This implies that there exists an optimal ratio of L^M to L^G, with $L^M < L$ for $s = s_0$. This follows immediately, if we add the equilibrium conditions for the two monies

$$M \leq PL^M \tag{6.7}$$

$$wG = PL^G \tag{6.8}$$

Note that (6.8) has been expressed in terms of the paper money (see (6.10)). In (6.7), we have taken into account that not enough paper money may be supplied to correspond to demand, since period one begins without any stock of paper money. Since, for $s =$ constant, the total real demand for both monies is constant according to (6.4), the real demand for gold money is greater than the optimal demand for it (for $s = s_0$) according to (6.6), if the optimal demand for paper money is greater than its supply. For then $L^G > L - L^M$. If, on the other hand, the equality holds in (6.7) then $L^G = L - L^M$, and the optimal composition of paper and gold money has been realised.

Finally we have to take into account that the small country is an open economy. For its balance of payments B we get in terms of the paper money

$$B = w(\dot{G} + \dot{G}^B) \tag{6.9}$$

The surplus (deficit) is equal to the increase (decrease) of the gold stock in terms of paper money held by the public and as official reserves. This definition is somewhat different from the usual one since it takes into account changes in 'reserves' held by the public. Further, the validity of the purchasing power parity and the open interest rate parity are postulated:

$$P = wP^* \tag{6.10}$$

$$r = r^* + \frac{\dot{w}}{w} \tag{6.11}$$

Note that $\dot{w} = \dot{w}^E$, that is the equality of actual and expected change of the exchange rate, has been assumed. The foreign price level P^* and the interest rate r^* are taken to be constant. Finally

$$w = q, \text{ if } wG^B > fM \qquad (0 \leq f < 1) \tag{6.12}$$

$$\pi \equiv \frac{\dot{P}}{P} \tag{6.13}$$

$$G_0 \geq 0, \ G_0^B > 0, \ B_0 = 0, \ M_o > 0 \tag{6.14}$$

where q and f are constants. According to (6.12), the exchange rate and thus the parity among the two monies is fixed so long as official reserves cover a certain percentage of the paper money in circulation.

6.4   *FIRST PERIOD: INTRODUCTION OF PAPER MONEY

We start at $t = 0$ with a situation in which $M_o = 0$, $wG_o^B > fM_0$ and $B_0 = 0$. Now the government begins with the help of the monetary authorities to issue paper money to finance the budget deficit. Since $M_0 < P_0 L_0^M$ the public is ready to take up this paper money until equality holds in (6.7). Assume that this happens in $t = T_1$ and that $G_{T_1}^B \geq fM_{T_1}$. (If the latter condition were not fulfilled, the system would move directly to the third period before T_1.) Since L is constant and the same is true for P because of (6.10) and (6.12), it follows from (6.8) and (6.6) that

$$wG = PL^G = PL - M \tag{6.2.1}$$

But then, because of (6.9), (6.3) and (6.2)

$$B = -\dot{M} + w\dot{G}^B = -w\dot{G}^B - D + w\dot{G}^B$$

$$B = -D = -PA \tag{6.2.2}$$

Finally, the newly created money corresponds to the budget deficit, $\dot{M} = D$, and thus from (6.3)

$$\dot{G}^B = 0 \tag{6.2.3}$$

In the first period all the newly issued paper money is taken up by the public, who gets rid of a corresponding amount of gold. This amount flows out of the country and gives rise to an equal balance of payments deficit, which is again equal to the budget deficit. This process comes to an end when at time T_1 the public has acquired an optimal amount of paper money (see Figure 6.1), so that for $r = r^*$, $w = q$ and $\pi = 0$, equality holds in (6.7).

It should be noted that up to this time the issue of paper money cannot be considered to be an issue of bad money, quite the contrary. Then public prefers the new paper money to gold and this is used to buy more goods and services abroad, so that the issue of paper money increases welfare in two respects.

6.5   *SECOND PERIOD: FIXED EXCHANGE RATE AND LOSS OF OFFICIAL RESERVES

In this period the government goes on to finance the budget deficit by issuing paper money. Official reserves $wG^B > f M$, so that $w = q$ according to (6.12) and thus $P = $ constant and $r = r^*$ because of (6.10) and (6.11). But now equation (6.7) holds and L and L^M are constant according to (6.4) and (6.5). It thus follows from (6.6) and equations (6.7) and (6.8):

$$wG = PL^G = PL - PL^M \tag{6.3.1}$$

so that wG is also constant. As a consequence $-\dot{M} = w\dot{G} = 0$ from (6.7) and (6.3.1). Taking (6.2), (6.3) and (6.9) we thus get:

$$0 = w\dot{G}^B + D = w\dot{G}^B + PA$$

$$D = -w\dot{G}^B = PA \tag{6.3.2}$$

$$B = w\dot{G}^B = -D = -PA \tag{6.3.3}$$

In this period the public adheres to its optimal portfolio of the two monies. The additional amount of paper money issued is converted through the monetary authorities into gold, which flows out of the country. The budget deficit is equal to the balance of payments deficit and to the loss of official reserves. The stock of money in the hands of the public remains unchanged. Since these are well-known results of the monetary approach to the balance of payments, no further comment is necessary. Finally, denote as T_2 the time at which $wG^B = fM$, so that period two extends from T_1 to T_2.

6.6   *THIRD PERIOD: GRESHAM'S LAW AT WORK

Since official reserves have now reached their minimum, the fixed exchange rate can no longer be maintained by official interventions in the exchange market but only by government regulations. Foreign credit to monetary authorities is excluded in our model, and anyway would merely postpone the date at which official interventions must be ended, given that more paper money is continually being issued.

Suppose then that the government makes the paper money legal tender and introduces and increases, if necessary, penalties against a discount of the paper money or a premium on gold or, what amounts to the same thing, a change of the exchange rate between gold and paper money. In our model this means changing s in equations (6.5) and (6.4) in such a way that w and thus r and P remain unchanged (equations (6.10) and (6.11)). It implies, moreover, that the real demand for paper money grows, whereas the demand for gold money decreases (see also (6.5a) and (6.6)).

Note first that now $\dot{G}^B = 0$, that is interventions in the exchange market have ended. Then, from (6.2), (6.3) and (6.9):

$$\dot{M} = D = PA \qquad (6.4.1)$$

$$B = w\dot{G} \qquad (6.4.2)$$

From equations (6.7), (6.5) and (6.5a) we get, since $\pi = r - r^* = 0$ according to (6.10)–(6.13),

$$\frac{M}{P} = CL \qquad (6.4.3)$$

$$\dot{M} = (\dot{C}L + C\dot{L})P$$

$$\frac{\dot{M}}{M} = \frac{\dot{C}}{C} + \frac{\dot{L}}{L}$$

Thus because of (6.4) and (6.5a):

$$\frac{\dot{M}}{M} = (k - d)(1 + s)^{-1} \dot{s} > 0 \tag{6.4.4}$$

The absolute increase in transfer costs and (or) penalties must be proportional to the relative growth of the minimal stock of paper money to force the public to hold the paper money. Note that $\dot{s} > 0$ because of (6.4.1) and of $k - d > 0$.

Let us look at the development of wG. From equations (6.5)–(6.8) it follows that

$$wG = PL^G = PL - PL^M = P(L - CL)$$

$$w\dot{G} = P(\dot{L} - \dot{L}^M) = P(\dot{L} - \dot{C}L - C\dot{L})$$

$$\frac{w\dot{G}}{PCL} = \frac{1}{C}\frac{\dot{L}}{L} - \frac{\dot{C}}{C} - \frac{\dot{L}}{L} = \left(\frac{1}{C} - 1\right)\frac{\dot{L}}{L} - \frac{\dot{C}}{C}$$

so that because of (6.5), (6.5a) and (6.4)

$$\frac{w\dot{G}}{PCL} = -\left(k - d + \frac{d}{C}\right)(1 + s)^{-1}\dot{s}$$

By using (6.10) this can be written as

$$\dot{G} = P * L^M \left(k - d + \frac{d}{C}\right) \qquad (1 + s)^{-1}\dot{s} < 0$$

This implies, because of (6.4.2), a negative balance of payments.

Summing up, the bad paper money drives out the good money because the government further issues paper money to finance the budget deficit and takes measures to force it on the public at a fixed parity with gold. The public reduces its gold stock, the gold leaves the country and the balance of payments is negative. This process goes on until the gold has completely vanished at time T_3 (see Figure 6.1).

In reality, of course, the government may not be able to increase the penalties adequately or to find out whether its rules are being violated. In this case

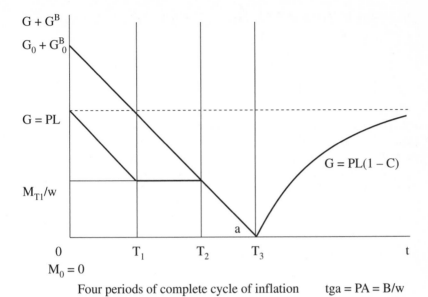

Four periods of complete cycle of inflation $tga = PA = B/w$

Figure 6.1   *Development of gold held by domestic public and monetary authorities*

transactions with gold may be undertaken secretively, at an increased exchange rate (premium or agio), or part of the gold holdings be hidden. But even then the higher transaction costs for using gold as a medium of exchange should lower the real demand for it and lead to an outflow. If s is not increased sufficiently, the exchange rate, price level and interest rate begin to rise. In this case periods three and four are interwoven. But there is still first an outflow of gold because the exchange rate is held below its equilibrium level.

We note that there is good reason for the government to make the paper money legal tender and to force its use on the public at a fixed parity with gold. For by doing so it increases the base for the later inflation tax. Moreover, in the third period it can prevent or at least lower – outside the model – the inflation tax and get the resources corresponding to the budget deficit from abroad without seeming to burden the public.

Let us stress finally that the developments of period three are parameter-driven in our model. They depend fully on adequate increase of s. This corresponds, however, to reality since regulations and penalties are legal measures of the government. An incorporation of such policies into our model would require a political-economic model not presently available.

6.7　*FOURTH PERIOD: THE RETURN OF GOOD MONEY

> ... *the paper money quickly disappeared from circulation* [in Mexico] *in November 1916, and gold and silver came back into general circulation almost as if by magic.*
> (Banyai 1976, p. 76)

If government policy in raising s is successful, G decreases until all gold formerly held by the public has left the country. Thus in T_3 $G = 0$ and $wG^B < f M$ so that, with additional paper money still issued to finance the budget deficit, it is impossible to keep w fixed. Let us consider the consequences.

Recall that $\dot{G}^B = 0$, so that because of (6.2) and (6.3)

$$\dot{M} = PA \tag{6.5.1}$$

From equations (6.7), (6.4), (6.5) and (6.5a)

$$\frac{M}{P} = L^M = CL \tag{6.5.2}$$

Here s is assumed again to be constant,[2] whereas w is now variable. It follows then from (6.10)–(6.13) that

$$\ln P = \ln w + \ln P*$$

$$\pi = \frac{\dot{P}}{P} = \frac{\dot{w}}{w} \tag{6.5.3}$$

$$r = r* + \pi \tag{6.5.4}$$

$$\dot{r} = \dot{\pi} \tag{6.5.5}$$

Differentiating (6.5.2) with respect to t and using (6.5.3) and (6.5.5) we derive

$$\frac{\dot{M}P - M\dot{P}}{P^2} = \dot{L}^M = \dot{C}L + C\dot{L} \tag{6.5.6}$$

Multiplying by $P/M = 1/L^M = 1/CL$ it follows that

$$\frac{\dot{M}}{M} - \pi = \frac{\dot{C}}{C} + \frac{\dot{L}}{L}$$

Thus because of (6.4) and (6.5a)

$$\frac{\dot{M}}{M} = \pi - h(1 + \pi)^{-1} \dot{\pi} \qquad (6.5.7)$$

so that

$$\frac{\dot{M}}{M} < \pi \qquad (6.5.8)$$

if $\dot{\pi} > 0$, and $\pi > -1$ which should be true to be in accord with the empirical evidence. Now (6.5.8) has been well confirmed for all advanced inflations (Bernholz, Gaertner and Heri, 1985; for Austria, Germany, Hungary, Poland and Russia in the early 1920s and France in the 1790s see Bresciani-Turroni, 1937, pp. 160–5). It means that the real stock of paper money M/P, approaches zero with $t \to \infty$. The base of the inflation tax shrinks towards zero, thus implying an ever increasing inflation tax rate π to finance the constant real budget deficit.

We will discuss the meaning of the condition $\dot{\pi} > 0$ in the setting of the model in a moment. Before doing so, let us complete our derivations.

Inserting (6.5.1) and (6.5.2) into (6.5.7) we get

$$\frac{A}{CL} = \pi - h (1 + \pi)^{-1} \dot{\pi}$$

Using (6.5a) it follows that

$$\frac{A}{g(1 + s)^k L}(1 + \pi)^h = \pi - h(1 + \pi)^{-1} \dot{\pi}$$

$$(1 + \pi)[\pi - B(1 + \pi)^h] = h\dot{\pi} \qquad (6.5.9)$$

with

$$B \equiv \frac{A}{g(1 + s)^k L} \text{ , a constant.} \qquad (6.5.10)$$

The differential equation (6.5.9) determines $\pi(t)$. It is obviously critically dependent on A, g, L, s, k and h, that is especially on the real budget deficit in relation to the optimal real demand for paper money and on the interest elasticity of the demand for money.

It has already been mentioned that the stylised facts of advanced inflations and of hyperinflations require that $\dot{\pi} > 0$. To see what this means within the model, let us analyse (6.5.9) and first set $\dot{\pi} = 0$. Obviously this is true if either

$$1 + \pi_1 = 0$$

$$\pi_1 = -1$$

or if $\pi = B(1 + \pi)^k$

The corresponding solution is denoted by π_2.

The first result is useless for our purpose, since it does not correspond to any empirical facts for inflation. The second equation can be analysed by considering function $x \equiv \pi$ and $y \equiv f(\pi) = B(1 + \pi)^h$ in Figure 6.2. Note that $d\pi/dt > 0$ if and only if $\pi > f(\pi)$.

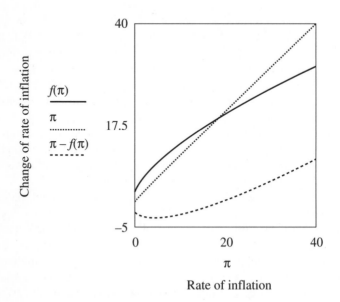

Figure 6.2   Development of inflation I

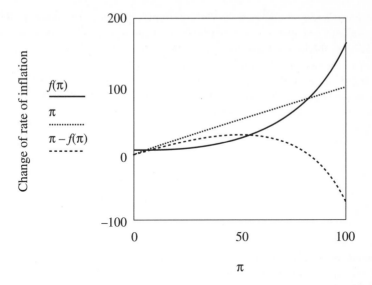

Figure 6.3   Development of inflation II

For $0 < h < 1$, which is a reasonable assumption considering available econometric estimations, there exists one inflation equilibrium, that is $\dot{\pi} = 0$, for a positive rate of inflation, namely π_2. For all $\pi > \pi_2$, $\dot{\pi}$ increases with π, which implies a π growing beyond all bounds. By contrast, if $h > 1$ there exists also an upper, stable equilibrium for π, which determines its highest value (Figure 6.3). In both cases, however, it follows that $\dot{\pi} < 0$ for $\pi < \pi_2$. This means that the rate of inflation decreases and finally becomes negative, ending up at $\pi = \pi^1 = -1$.

The latter result makes no sense empirically. The conclusion must therefore be that in the present model, to explain growing inflation caused by a constant real budget deficit, the rate of inflation $\pi = \dot{w}/w$ has to jump at time T_3 to a value greater than π_2. This implies, of course, a corresponding jump in the exchange rate and the price level, a trait of models of the type postulating rational expectations, as has been noted by several economists (Sargent and Wallace, 1973; Black, 1974).

If the real budget deficit financed by issuing paper money is not too high, the jump in the rate of inflation required in the beginning may not appear unreasonable. Still, looking at the empirical evidence for some advanced inflations and hyperinflations, this characteristic of the model appears to be doubtful. Given high initial real budget deficits financed by issuing money and a gradual rise of the rate of inflation from zero in several cases, the assumption of rational expectations seems to be clearly inadequate.[2] In spite of this we stick to the model for simplicity and do not introduce adaptive expectations or some form of learning implying changes in the expectation formation mechanism, especially since we have already done so in an earlier paper (Bernholz, Gaertner and Heri, 1985).

We conclude that if π and $\dot{w}/w$ jump to a value greater than π_2 at time T_3, $\dot{\pi}$ is positive, and π grows beyond all bounds. But then from (6.5) $L^M \rightarrow 0$ as $t \rightarrow \infty$. Let us now look at the development of the gold stock held by the public. From (8), (6), equations (6.7) and (6.10)

$$G = P*L^G = P*(L - L^M)$$

so that because of (6.5.5) and (6.6.5a)

$$G = P*(1 - C)L \qquad (6.5.13)$$

$$\dot{G} = P* (\dot{L} - \dot{C}L - C\dot{L}) = - P*\dot{C}L \qquad (6.5.14)$$

since $\dot{L} = 0$ according to (6.4). Using (6.5) and (6.5a) it follows that

$$\dot{G} = ghP* (1 + s)^k L(1 + \pi)^{-(1+h)} \dot{\pi} \qquad (6.5.15)$$

Since $\dot{G}^B = 0$, we derive from (6.9)

$$B = w\dot{G} > 0 \qquad (6.5.16)$$

In period four, therefore, the balance of payments turns into surplus, gold flows into the country and the public substitutes gold for paper money. What is the intuitive explanation for this process, reversing the balance of payments deficit of the earlier periods? Obviously, in a monetised economy the public is adapted to the advantages of using money compared to barter. But with the rate of inflation of the paper money increasing beyond all bounds, the real demand for paper money decreases and approaches asymptotically zero, since the cost of holding paper money is rising with inflation. But the public still prefers to use money for its purchases and sales. Thus the real demand for gold money increases. But to this excess demand there must correspond an excess supply of goods, services and financial assets of the same value. Since this relates to the whole domestic economy, the excess supply necessarily corresponds to the balance of payments surplus. The outside world pays with its stable money for its deficit which is equal to the domestic surplus. As a consequence, the excess demand of the public for stable money is satisfied. Thiers' Law is at work, with

$$\frac{M}{P} = LM$$

approaching asymptotically zero with t → ∞. Then G/P* approaches *L*, the total real demand for money (see Figure 6.1).

In the model inflation can go on indefinitely with an increasing rate sufficient to finance the budget deficit at an always decreasing base (that is, of the real stock of paper money) for the inflation tax. This is certainly not true in reality, in which paper money will be totally repudiated at some time T_4, depending on several factors like the technical sophistication of the payments system, the patience of the public, the damages wrought by the inflation and so on. It seems in fact that the highest possible rate of inflation has risen substantially from the French assignat inflation, to the German inflation in the 1920s and the Hungarian inflation in the 1940s.

Let us finally look at the rate of growth of *G*. It follows from (6.5.13) and (6.5.14) that

$$\frac{\dot{G}}{G} = \frac{-\dot{C}L}{(1 - C)L}$$

Using equations (6.5) and (6.7) we get

$$\frac{\dot{G}}{G} = \frac{-\dfrac{d}{dt}\left(\dfrac{M}{P}\right)}{L - \dfrac{M}{P}} > 0 \qquad\qquad (6.5.17)$$

As had to be expected, the growth of the gold stock held by the public corresponds exactly to the decrease of its real stock of paper money.

6.8   CONCLUSIONS

The model used in this chapter to explain widespread historical events is a simple one. For example, purchasing power parity and open interest parity certainly do not always hold. The same is true for the implied Fisher relation stating that the real rate of interest (in our case r^*) equals the nominal interest rate minus the rate of inflation.

In fact, as shown in earlier chapters, there seems to be a systematic undervaluation of the inflating currency with flexible exchange rates, until either a stabilisation or hyperinflation removes it (Bernholz, 1982; Bernholz, Gaertner and Heri, 1985). Also, the expected rate of inflation is not equal to the actual rate. Perfect foresight is not present in reality. Often, moreover, foreign countries experience inflation themselves, so that the relative increase of their money supplies together with growing (not constant, as in the model) real national incomes have to be taken into account. Finally, real deficits are not constant, inflation usually even increases them if it is high enough. And certainly not all countries are small.

We have seen, however, that the simplicity of the model has great advantages. It allows us to find the causes responsible for certain general events which can all be observed in some inflations studied, and of which some are present in all inflations studied. This is satisfying, for it is with this aim that general theories are developed.

Let us summarise some of the results:

1. A continuous flow of new money into the economy leads to inflation only after a more or less extended time, if the old money is also used abroad, which has historically been the case with gold and silver, but can also be true not only for different commodity monies but also for monies based on substantial foreign reserves.
2. A real budget deficit cannot be maintained permanently. The government must either reduce it or the inflating bad money will be substituted in time by the good money and the base of the inflation tax will be eroded. Here, of course, we neglect the asymptotical developments predicted by the model.
3. Because of the latter relationships, governments which find themselves unable or unwilling to control real budget deficit, are strongly motivated to try to preserve the basis of the inflation tax by making the bad money legal tender, forcing its use on the public, prohibiting the use of the old money and introducing exchange controls. All these measures will, however, in the end be inadequate to deal with the situation.
4. Gresham's Law works at an earlier period of the inflationary process, when the government tries to maintain the fixed parity between the two monies, in other words, with a double standard of currency (like the old bimetallism). Thiers' Law will only operate later when the increase of the now flexible exchange rate and of the rate of inflation lower the real demand for the inflating money.

It should be obvious how these results have to be modified if real national income grows, if the old money is also inflating but at a lower rate, and if the country considered is large.

NOTES

1. This chapter is based on Bernholz, Peter (1989), 'Currency Competition, Inflation, Gresham's Law and Exchange Rate', *Journal of Institutional and Theoretical Economics*, 145 (3), 465–88. Reprinted in Siklos, P.L. (ed.) (1995), *Great Inflations of the 20th Century: Theories, Policies and Evidence*, Aldershot, UK/Brookfield, USA: Edward Elgar, pp. 97–124.
2. There are other, much more fundamental problems with this type of model using the monetary approach with rational expectations together with a financing of the budget deficit by money creation. They cannot be discussed here. See Bernholz and Jaksch (1989) and especially Bernholz and Gersbach (1992) for a comprehensive critique.

REFERENCES

Banyai, R.A. (1976), *Money and Finance in Mexico During the Constitutionalist Revolution 1913–1917*, Taipei: Tai Wan Enterprises.

Bernholz, P. (1982), 'Flexible Exchange Rates in Historical Perspective', *Princeton Studies in International Finance*, 49, International Finance Section, Department of Economics, Princeton University.

Bernholz, P., Gaertner, M. and Heri, E. (1985), 'Historical Experiences with Flexible Exchange Rates', *Journal of International Economics*, 19, 21–45.

Bernholz, P. and Gersbach, H. (1992), 'The Present Monetary Theory of Advanced Inflation: A Failure?', *JITE (Journal of Institutional and Theoretical Economics)*, 148 (4), December, 705–19.

Bernholz, P. and Jaksch, H.J. (1989), 'An Implausible Theory of Inflation', *Weltwirtschaftliches Archiv*, 125 (2), 359–65.

Beusch, P. (1928), *Waehrungszerfall und Waehrungsstabilisierung*, Berlin: Springer.

Black, F. (1974), 'Uniqueness of the Price Level in Monetary Growth with Rational Expectation', *Journal of Economic Theory*, 7, 53–65.

Bordes, J. van Wide (1924), *The Austrian Crown*, London: King.

Bresciani-Turroni, C. (1937), *The Economics of Inflation*, London: Allen and Unwin, First edition, in Italian, 1931.

Connolly, M. (1978), 'The Monetary Approach to an Open Economy: The Fundamental Theory'. In Putnam, B.H. and Wilford, O.S. (eds), *The Monetary Approach to International Adjustment*, New York: Praeger.

Eagley, R.V. (ed. and transl.) (1971), *The Swedish Bullionist Controversy: P.N. Christiernin's 'Lectures on the High Price of Foreign Exchange in Sweden'*, Philadelphia: American Philosophical Society.

Frenkel, J.A. and Johnson, H.G. (eds) (1976), *The Monetary Approach to the Balance of Payments*, London: Allen and Unwin.

Garland, A. (1908), *Estudio Sobre los Medios Circulantes Usados en el Peru*, Lima: Imprenta la Industria.

Girton, L. and Roper, D. (1981), 'Theory and Implications of Currency Substitution', *Journal of Money, Credit and Banking*, 13(1), 12–30.

Hamilton, E. J. (1936/37), 'Prices and Wages at Paris Under John Law's System', *The Quarterly Journal of Economics*, LI, 42–70.

Jastrow, J. (1923), *Textbuch 4, Geld und Kredit*, 5th edition, Berlin.

Joerberg, L. (1972), *A History of Prices in Sweden*, 2 vols, Lund: C.W.K. Cleerup.

Luethy, H. (1959), *La Banque Protestante en France, vol. 1*, Paris: SEVPEN.

Mitchell, W.C. (1908), *Gold, Prices and Wages under the Greenback Standard*, Berkeley: University of California Press.

Sargent, T.J. and Wallace, N. (1973), 'The Stability of Models of Money and Growth with Perfect Foresight', *Econometrica*, 41(4), 1043–8.

Shun-Hsin Chou (1963), *The Chinese Inflation*, 1937–1949, New York and London: Columbia University Press.

Starbatty, J. (1982), 'Zur Umkehrung des Gresham'schen Gesetzes bei Entnationalisierung des Geldes', *Kredit und Kapital*, 15(3), 387–409.

Storch, H. (1823), *Cours d'Economie Politique*, ed. Say, J.-B., Aillaud, J.P. and Bossuage, P., Paris: Rey and Gravier.

Subercaseaux, G. (1912), *El Papel Moneda*, Santiago de Chile: Imprenta Cervantes.

Wagner, A. (1861), 'Zur Geschichte und Kritik der Oesterreichischen Bankozettelperiode', *Tuebinger Zeitschrift für die Gesamte Staatswissenschaft*, 17, 577–631.

7. Ending mild or moderate inflations

In this chapter we will try to answer the question how mild or moderate inflations can be ended, whereas in the next chapter the same question will be asked for high and hyperinflations. This separation into two chapters already suggests that the tasks to end these two types of inflation call for different answers (Ireland 1997, with comments by Blanchard 1997, and Sargent 1997). This is indeed the case. The reason lies in the fact that during high and hyperinflations the real stock of the national money has been strongly diminished, whereas this is not true for mild and moderate inflations, in which the real stock of money rises often even above the normal non-inflationary level. The effort, in many cases undertaken by monetary and fiscal authorities, sometimes with the support of international organisations, to end high inflations with the recipes adequate for moderate inflations has led several times to catastrophic consequences. We will return to this problem in the next chapter.

7.1 CONDITIONS FAVOURING THE STABILISATION OF MODERATE INFLATION

In Chapter 2 the inflationary bias of governments was analysed and historically documented. This led to the conclusion, supported by empirical evidence for different monetary regimes, that only monetary constitutions binding the hands of government can prevent or contain inflation over extended periods. The idea that sound monetary constitutions are necessary to limit the inflationary tendencies of unfettered government dates back to at least 1800, and has been favoured by economists like Jevons (1900, pp. 229–32) in England and Wagner (1868, pp. 46–8) in Germany. Ludwig von Mises stated it as follows (1912, p. 288):

> As soon as ever the principle has been accepted that the state is allowed [to influence] and has to influence the value of money, be it even only to guarantee its internal stability, then the danger of mistakes and exaggeration at once emerges again. These possibilities and the memories of the financial and inflationary experiments of the recent past have pushed into the background the unrealisable ideal of a money with an unchangeable intrinsic value as compared to the postulate that at least the state should refrain from influencing in any way the intrinsic value of money. (My translation)

Given the early insight into these relationships, it is surprising that the problem of how and under which conditions a sound monetary constitution can be introduced and maintained has attracted little attention. For if the political system has this inherent inflationary bias, why should politicians and governments be prepared to let their power be restricted by a monetary constitution binding their hands? Why should they agree and even promote the introduction of such a constitution to end or to limit inflation? It follows that these questions contain the very problem we have to address if we want to determine how and when inflation can be ended or strongly reduced for a longer future period. Possible answers may also throw light on which monetary constitution it is best to select when stabilising inflation. For though a certain constitution may be judged excellent for its consistency and potential to prevent inflation, it may be difficult or impossible to introduce it. In this case a less satisfactory but still helpful alternative must be envisaged.

When looking for historical patterns in the introduction of sound monetary constitutions, four different categories emerge:

1. The imitation of successful monetary constitutions like the gold standard in the 19th century or of independent central banks or currency boards in the 20th. This is an effort to reach a certain standard which is considered best during a given period. This category has already been mentioned and is sometimes connected with one or the other of the following categories.
2. The restoration of a stable monetary constitution at the old (gold or silver) parity following periods of war, during which convertibility has been abolished.
3. The introduction or reintroduction of a monetary constitution at a lower parity following moderate inflation.
4. The return to a stable monetary constitution following high, especially hyperinflation. In the next two sections categories 1–3 will be discussed, whereas category 4 will be taken up in the next chapter.

7.2 RESTORATION OF STABLE MONETARY CONSTITUTIONS AFTER WARS AT THE OLD PARITY

In the cases belonging to category 2, gold or silver convertibility at a fixed parity had been abolished during a war or during other dramatic upheavals, but was restored at the old parity afterwards. A number of examples are presented in Table 7.1. Here as for the other categories the question arises, which political forces allowed and would in the future permit such a return to the old standard. First, it seems that the most important factor working in this direction has

Table 7.1   Cases of restoration after moderate inflation at pre-war parity

Country	Period of inflation before stabilisation	Maximum of domestic/ foreign price level (normal = 100 for base year)	Year of maximum
Sweden	1750–1772	200	1764
United Kingdom	1797–1823	143	1813
United States	1861–1879	174	1864
United Kingdom	1914–1925	129	1921
Netherlands	1914–1924	233	1918
		160	1919
Sweden	1914–1922	141	1921
Switzerland	1914–1924	135	1919
Norway	1914–1928	165	1921
Denmark	1914–1926	139	1921

Notes:
1. Only the domestic price level has been used for Sweden in the 18th century.
2. In all cases except for the United Kingdom in the 19th century the ratio of cost of living indices has been used. For this exception wholesale price indices were applied.
3. Since the figure of 233 for the Netherlands in 1918 seemed to be rather high, the second highest for 1919 has also been given.

Sources: Mitchell (1976, pp. 735–47), US Dept. of Commerce (1975, part 1, pp. 199–202). For Sweden in the 18th and the USA in the 19th century see also the sources given with Figures 4.1 and 4.6.

been the perception of the population that the war period was an extraordinary event and that with its end everything, including the currency and consequently the monetary constitution, should return to normality. Obviously politicians responded to this widely shared feeling.

Second, national prestige has also often played a part in resurrecting the old system and parity. A leading power like the United Kingdom would have lost status if it had not returned to the pre-war parity after the Napoleonic Wars and after World War 1. Finally, for a world financial centre, as London had been at the outbreak of World War 1, the absolute trustworthiness of a stable international currency, the pound, employed in worldwide contracts was essential. We have already pointed out that for internationally dominant currencies of earlier times the preservation of monetary stability was much more likely than for less important currencies. Let us mention again the Florentine guilder or florin, the Venetian ducat and the Spanish piece of eight as examples. For Britain after World War 1 the competition with the emerging financial centre of New York was also an important consideration in this respect (Kindleberger 1984, Ch. 18).

But there exist also forces opposing the return to the old system at the pre-war parity. Especially industries and workers dependent on exports or who are competing with imports are mostly against the deflation necessary for a return to the old parity of the exchange rate, since the price level has risen because of the war. For as we have seen, such a policy removes the earlier undervaluation or even leads to an overvaluation of the domestic currency, and thus hurts the export and import-competing industries and those employed by them. But other sectors of the economy are also hurt, since the real effects of a deflationary policy usually precede the influence on the price level. The coal strike of 1925 in Britain and the General Strike in 1926 show which forces were aroused by the recession or depression that paved the way to the old parity. It is thus not surprising that David Ricardo (at least under certain conditions) and John Maynard Keynes favoured a lower than the pre-war parity. Keynes, in contrast to Ricardo, even preferred the replacement of the gold standard by a more discretionary monetary system (Silberling 1924, 437–8; Kindleberger 1984, pp. 337–42).

The strength of the political and social forces opposing reform is related to the necessary degree of disinflation. Consequently, a return to the old parity is only possible if the rise of the price level and the devaluation of the currency are not too far out of line with the cost and price levels of the main trading partners who have not given up or reintroduced the stable monetary constitution and the old parity. This evaluation is confirmed by the League of Nations (1946, p. 92) in a report on the monetary experiences of various countries following Word War 1:

> *Of the six countries which ultimately stabilised their currencies at the pre-war gold parity, five, namely Sweden, Norway, Denmark, the Netherlands and Switzerland, were neutral during the war and had been spared such fundamental dislocations of their national economies and finances as were experienced by most of the belligerent countries. All of them, including the United Kingdom, were countries whose currencies had not depreciated by more than one-half in relation to the dollar.*

As can be seen by looking at the maxima of relative price indices (Tables 7.1 and 7.2), only the countries with relatively low maximal indices returned to their pre-war parities.

7.3   PRECONDITIONS FOR RETURNING TO A STABLE MONETARY REGIME AT A NEW PARITY

In this section cases contained in the third category (end of Section 7.1) will be analysed. Here a return to or the new introduction of a stable monetary regime takes place after moderate inflation. In contrast to those of the second category,

Table 7.2 Cases of moderate inflation and stabilisation at new or lower parity than before

Country	Period of inflation before stabilisation	Historical comment	Maximum of domestic/foreign price level (normal = 100 for base year)	Year of maximum
Netherlands	1864–1875	No real inflation. Fall of silver price leads to abandonment of silver standard (1873) and adoption of gold standard (1875).	103.58	1873
Austria–Hungary	1864–1896	No real inflation. Fall of silver price leads to abrogation of private rights to demand minted silver coins at parity (1879) and to adoption of gold standard (1892/1896).	130 121 144	1887 1890 1896
Argentina	1884–1896		255 161	1891 1896
Czechoslovakia	1914–1927		818	1921
France	1914–1928		290	1916
Belgium	1914–1927		459	1927
Poland	1914/1924–1927		235.1	Dec. 1924

Notes:
For the Netherlands: Price of silver in terms of gold (exchange rate). The price of silver fell further after 1873, so fears of future devaluation and of an inflation would have been justified if the country had remained on the silver standard.
For Austria–Hungary: The first figure gives the maximum until 1892, the year of the currency reform. The second figure is the lowest price index between 1892 and 1896. The third figure is the maximum for the 1864–1904 period.
In 1896 the new gold parity became effective in setting a lower limit to the value of the Austrian guilder which was equal to two new crowns of 1892.
Argentina: Indices for domestic prices only. The first index refers to export prices, the second to wages.

Sources: See Table 7.1 and Figures 7.1–7.3

some of the historical cases considered were not connected with wars or other traumatic experiences. Also, in cases of a restoration of a former monetary regime, not the pre-inflation parities but lower ones were selected. These two facts are not unrelated. In the absence of an earlier war, revolution or whatever, no necessity was perceived to return to normality and to restore national prestige after an extraordinary period.

But given these facts, why has it been possible to introduce sound monetary constitutions after moderate inflations not connected with wars or other traumatic experiences? And in the case of wars: why could such monetary regimes be introduced with a lower than the old pre-war parity, given the fact that a restoration of the old parity was politically not feasible?

The answer seems to be that the same political forces that opposed a return to a pre-war parity, or are normally opposed to a stable monetary regime, favoured a restoration or an introduction of a sound monetary regime in the cases of the third category. And in those third-category examples which were connected with wars, the same political forces were strong enough to prevent a return to the old parity because inflation had raised the price level so much that a drastic disinflation would have been required. Indeed, Table 7.2 shows that the relative cost of living index for all countries with war-connected inflations rose to higher levels than for the cases belonging to the second category (compare Table 7.1).

Moreover, to understand better the political forces leading to a stable monetary constitution in the cases of the third category, it is necessary to recall the economic and political characteristics connected with moderate inflations and their stabilisation. If after a period of monetary stability, a country embarks on a moderate inflation, the first consequences are felt in the markets for goods, services and labour. Demand rises, production and incomes increase and unemployment tends to fall (see also Section 2.4). In spite of a few bottlenecks which may emerge in one or the other sector of the economy, no general rise in prices occurs, and none is expected in this early stage of the process, if people have no previous inflationary experiences. A rise of the price level begins only later and a demand for compensating wage increases is slow to come. All these facts are usually reflected in the statistical observation that even when the price level begins to rise, it increases less and later than the nominal stock of money (compare Figures 4.1–4.3, 4.6, 7.1–7.3).

But whereas domestic prices and wages react slowly in the early years of an unexpected moderate inflation, foreign exchange rates move up more quickly and strongly, though often less than the supply of money. Exchange markets are better organised and market participants are usually better informed about changes affecting the whole economy. It follows that the beginning of a moderate inflation (if it is higher than that experienced by the main trading partners) leads to an undervaluation of its currency.

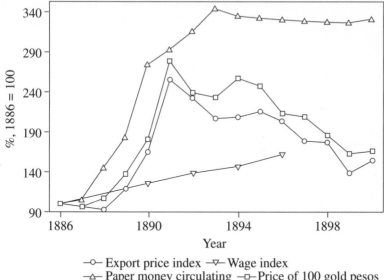

-o- Export price index -▽- Wage index
-△- Paper money circulating -□- Price of 100 gold pesos

Source: Williams (1920)

Figure 7.1   Argentinian inflation and stabilisation, 1886–1900

Consequently, export industries benefit from prices (expressed in domestic currency) that have increased more strongly than the prices of most of their domestic inputs. Similarly, import-competing industries enjoy better competitive positions in domestic markets than before the inflation. On the other hand, the stronger rise of import prices than of the prices of goods produced at home leads to a positive feedback on inflation, to so-called *imported inflation*. These relationships are rather long lasting, as can be seen from several historical experiences (Figures 4.1–4.3, 4.6, 7.1–7.3).

Let us turn now to stabilisation. To stabilise inflation relative to other countries requires a reduction of the growth of the domestic stock of money, at least compared to that of these countries. Such a development took place in all cases shown in Figures 4.1–4.3, 4.6 and 7.1–7.2. The respective foreign countries were either on a gold or on a silver standard, and in some of these cases the gold or silver premiums were used to measure the movement of the exchange rate when convertibility of the domestic currency had been abolished. Note that though in the case of Figure 7.3 the average annual index for the ratio of the money stock fell only in 1923, the monthly figures for the first half of 1927, when the stabilisation took place, in fact also show a reduction of the amount of banknotes and coins circulating compared to 1926 (Statistisches

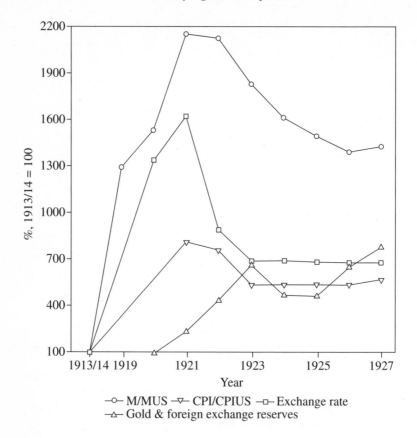

Notes:

M = Notes in circulation in Czechoslovakia; MUS: Currency held by public plus demand deposits in the USA; CPI/CPIUS: Cost of living index for Czechoslovakia divided by US index. Exchange rate: Czech (before: Austro–Hungarian) crowns per US $. The figure for M for 1914 is estimated as a percentage of the Austrian–Hungarian circulation, as corresponding to the figures given by Ammonn (1923), Alfred, 'Die Tschechoslowakische Währung und Währungsreform', *Schriften des Vereins für Sozialpolitik*, 165, 1–21, for this year and 1919.

The Czech crown was stabilised in 1923.

Figure 7.2   Czech inflation and stabilisation, 1914–1927

Reichsamt 1928, pp. 158*f.). These developments cannot be seen in the figure, since only annual averages have been used. Similarly, in the case of Figure 7.4, whereas the Belgian average annual index for the relative money stock declines only in 1925, the monthly figures show a decline also for the second half of 1926, when the stabilisation occurred (Statistisches Reichsamt 1927).

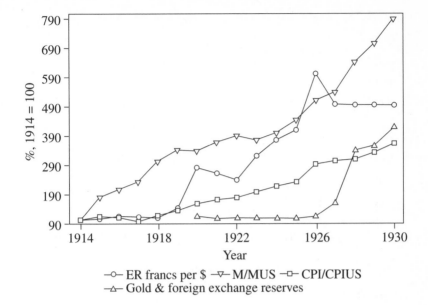

-○- ER francs per $ -▽- M/MUS -□- CPI/CPIUS
-△- Gold & foreign exchange reserves

Notes:
M = Banknotes in circulation in France; MUS = Currency held by public plus demand deposits in the USA, end of year; CPI/CPIUS: Consumer price indices of France and USA, respectively, for France from 1914–1918 index for food only.
On 25 June 1928, France returned to the gold standard with a gold parity equivalent to a parity with the US $ of 25.52 francs per $.
The CPI index figure for 1928 is an average of the first half of this year.

Source: Statistisches Reichsamt (1921/22, 1924/25, 1936)

Figure 7.3   Inflation and stabilisation in France, 1914–1930

Taking everything together, the following picture emerges as a conse-quence of the reduction of the growth (sometimes even the decline) of the (relative) stock of money. First, the rise of the (relative) price level slows down (Figures 4.3, 7.3) or even turns into a decline (Figures 4.1, 4.6, 7.1 and 7.2). Second, the exchange rate reacts more quickly and more strongly, that is, the external value of the domestic currency increases in all these cases, except for the case of Massachusetts (Figure 4.3). Only Belgium (Figure 7.3) seems to provide an exception, but there monthly averages of exchange rates declined during 1926, when stabilisation took place.

These results imply that undervaluation is reduced and threatens to turn into an overvaluation, so that a kind of stabilisation crisis occurs. For the disinfla-tionary effects on production and employment stemming from the decrease in the growth rate of money are reinforced by the stronger effect on foreign

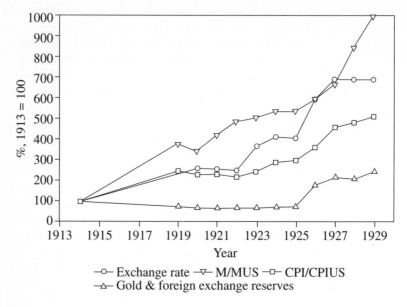

Legend:
—o— Exchange rate —▽— M/MUS —□— CPI/CPIUS
—△— Gold & foreign exchange reserves

Notes:
Exchange rate: Belgian francs per US $.
M/MUS: Banknotes in circulation in Belgium, and currency held by public plus demand deposits in USA, end of year. CPI/CPIUS: Cost of living indices, Belgium and USA, respectively.

Sources: Statistisches Reichsamt (1924/25, 1928, 1934)

Figure 7.4   Inflation and stabilisation in Belgium, 1913–1929

exchange rates, which usually even fall. Export and import-competing industries lose the advantage of undervaluation to which they had accustomed themselves. They and their employees feel the disciplining forces of foreign competition.

Politically, it follows that interest groups now begin to lobby for protection against foreign competition, for price support and (or) subsidies. Politicians respond to these pressures in the hope of gaining or preserving the votes of the people employed in these sectors of the economy. Although consumers will be hurt by measures restricting trade, the costs are widely dispersed and are usually not perceived as being related to these measures. Given this situation, governments can take quite different actions. For example, intervention could take the form of protective tariffs, import quotas, and anti-dumping duties, or it could take the form of interventions in foreign exchange markets combined with a new increase of the money supply. Interventions of this latter kind were pursued by the German Bundesbank and the Swiss National Bank in 1978, when their currencies were overvalued against the US dollar, and by the British Exchange Equalisation Account after April 1932 to depress the external value of the pound (Kindleberger 1984, pp. 382–4). A successful move to lower the external value of the domestic currency has the advantage of favouring not only the import-competing industries but also the export industries, which is not the case if the other protective measures mentioned above are taken.

But there is still another course of action available, namely to introduce a stable monetary regime at a fixed but still undervalued exchange rate. Such a proposal would readily gain support from export and import-competing industries, which would be hurt by a further strengthening of the foreign exchange rate and thus a fall of the degree of undervaluation. As explained, export industries would prefer such a solution to import duties or quotas. And politicians could even boast that they had finally provided an inflation-proof currency, provided that the exchange rate is fixed to a stable foreign currency or by a return to convertibility at a corresponding gold or silver parity.

It follows that the very forces usually favouring mild inflation and undervaluation of the currency are in this way harnessed to introduce monetary stability in the long run. The short-term interest of these forces in preventing a further reduction of the undervaluation or even an overvaluation induces them and, as a consequence, the politicians, to work for the implementation of a stable monetary constitution. This leads for some years to an inflow of gold and foreign exchange reserves and thus to an increase of the domestic money supply (Figures 7.2–7.4). And the price level continues to rise slowly until purchasing power parity for traded goods is reached. But afterwards this process ends and the price level is stabilised.

To complete the explanation of how political forces can under such conditions be motivated to bind their own hands for the future by a stable monetary constitution, it remains to explain why politicians try at all to stabilise a moderate inflation by a more restrictive monetary policy. And this even in cases when there has been no war or other upheaval after which a return to normality is wanted by the population. We have already touched on this question in Section 2.4.

The realisation by politicians that the inflationary process is or may be getting out of control seems to be a major motive against pursuing expansionary monetary policies any further. As inflation proceeds, more and more people, including wage earners and their unions, will begin to perceive inflation. Consequently, spending increases, bottlenecks develop, and workers and unions begin to include the expected rate of inflation in their wage demands. People become dissatisfied because of rising prices, which reduce their fixed or lagging nominal incomes in real terms, and since their savings are losing value. Creditors demand higher nominal interest rates for new loans.

The political party (parties) in power are held responsible for these developments. As a consequence, government and opposition leaders now find it politically feasible or rewarding to propose and to enact disinflationary measures. A comparison with other countries enjoying greater stability may also engender a widespread public belief that stabilisation policies are necessary. The prevention of capital flight, moreover, induced by outside stability, may be an additional motive to turn away from expansionary monetary and fiscal policies.

Although stabilisation efforts can thus be expected after the main advantages of moderate inflation have been exhausted, this does not mean that politicians will persist in stabilisation efforts until an inflation-free situation has been reached. Indeed, as already discussed in Section 2.4, disinflation itself awakens political forces opposing the further pursuit of stabilisation policies. It follows that another turnaround has to be expected, if the propitious moment of mounting pressures on export and import-competing industries is not used to introduce a stable monetary constitution acceptable at this time to the political forces opposing further stabilisation.

7.4   FURTHER DISCUSSION OF HISTORICAL EXAMPLES

In this section we want to show that the factors discussed above were indeed instrumental in creating sound monetary constitutions in the cases of category 3 (Table 7.2). Let us begin with Argentina in the 1890s (Bernholz 1984), a case not connected with war. After years of inflation and rising foreign debts used to finance an unsustainable development boom, a general collapse in Argentina resulted in London in the crisis of the Baring Bank in 1890. The Argentine national Government, the fourteen provinces, and many municipalities defaulted. Bank runs in 1890 ended with the liquidation of the Banco Nacional and the Bank of the Province of Buenos Aires in April. The panic reached its high-water mark that summer, and a general moratorium was declared from 4 July to 18 October.

After stabilising measures were taken the situation changed swiftly for the better. The Rothschild Committee and the Argentine federal Government agreed on a moratorium on the payment of foreign debt for several years; a funding loan in the amount of $15 million; the Argentine Government undertook not to incur any new foreign debts; no increase in national obligations would take place through any arrangements with the provinces; and the Government would reduce the amount of banknotes in circulation. Some consequences of these measures can be seen in Figure 7.1. The exchange rate and the export price index declined sharply as a consequence of some reduction of banknote circulation. Unfortunately no cost of living index is available. But we can be sure that the latter declined less than the exchange rate. Some evidence for this comes from the still rising wage level. As a consequence, the degree of undervaluation decreased. Agriculture and such new industries as sugar, paper, and textiles, which had benefited from the undervaluation, were now hurt by this reversal.

In this situation, in which a further revaluation of the peso or even an over-valuation were expected, banker Ernest Tornquist proposed a return to the gold standard and to fix the parity (and thus the exchange rate) between the paper and the gold peso at 2.5:1 in 1898. His suggestion was taken up by the Government, and Congress passed the Conversion Law in 1899, in which the parity was set at 227.27 paper pesos for 100 gold pesos (the paper peso had risen further since Tornquist's proposal). President Rocca's message accom-panying the Conversion Law revealed the political motivations behind the return to the gold standard:

> [T]*he instability of all values caused by the rapid increase of the values of the paper currency ... strongly damages our most important branches of production. ... These disadvantages are especially felt by the producers and manufacturers. The rise in the value of the currency changes the economic conditions under which we have lived for years, and disturbs the equilibrium of the value relationships, espe-cially between wages, rents and production costs, which are changing extremely slowly, and the prices of products following world market prices.* (Quoted from Wolff 1905, pp. 56–7, my translation)

At this new parity the Caja de Conversion was obliged to exchange gold against paper in unlimited amounts. Scarcely any gold was available to secure the conversion of paper pesos into gold. But this fact did not matter, since the parity had been fixed at a still undervalued level. A balance of payments surplus resulted, gold had to be bought with paper money to maintain the parity, and the amount of paper money in circulation began to increase. Argentina embarked on a period of remarkable economic growth and had accumulated the highest per capita gold stock in the world by 1914.

France in the 1920s is another example of the reintroduction of the gold standard. Inflation and undervaluation relative to the US dollar resulted from the events of World War 1 (Figure 7.3). Finally in 1926, after a renewed crisis, especially in foreign exchange markets, the new Poincaré Government took decisive action. It eliminated the low fixed interest rate on the floating debt, increased taxes, cut expenditures, and began to refund the floating debt. The amount of banknotes in circulation was reduced from 56 billion francs in July 1926 to 52.8 billion a year later. As a consequence, the exchange rate with the dollar fell from 793.3 in July 1926 to 487.4 in January 1927. The undervalua-tion of the French franc dwindled quickly.

Given this reversal, political forces in France began to act to limit the revaluation of the franc. According to Kindleberger (1984, p. 358):

> *Pressure began to come from businessmen, especially in the exporting automobile industry, not to let the rate get too high. In its report of 3 July, the Committee of Experts had warned against a high rate (of exchange or parity) which would produce a deflation like that being experienced in Britain. . . . In November, when Léon Juhaux, head of the Conféderation Générale de Travail, the national trade union federation, protested about rising unemployment in export industries, the franc was stabilised **de facto** at close to the rate recommended by Rueff, 124 francs to the pound and 25.51 to the dollar. . . . At this rate, however, the franc was seriously undervalued.*

The return to the gold standard in June 1928 did not change the *de facto* parity established in 1927, which was indeed still substantially undervalued (Figure 7.3). The balance of payments remained in surplus for years, since the domestic price level moved up only slowly. Gold and foreign exchange reserves, banknotes in circulation, and the price level all increased until 1933.

Similar developments took place in Belgium, Czechoslovakia and Poland about the same time. The return to the gold standard at undervalued parities occurred in these countries with results similar to those observed for France. Belgium (Figure 7.4), however, allowed only a drop of the index of the exchange rate with the dollar from 794 in July 1926 to 693.96 in October, much less than the corresponding drop in France. In Czechoslovakia (Figure 7.2), on the other hand, the index of the exchange rate fell even more than in France, from 1628 in 1921 to 691 in 1923, when stabilisation took place. The Polish experience (Figure 7.5) was different since Poland had suffered a hyperinflation before, which was ended by a successful currency reform in 1924. But the reform had not wiped out all sources of inflation. As a consequence, a moderate inflation followed the stabilisation, which was finally ended in 1926. The rise of the price level from 1926 until 1929 cannot be seen in the figure, since the price level of the USA rose more than the Polish one during this time. Moreover, the price level decreased from 1924–1926, presumably because of the currency reform ending hyperinflation in 1924. But since the real stock of money rose strongly, nearly one half of the gold and foreign exchange reserves were lost in 1925. As a consequence the gold parity of the zloty was lowered, a measure which was politically feasible because of the reasons given above and since the relative price level with the USA was under pressure. Obviously, the new exchange rate fixed at 8.917 zloty to the US dollar (the rate selected during the reform of 1924 had been 5.184 zloty to the dollar) implied an undervaluation. This led until 1928 to a substantial increase of gold and foreign exchange reserves (League of Nations 1946, pp. 108–11).

Patterns in agreement with our arguments can also be found in the cases of

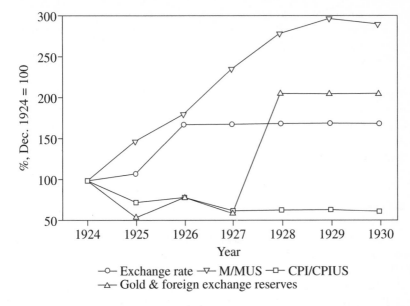

-○- Exchange rate -▽- M/MUS -□- CPI/CPIUS
-△- Gold & foreign exchange reserves

Notes: Exchange rate: Polish zlotys per US $, annual averages. M/MUS: Currency in circulation in Poland and the USA, respectively. CPI/CPIUS: Cost of living indices for Poland and the USA, December for Poland and annual average for the USA.

Sources: Statistisches Reichsamt (1924/25, 1928, 1934). For exchange rates also: Young (1925)

Figure 7.5   Polish moderate inflation and stabilisation, 1924–1930

Austria–Hungary (1872–1892) and the Netherlands (1864–1875). The former case had already been discussed along the lines of our analysis in a pioneering work by von Mises (1906, 1912). Also, in the case of the Netherlands the work of Bamberger (1876), Haupt (1886) and Kalkmann (1901) has to be mentioned. Although the movements of the exchange rates were rather small, they led to strong political reactions. For example, the Austrian guilder rose by only 8.4 per cent compared to the pound between 1886 and 1891. The increase of the real exchange rate was somewhat stronger, namely 14.6 per cent, from 1882–1891. But even this figure is small compared to the magnitudes to which we are accustomed today. The movement of the Dutch exchange rate that led to the currency reform of 1875 was even less pronounced, at 3.1 per cent. One explanation of why such small movements of exchange rates were able to generate such strong political reactions is that people in the second half of the 19th century were accustomed to relative monetary stability and therefore quite sensitive to changes of the real exchange. More importantly, von Mises (1906, pp. 561–2) points out that all experts expected a further revaluation of the Austrian guilder: *'The generally shared belief in a persistent "advance" of the Austrian currency was one of the most effective motives of the rapid beginning of the reform'* (see also Menger 1892).

The introduction of the gold exchange standard in British India seems to have followed the same pattern. Silver convertibility of the rupee was abolished by the colonial Government in June 1893, after the exchange rate had fallen from 22.5 pence sterling in 1873 to 14.625 pence in May 1893. At the same time the Government announced that it would buy gold in any amount against rupees at 16 pence per rupee, but would not buy rupees with gold. Taking into account that the fall of the rupee, similar to that of the Dutch guilder before, was the result of the declining price of silver, it is remarkable that the new gold parity was not set higher, and that no convertibility of the rupee into gold was guaranteed. It is at least probable that even the colonial Government reckoned with the interests of the export and import-competing industries (Heyn 1904).

After the end of silver convertibility, the exchange rate of the rupee fluctuated for some time and reached a low of 12.5625 pence sterling in January 1894. But it soon became clear that an undervalued gold parity had been selected as the upper limit of the rupee rate. After 1898 the exchange rate reached 16 pence, and did not move higher than a little above this parity only because of Government intervention (Heyn 1904, pp. 163–5). Gold and sterling exchange reserves were accumulated, the balance of payments showed a surplus (Heyn 1904, pp. 314–15).

It is revealing that legislation in Austria–Hungary (1892), the Netherlands (1875), and in British India (1893) merely set an upper limit on the parity for the value of the domestic currency. For only the purchase of gold with domestic currency was guaranteed by law at the legal parity. As von Mises explained (1906, pp. 581–2):

> [I]t seems certain that the victory of the reform project was assisted by just the fact that accepting the bills of the Government [the paper money] only prohibited, at the moment, a further increase of the value of the currency and that the chance of its eventual decrease, if such existed, was left open. By agreeing to the currency reform the friends of easy money lost nothing but gained much, namely the fixation of an upper limit for the currency.

In Austria–Hungary full *de facto* convertibility was reached only when the Austrian–Hungarian Bank began, in 1896, to follow the initiative of the Government and the wishes of the business world, to sell gold at the new parity (von Mises 1906, p. 582). The political situation in the Netherlands and India was probably similar. The Bank of the Netherlands began as early as 1875 to sell gold at 1653 guilders per kilogram of fine gold (Kalkmann 1901, p. 56). Finally, the British Indian Government was also ready, if not legally bound, to exchange rupees into gold at parity in 1899 (Heyn 1904, p. 316).

7.5 MORE RECENT HISTORICAL EXAMPLES

After the breakdown of the Bretton Woods system in 1971, when President Nixon abolished the gold convertibility of the US dollar at a fixed parity, which had only existed for monetary authorities, all countries found themselves with discretionary paper money regimes. The introduction of a stable monetary regime under these conditions meant either the creation of an independent central bank or the establishment of a fixed exchange rate with one of the more stable currencies, mainly the dollar and to a much lesser degree the Deutschmark (DM) (Section 2.2). The introduction of a fixed exchange rate can also take the form of the creation of a currency board instead of a central bank in the proper sense. A currency board is only permitted to issue the national currency in exchange for the stable foreign currency to which its exchange rate is pegged at a fixed parity.

For our comparative analysis concerning the introduction of a stable monetary regime after moderate inflation, the European Exchange Rate Mechanism of 1972–1978 (the so-called 'Snake') and the European Monetary System of 1979–1998 are of interest. In spite of several credit provisions and some intervention rules for foreign exchange markets, especially in the latter system, both were *de facto* arranged around the DM as the stable reserve currency managed by the German Bundesbank (for a detailed discussion see Bernholz 1999). This means that all other participating countries had in fact fixed the exchange rates of their currencies to the DM. For our analysis it is relevant to check whether countries joining these two systems after moderate inflation did so at an undervalued exchange rate, similar to the cases discussed in Section 7.3.

A first case to be studied are the countries which joined the European 'Snake' when it was formed in 1972. It has however to be admitted that the comparison of their purchasing power parities and their exchange rates with the DM cannot be taken as conclusive evidence for our hypothesis. This follows because the respective countries were also members of the tottering Bretton Woods system with its fixed exchange rates, so that the exchange rates with the DM were just implied by this system. Still, the comparison is not without relevance. For first, several currencies had been devalued during the Bretton Woods system. From this it is obvious that some adaptation of exchange rates compared to the DM either was or could have been undertaken. Thus, if for the countries joining the 'Snake' at its formation an undervaluation of the currencies compared to the DM can be observed, this can be interpreted as weak evidence for the above hypothesis (Table 7.3).

In Table 7.3 absolute purchasing power parities have been taken. They were calculated by the German Statistisches Bundesamt applying the goods and their weights in the German and domestic baskets used for constructing the

Table 7.3 Undervaluation of several currencies entering the European 'Snake' (compared to the DM in 1971)

	Baskets	France	Denmark	Netherlands	Belgium	Norway
Cost of basket in DM = purchasing power	German	0.7	51.56	1.1	7.5	46.27
	Domestic	0.79	53.56	1.22	8.57	52.55
	Average	0.745	52.56	1.16	8.035	49.41
Exchange rate, DM with domestic currency		0.63	47.02	1	7.17	49.59
Undervaluation: < 1		0.846	0.895	0.862	0.892	1.004

Note:
The baskets refer to the goods and their weights used in calculating the German and the domestic cost of living indices, respectively. The calculation is performed by the German Federal Statistical Office (Statistisches Bundesamt)

Source: Statistisches Bundesamt, *Statistisches Jahrbuch fuer die Bundesrepublik Deutschland, 1977.*

cost of living indices. We have also taken the averages of these two measures. By dividing the nominal exchange rate by them, the degree of under- or overvaluation of the currency has been obtained. The year 1971 has been selected, since the countries discussed decided to participate in the 'Snake' in mid-1972. As can be seen, only the Norwegian exchange rate corresponded to purchasing power parity. All other currencies were undervalued in relation to the DM by more than 10 per cent. It follows that all cases except that of Norway correspond to our hypothesis. It may also be mentioned that France left the 'Snake' in early 1974, re-entered it in July 1975 and left it again in March 1976. It suffered from much higher rates of inflation during the years 1973–1977 than Germany. The average annual rate of inflation amounted to 10.24 per cent for France and to 5.34 per cent for Germany during this period.

For our hypothesis it is even more instructive to check whether the currencies of the countries later entering or re-entering the 'Snake', or afterwards the European Monetary System (EMS) or the unified Euro Currency Zone, were undervalued at the respective dates. So let us turn to exploring the respective empirical evidence (Table 7.4). We again use the absolute purchasing power parities as calculated by the German Statistisches Bundesamt according to the baskets of goods used for determining the cost of living indices. Unfortunately, however, for most of the countries only the calculations using the German basket are available for these years. This biases the results against our hypothesis since the purchasing power using the domestic basket of goods is usually greater than that using the German basket (compare Table 7.3).

Let us now analyse Table 7.4. We find that during the year in which the different countries entered the stable monetary system we observe an undervaluation in seven cases, but an overvaluation in the remaining three. In three cases the undervaluation and in two the overvaluation diverges less than five per cent from purchasing power parity. But we have to look at the sample more closely. Let us first consider the cases in which the respective countries joined the stable system during the first half of the year. Then the politicians and interest groups were presumably not yet informed concerning the developments of prices during that year. Their information rested on the situation of the preceding year. Looking at the evidence for the year before entering in these cases the number of undervaluations increases to eight, and only two overvaluations remain, namely that of Sweden in March 1973 and that of Norway in October 1990. But Sweden in fact entered with an undervalued currency. For in its case we cannot take the figures of the preceding year, since a devaluation of its currency occurred before entering the 'Snake'. As one can see, the average annual exchange rate fell from DM 67.06 to 100 crowns in 1972 to DM 60.96 in 1973. This leaves us with only one exception, Norway. But this country enjoyed or suffered an oil boom, and since much of the North

Table 7.4 Undervaluation of several currencies compared to DM and Euro when entering the 'Snake', the EMS or the Euro Zone

Country	Date of entry	Purchasing power: basket	Average of year	Average of year	Average of year
Sweden	March 1973		1973	1972	1988
		German	0.6	0.598	1.62
		Domestic	0.634	0.632	
		Average	0.617	0.615	1.62
		Exchange rate	0.61	0.671	1.59
		Undervaluation	0.988	1.091	0.981
France	Oct. 1975		1975	1974	1989
		German	0.56	0.59	2.92
		Domestic	0.62	0.66	3.42
		Average	0.59	0.625	3.17
		Exchange rate	0.57	0.54	3.08
		Undervaluation	0.966	0.864	0.972
	March 1979		1979	1978	
		German	0.45	0.48	
		Domestic	0.5	0.53	
		Average	0.475	0.505	
		Exchange rate	0.43	0.45	
		Undervaluation	0.905	0.891	

Italy

March 1979	1979	1978	1991
German	0.31	0.34	11.68
Domestic	0.38	0.41	
Average	0.345	0.375	11.68
Exchange rate	0.22	0.24	11.49
Undervaluation	0.638	0.64	0.984

Nov. 1996	1996	1995	1998
German	10.95	11.29	5.98
Domestic			
Average	10.95	11.29	5.98
Exchange rate	9.75	8.81	5.96
Undervaluation	0.89	0.78	0.99

Spain

June 1989	1989
German	1.55
Domestic	
Average	1.55
Exchange rate	1.59
Undervaluation	1.026

UK

Oct. 1990	1990
German	2.74
Domestic	3.21
Average	2.975
Exchange rate	2.88
Undervaluation	0.968

Table 7.4 (continued)

Country	Date of entry	Purchasing power: basket		Average of year	Average of year	Average of year
Norway	Oct. 1990			1990		
		German		17.64		
		Domestic				
		Average		17.64		
		Exchange rate		25.82		
		Undervaluation		1.464		
Portugal	April 1992			1992		
		German		11.02		
		Domestic				
		Average		11.02		
		Exchange rate		11.57		
		Undervaluation		1.05		
Greece	Jan. 1999			1999		
		German		6.14		
		Domestic				
		Average		6.14		
		Exchange rate		6.004		
		Undervaluation		0.978		

Notes: Purchasing power: cost of basket in DM. Undervaluation: < 1

Sources: Statistisches Bundesamt (1980, 1994, 1998, 2000)

Sea oil was exported, an overvaluation of its currency had developed and could be maintained.

Finally, we have to take into account that politicians and interest groups were presumably guided by their domestic cost of living indices and not by the German index. Unfortunately, the former indices are not available in all cases. But in all cases in which they are present, they imply a stronger undervaluation than the German index. The domestic figures in Table 7.4 are always higher than the German ones. In two cases, a slight undervaluation of less than five per cent is turned into a higher one. The undervaluation figure for France (Oct. 1975) is 0.92 and for the United Kingdom (Oct. 1990) 0.897 when using the domestic cost of living index instead of its average with the German index. We conclude that the developments in Europe from 1971 to 2001 demonstrate again that countries tend to join stable monetary systems at an undervalued exchange rate.

7.6 CONCLUSIONS

The results of this chapter can be summarised as follows. In stabilising moderate inflation the hands of government have to be bound with the help of institutional reforms for the reasons explained in Section 2.4. The institutional measures can take different forms: the introduction of a metallic standard with a fixed (gold or silver) parity and full convertibility; the creation of an independent central bank; the fixing of the exchange rate to a (relatively stable) currency; and a further strengthening of this latter measure by creating a currency board. But since politicians and governments are not inclined to allow their influence to be restrained, special circumstances have to be present to make such measures palatable to them. The following environments have been found to be favourable for the introduction of stable monetary regimes after moderate inflations.

1. Imitation of the example of more stable currencies. Political pressure for such a step may arise since the population compares the unfavourable performance of its own currency with that of the former. This factor may, however, also play a role in conjunction with those mentioned below. It can be assumed that political pressure for imitation is the stronger the more foreign countries are following stable policies, as during the gold standard.
2. After wars or other upheavals a return to 'normal conditions' is favoured by the population. But a restoration of the old system at an unchanged former parity can only happen if the moderate inflation has not increased the price level too much out of line with that of the main trading partners.

3.	If after a period of moderate inflation, a reduction of the growth rate of the money supply is initiated to reduce inflation, the undervaluation of the (flexible) exchange rate decreases and may after some time even turn into an overvaluation. This, however, weakens the economic situation of the export and import-competing industries and endangers the jobs of workers employed by them. As a consequence, politicians are asked by the respective interest groups, including the unions, to take measures against this development. One such measure is the stabilisation of the exchange rate at a still undervalued level. This leads to some further mild inflation during the next years, but finally stabilises the system because either a metallic standard or a fixed exchange rate with a stable currency has been introduced.

REFERENCES

Bamberger, Ludwig (1876), *Reichsgold*, Leipzig: Brockhaus.
Bernholz, Peter (1984), 'Inflation, Over-indebtedness, Crisis and Consolidation: Argentina And the Baring Crisis (1884–1900)', *Zeitschrift fuer die Gesamte Staatswissenschaft (JITE)*, 140, 669–84.
Bernholz, Peter (1999), 'The Bundesbank and the Process of European Monetary Integration', in Deutsche Bundesbank (ed.), *Fifty Years of the Deutsche Mark: Central Bank and the Currency in Germany since 1948*, Oxford and New York: Oxford University Press, pp. 731–89.
Blanchard, Olivier Jean (1997), 'Comment on Stopping Inflations, Big and Small', *Journal of Money, Credit and Banking*, 29 (4), Part 2, November, 778–82.
Haupt, Ottomar (1886), *L'Histoire Monétaire de Notre Temps*, Berlin and Paris.
Heyn, O. (1904), 'Das Steigen des Rupienkurses nach der Aufhebung der Indischen Silberwaehrung und seine Ursachen', in *Jahrbuecher fuer Nationaloekonomie und Statistik*, 38, 3rd series, pp. 160–79, 289–318.
Ireland, Peter N. (1997), 'Stopping Inflations, Big and Small', *Journal of Money, Credit and Banking*, 29 (4), Part 2, November, 759–75.
Jevons, William St. (1900), *Money and the Mechanism of Exchange*, New York: D. Appleton & Co.
Kalkmann, P. (1901), Hollands Geldwesen im 19. Jahrhundert, in *Jahrbuch fuer Gesetzgebung, Verwaltung und Volkswirtschaft im Deutschen Reich*, 25, pp. 33–66.
Kindleberger, Charles (1984), *A Financial History of Western Europe*, London: George Allen & Unwin.
League of Nations (1946), *The Course and Control of Inflation: A Review of Monetary Experience after World War I*, Paris.
Menger, Carl (1892), 'Aussagen vor der Waehrungs-Enquête-Kommission', in *Gesammelte Werke*. 2nd ed., vol. 4. Reprint, Tuebingen: J.C.B. Mohr, 1970.
Mises, Ludwig von (1906), Die Wirtschaftspolitischen Motive der Oesterreichischen Valutaregulierung, *Zeitschrift fuer Volkswirtschaft, Sozialpolitik und Verwaltung* 16, 561–82.
Mises, Ludwig von (1912), *Theorie des Geldes und der Umlaufmittel*, Munich and Leipzig: Duncker and Humblot.

Mitchell, Brian R. (1976), *European Historical Statistics 1750–1970*, New York: Columbia University Press.

Sargent, Thomas (1997), 'Comment on Stopping Inflations, Big and Small', *Journal of Money, Credit and Banking*, 29 (4), Part 2, November, 776–7.

Silberling, Norman J. (1924), 'Financial and Monetary Policy of Great Britain during the Napoleonic Wars', *Quarterly Journal of Economics*, vol. 39, 214–33, 397–439.

Statistisches Reichsamt (1921/22, 1924/25, 1927, 1928, 1934 and 1936), *Statistisches Jahrbuch fuer das Deutsche Reich*, Berlin.

Statistisches Reichsamt (1928), *Die Wirtschaft des Auslands 1900–1927*, Berlin: Reimar Hobbing.

Statistisches Bundesamt (1980, 1987), *Statistisches Jahrbuch fuer die Bundesrepublik Deutschland*, Stuttgart und Mainz: W. Kohlhammer.

Statistisches Bundesamt (1994, 1998, 2000), *Statistisches Jahrbuch fuer das Ausland*, Wiesbaden: Metzler/Poeschel.

US Department of Commerce, Bureau of the Census (1975), *Historical Statistics of the United States*, Bicentennial ed., Washington, D.C.: Government Printing Office.

Wagner, Adolph (1868), *Die Russische Papiergeldwaehrung*, Riga.

Williams, John H. (1920), *Argentine Trade Under Inconvertible Paper Money 1880–1900*, Cambridge, Mass.: Harvard University Press.

Wolff, J. (1905), 'Die Argentinische Waehrungsreform von 1899', *Staats- und Sozialwissenschaftliche Forschungen*, 24 (5), I–XV, 1–131.

Young, J.P. (1925), *Foreign Currency and Exchange Investigation*, Prepared for the US Senate Commission of Gold and Silver Inquiry, Serial 9, vol. 2, Washington, D.C.: Government Printing Office.

8. Currency reforms ending hyperinflations

Then something strange happened [in Germany in November 1923]. *One day the incredible story began to circulate that soon there would again be money of a 'stable value', and this became reality some time later: small ugly green-blue notes with the inscription 'eine* [one] *Rentenmark'. When somebody first used them for payment, he waited somewhat surprised to see what might happen. But indeed they were accepted and he received his goods – goods with a value of one billion* [marks]. *The same happened the following day and the subsequent days. Incredible.*

The dollar no longer rose, nor did share prices. And if one changed the latter into Rentenmark, behold, they amounted to nothing, like everything else. ... But suddenly wages and salaries were paid in Rentenmark, and what a miracle, there even appeared ten and five pfennig pieces, strong, shining coins which maintained their value. It became possible to still buy something on Thursday with the money which one had received last Friday. The world was full of surprises.
(Sebastian Haffner, German political journalist writing in early 1939; posthumously published in 2000, pp. 65f., my translation)

8.1 INTRODUCTION

We turn now from the problem of ending moderate inflations to that of stabilising currencies which have suffered hyperinflation. Hyperinflations are, as mentioned, according to the definition by Cagan (1956), high inflations in which the *monthly* rate of inflation reaches 50 per cent or more at least during one month. The borderline drawn by this definition is of a somewhat dubious quality, since other high inflations show the same qualitative characteristics as hyperinflations, characteristics which have been described in Chapter 5: especially that hyperinflations are mainly caused by budget deficits which are financed by money creation; that an undervaluation of the domestic currency takes place; that currency substitution plays a decisive role; and that the real stock of domestic money falls strongly below its normal level.

In spite of this critique we will discuss reforms ending hyperinflations for the following reasons. First, we want to have a definite sample of empirical cases from which to draw conclusions; a sample, moreover, which is not determined by our own choice, so that there is no temptation to define its range according to our own hypotheses or prejudices. Second, since hyperinflations are extreme cases of high inflations, the conclusions to be drawn concerning the necessary and sufficient conditions for ending them may be more transparent than for other high inflations.

It should be apparent that in the social sciences it is very difficult to formulate necessary or sufficient conditions for certain events to happen or for the success of certain measures. It is almost impossible to obtain necessary *and* sufficient conditions. We know, for instance, that budget deficits seem to be a necessary condition for a hyperinflation to occur. But they need not be a sufficient condition since they may be financed out of savings, especially if a highly developed capital market exists, and if the growth rate of the public debt is not permanently higher than that of the gross domestic product (GDP). Similarly, a continuous increase of the stock of money is certainly necessary for an inflationary development. But it is not sufficient, as long as real GDP rises at least as strongly as the money supply. On the other hand, a substantial fall in the growth rate of the money supply may be sufficient to end high inflation, but is certainly not necessary, as will be shown below. Moreover, even if we can postulate on the one hand necessary and on the other sufficient conditions which are met by all historical cases considered, there may still occur later other cases which contradict these hypotheses. This is true for all empirical sciences, quite in contrast to mathematics, for example.

In spite of these problems we will try to formulate hypotheses concerning necessary as well as sufficient, but not necessary *and* sufficient, conditions to end hyperinflations for the sample of historical cases to be considered. No doubt these hypotheses may be contradicted by later evidence. But even in this case their formulation would be a stepping stone towards further theoretical developments in this field.

We have tried to assemble all hyperinflations in history. If we have been successful in discovering them all, their number amounts to twenty-nine up to the year 2001 (see Table 2.1). All of them had ended by that year, though some of the respective countries are still suffering from high inflation in 2002. Let us recall here that Cagan's definition also contains the dictum that a hyperinflation ends one year after a monthly inflation of at least 50 per cent has last taken place.

Our efforts to find the conditions for successful currency reforms after hyperinflations also encounter the problem that it is sometimes hard to get the necessary information on the nature of the reforms. This is especially true for several successor states of the former Soviet Union. The information can be unreliable or somewhat vague since it has not been assembled or presented by using the categories which are important for our analysis.

8.2   POLITICAL-ECONOMIC PRECONDITIONS FOR INITIATING SUCCESSFUL REFORMS

The prevailing economic situation during high inflations is quite different from that during moderate inflations. The public no longer has any illusions about the further development of the price level. As a consequence, the real stock of the national money has fallen drastically and currency substitution progressed widely. The domestic money was, first, no longer used as a unit of account for major transactions, especially for those implying deferred payment. Somewhat later it was no longer used as a store of value. Finally, it was substituted increasingly by stable (metallic or foreign) money even in cash transactions. For instance, when the Serbian hyperinflation was ever accelerating during the last months of 1993 and the beginning of 1994, even taxi drivers declined to accept dinars. Coins, especially ten pfennig pieces (= 0.1 DM) were bought at a premium compared to German banknotes, since the Yugoslav public needed them urgently for small transactions. As a consequence:

> . . . it has to be stated that the return to a stable monetary regime is inescapable as soon as the system has entered the phase of hyperinflation. For continuous hyperinflation has to end in a collapse so that either a reform or the substitution of the inflating currency by a stable money or by barter has to follow. In highly organised modern states usually the path of reform has been chosen. (Bernholz 1986)

In fact, as has been shown before (Section 5.3), the government is in imminent danger of losing its monetary authority, since currency substitution has progressed to a point at which it has to be expected that the real stock of the inflating money will soon reach a negligible part of total money circulation (Rostowski 1992). But this implies that the revenues from the inflation tax are dwindling because its base, the real stock of the domestic money, is falling to a very low level. At the same time ordinary revenues are also decreasing because of the misallocation of resources resulting from inflation and because of the time lag between declaration of taxes and their expenditure, that is because of Tanzi's Law (Section 5.2). Government expenditures have to fall. If no currency reform is undertaken at this juncture, the domestic currency is driven out of circulation (see the examples of Table 5.2). But then the government would have to legalise the stable money and to denominate taxes in this (these) stable currency (currencies). For otherwise revenues would fall to zero, which would mean the end of its rule.

It follows that the probability that monetary reform efforts will become politically feasible increases with the degree of inflation and that these reforms become almost inescapable during accelerating hyperinflation. Moreover, there are other events calling for reform. Since the population has learned about the mechanisms of inflation, any expansionary effect on the economy by increasing the rate of growth of the money supply is absent or negligible. The demand for labour falls and the misallocation of resources leads to rising unemployment. In such a situation government or opposition parties can gain a broad majority of voters if they propose a monetary reform. But at the same time scarcely anybody believes in proposals made by the discredited government or monetary authorities to change the monetary situation. As a consequence, the introduction of a new monetary regime, usually by a new government, which seems to be a credible safeguard against further inflation, is inescapable. Without the introduction of such a stable regime the reform would falter or be only partially successful. This happened for instance in the cases of the substitution of the French *assignats* by the *mandats* in 1796, the Chinese currency reform of 1948 and the Brazilian reform (Plan Cruzado) of 1986.

We conclude that a hyperinflation itself creates sufficient political conditions for at least trying to take monetary and fiscal measures to substantially reduce the rate of inflation. Whether the measures taken are sufficient to bring about a stable money is, however, a different question. For this purpose new institutions guaranteeing a stable monetary regime have to be introduced. It will be shown below which conditions are necessary and which are sufficient to guarantee a successful reform.

At the moment we are content to support our hypothesis that a hyperinflation is sufficient to engender a change of monetary policy with the empirical statement that in all cases of hyperinflation described in Table 2.1, with the possible exception of Belarus and Congo (Zaire), measures to substantially reduce hyperinflation have been taken. Even in these two exceptional cases hyperinflation seems to have ended for the time being. It is, however, not clear from the information available whether this is the result of monetary and fiscal measures undertaken by the governments. The monetary and fiscal measures taken by the other countries will be analysed in detail below.

8.3 SUFFICIENT ECONOMIC AND INSTITUTIONAL CONDITIONS FOR SUCCESSFUL CURRENCY REFORMS

It is relatively well known today which bundle of measures is sufficient to end a hyperinflation, that is which measures are sufficient for a successful currency reform given high inflations (Bruno et al. 1988, Bruno et al. 1991, Siklos 1995a, Vegh 1995, Ireland 1997, with comments by Sargent, 1997, and Blanchard, 1997). This fact has been proven again during the last decades by the successful reforms even in rather poor countries like Bolivia (1985), Argentina (1990) and Bulgaria (1997). Also, it is clear from the different situation during high compared to moderate inflations (see Chapters 4 and 5) that the reforms to be undertaken should take into account the respective differences.

We recall that high inflations are nearly always caused by huge budget deficits and that this need not be the case in moderate inflations. Similarly, whereas in the latter inflations the real stock of the national money is often above normal, it always falls far below this level in the former. Moreover, currency substitution reaches a high level in contrast to moderate inflations. The expectations of the public are highly inflationary. Government and central bank are not trusted any longer. Or as a Brazilian expressed it in 1984 to the author: *'If our ministers express some opinion, we just believe the contrary.'*

These characteristics of high and hyperinflations already suggest certain ingredients of promising reforms. First, in contrast to moderate inflation the nominal stock of the national currency has to be increased strongly to bring the real stock back to its normal level. The alternative to reach the latter objective would be a substantial fall of the price level at a constant nominal stock. This would certainly be an economically feasible solution. But it would usually lead to a severe depression and to such pronounced unemployment that the measures would soon have to be repealed in most cases for political reasons. It is because of this fact that one has to be critical concerning recommendations (which were also sometimes proposed by the International Monetary Fund) to reduce the rate of growth of the money supply and to diminish the budget deficit gradually in countries experiencing high inflation.

Second, the nominal stock of money should be increased, at least partly, by motivating the public to exchange its balances of foreign exchange into the national currency. Third, to reach these two aims it is necessary to restore the confidence of the population in the stability of the national currency with the help of adequate measures (Dornbusch 1991, Agenor and Taylor 1992, Miller and Zhang 1997). For otherwise the public would not be prepared to hold greater stocks of the national money and to exchange their foreign exchange holdings.

Finally, it should be mentioned that if these measures prove successful, then the budget deficit will decrease, since Tanzi's Law will work in reverse, as inflation no longer devalues the revenues of the government until they are disbursed.

At first sight, it seems to be impossible to introduce these ingredients of a successful currency reform together at the same time. A solution appears to be as impossible as squaring the circle. But fortunately this is not the case, if the right institutions are created, and the right monetary regime (Sargent 1982).

Let us turn now to describing an adequate bundle of such reforms. The empirical evidence that they will be successful will be presented in the following sections. The bundle of reforms which are sufficient to end high inflations contains the following measures:

1. Absolute limitation of the amount of credit which can be lent by the central bank or by other monetary authorities to the government in the future to cover its budget deficit, or the losses of government-owned or subsidised enterprises. This rule has to be anchored either in international treaties or in a constitution which can be changed only by a qualified majority of parliament. Independence of the central bank from other government agencies has to be introduced.
   a. In order to realise point 1 it may be necessary to reduce the domestic debt of the government, to bring down expenditures for interest payments to a feasible amount.
   b. Note that this measure is only necessary if the domestic debt has been indexed or been expressed in stable value terms, such as in foreign currency, gold or wheat. Otherwise the debt has long been wiped out by inflation.
   c. The same may be necessary concerning foreign debt (denominated in foreign currency). In this case, however, only a moratorium on repayments and (or) interest payments extending over five to ten years is preferable, to maintain future creditworthiness.
2. If the problem of restoring creditworthiness abroad can be solved (point 1c), it will be possible to obtain a foreign bridging loan, which can be used to finance short-term balance of payments and budget deficits, until the balance of payments has improved and the budget reforms lead to higher revenues and (or) lower expenditures (point 1b).
3. The real stock of money has to be increased to a normal level, since it fell to a very low level during the hyperinflation. To prevent a depression in reaching this end, the nominal stock of money has to grow adequately. Otherwise the price level would have to fall substantially. Obviously these aims can only be reached together if it is possible to remove inflationary expectations as much as possible at one blow, once and for all, by the reforms. For this purpose the following measures are to be recommended, besides those mentioned under points 1a and 1b:
   a. a new government implementing the measures;
   b. a new directorate of the central bank or, even better, a new central bank with different personnel;
   c. a new currency unit.
4. To make the reform more acceptable socially all private long-term credits which lost their value should be partially revalued at the cost of debtors.

5. Confidence in reforms could be gained by removing, as soon as possible, exchange controls and obstacles to imports. Excessive import duties and subsidies for exports should be lowered and slowly be abolished. During a limited period, adequate import duties could be introduced for goods which have been sheltered before by exchange controls or import quotas.
6. Instead of or together with an independent central bank a fixed exchange rate to a stable currency may be introduced. This measure can be further strengthened by the creation of a currency board instead of an independent traditional central bank. Safeguarding these reforms by anchoring them in the constitution would be helpful.

It should be clear that certain of these measures are not necessary for a successful currency reform. For instance, it is not necessary to introduce a new currency unit even though this may prove helpful to subdue inflationary expectations. Also, an independent central bank or currency board is only necessary if it is expected that the government would not be able, after the currency reform, to resist political pressures to finance part of its expenditures by money creation. But because of recent experiences of the public with inflation and the inflationary bias of the government, an independent central bank or currency board is also important to subdue inflationary expectations.

8.4   CHARACTERISTICS OF MOST SUCCESSFUL CURRENCY REFORMS: EMPIRICAL EVIDENCE

Let us first analyse the most successful currency reforms ending hyperinflation. With some reluctance those nine out of the total of the twenty-nine cases of Table 2.1 have been included in this category, in which the annual inflation in the year after the reforms remained below 25 per cent. Reluctantly, since another categorisation asking for less than ten per cent would still have included seven cases. Some characteristics of these cases are described in Tables 8.1 and 8.2. The first table contains mainly economic, the second mainly institutional characteristics of the reforms and of their consequences.

It is the task of the present section to analyse whether the empirical traits characteristic of the most successful reforms ending hyperinflations correspond to the conditions mentioned in Section 8.3. In the following section a comparison with the traits of less successful or unsuccessful currency reforms will be undertaken.

Let us first look at the annual rates of inflation after the reforms. They are below four per cent for seven of the nine countries. Three of them are even negative. Only Bolivia and Poland 1 show rates of inflation of 19.4 and of 24.48 per cent. For Poland a remaining budget deficit of 12.49 per cent in 1924

Table 8.1 Economic characteristics of the most successful currency reforms

Country	Date of reform	Annual rate of inflation in year after reform, %		Real stock of national money (100% = Normal)			
				Minimum before reform		After reform	
Austria	Oct./Nov.1922	3.83	till 9.1923	37.22	9.1922	104.83	8.1923
Bolivia	August 1985	19.4	till 9.1986	36.45	1.1985	61.69	2.1986
Bulgaria	July 1997	2.93	till IV.1998	12.9	4.1997	47.22	11.1998
Germany	Nov. 1923	-1.68	1924	4.93	15.11.1923	44.5	12.1923
Greece 2	January 1946	1.27	till 1.1947	0.3	10.11.1944	242.85	2.1946
Hungary 1	June 1924	-6.33	till 7.1925	18.41	8.1923	60.15	6.1926
Nicaragua	March 1991	3.5	1992	1.82	12.1990		
Poland 1	January 1924	24.48	till 1.1925	18.9	12.1923	122.78	6.1927
Soviet Union	Feb. 1924	-0.5	till 12.1924	3.71	1.1923	14.48	12.1924
						24.73	12.1925

	Real interest rate (ex post) %		Unemployment (Before reform = 100)		Government deficit/expenditure			
					Before reform %		After reform %	
Austria	3.821DK	1923	248.04	11.1923	51.36	7-12.1922	15.6	1923
Bolivia	36.87	5.1987	133.03	IV.1986	92.16	1984	-14.7	1986
Bulgaria	10.37LR	1998	97.16	1998	32.07	1996	-16.23	1997

Table 8.1 (continued)

	Real interest rate (ex post) %		Unemployment (Before reform = 100)		Government deficit/expenditure			
					Before reform %		After reform %	
Germany	11.13	12.1924	130.23	1924	88.86	1923	-12.19	1924
Greece 2			91.9	31.12.1947	99	4–11.1946	50	3.1946
Hungary 1	20.87	1924	137.68	6.1925	27.28	1–6.1924	8.45	7.1924–6.1925
Nicaragua	13.06 LR	1993	175	1992	44.96	1990	27.3	1992
Poland 1	-12.913DK	1924	174.26	1.1925	61.92	2.1923–1.1924	12.49	1924
Soviet Union	7.5DK	1924			84.12	1921	5.5	10.1923–9.1924
					26.93	10.1922–9.1923		

Notes:
Inflation measured with cost of living indices. 'till 9. 1923' means year ending with September 1923. '5.1987' and 'IV. 1986' refer to May 1987 and to the fourth quarter of 1986. DK discount, LR lending rate.
'Hungary 1' and 'Poland 1' refer to the first Hungarian and Polish hyperinflations.
'Greece 2' refers to the second reform of the only Greek hyperinflation. A first reform undertaken at the end of 1944 failed (see below).
Germany: Government deficit/expenditure for 1924: Only Reich.
Nicaragua: Open unemployment together with hidden unemployment amounted to 121.74%.

Sources: See Appendix

168

(Table 8.1) offers an explanation. Indeed, the remaining inflation was caused by the fact that the reform had only ended the creation of money to finance the budget deficit by the central bank, but not by the Treasury (this has been described in Table 8.2 by the expression 'partly' in the column 'Legal safe-guards, Budget'). The Treasury made full use of its remaining right to issue token money (small coins) to finance the budget deficit. Because of this, it does not come as a surprise that the ex post interest rate turned out to be nega-tive (Table 8.1). As a consequence a second reform was undertaken in July 1926 (Heilperin 1931) which closed this loophole and reduced the annual rate of inflation to 11.52 per cent in the year until June 1927.

Let us look now at the budget deficits of the other countries before and after the reforms. This is especially important since three countries which were more successful in ending inflation than Poland, namely Austria, Greece 2 and Nicaragua, experienced higher budget deficits. Moreover, Bolivia suffered from a much higher remaining rate of inflation than these three countries in spite of a budgetary surplus (as shown by the minus sign). Before trying to explain these differences let us however observe that all budget deficits as a percentage of total expenditures were strongly reduced by the reforms compared to the time before. This means that point 1a has been fulfilled in these cases, provided that normal credits covered the remaining deficit. As a consequence we have to analyse whether normal grants or credits covered most of the remaining budget deficit. We have already discussed the case of Poland. This leaves us with the Austrian, Greek 2, Nicaraguan, Hungarian 1 and Soviet cases, in which budget deficits remained. In the Austrian stabilisa-tion the budget deficit decreased from 15.5 per cent of expenditures in 1923 to a trivial 1.11 per cent in 1924. In the meantime the Government was able to finance the budget deficit by selling foreign exchange to the new Austrian National Bank. This foreign exchange stemmed mainly from foreign credits which, therefore, were finally used to cover the deficit (League of Nations 1946, Bordes 1924). The case of Hungary 1 is similar. Here again foreign credits arranged with the help of the League of Nations were used to finance the much reduced budget deficit.

Let us next look at Nicaragua. Here two-thirds of the remaining deficit were financed by foreign grants in 1992 (Kalter et al. 1998). The deficit after grants amounted to 6.69 per cent of expenditures and 2.2 per cent of GDP. In 1993 a budget surplus after grants developed. In considering these figures one should also take into account that the real stock of the national money increased very strongly, which implies a strong rise of the nominal stock, given the low rate of inflation. It is obvious that part of this increase could be used to finance the small deficits remaining after taking into account grants and credits. This fact may also explain events in the Soviet Union, given the small remaining budget deficit.

Table 8.2   Institutional characteristics of the most successful currency reforms

Country	New currency unit	Reform credits and grants	
		Domestic	Foreign
Austria	1 schilling = 15 000 kronen (after success)	Yes	Yes
Bolivia	1 boliviano = 10 mill. pesos (after success)	No	Negligible
Bulgaria	No	Yes	Yes
Germany	1 rentenmark = 1000 billion mark	No (Credit line of 1.2 billion rentenmark at Rentenbank)	Yes (but after success)
Greece 2	1 new drachma = 50 mill. drachma	No (Credit line of 1 bill. new drachma at Central Bank)	Support through grants in kind
Hungary 1	1 pengoe = 12 500 kronen (after success)	Yes?	Yes
Nicaragua	1 gold cordoba = 5 mill. old cordoba	No	Yes
Poland 1	1 zloty = 1.8 mill. Polish mark	Yes (Credit line of 50 mill. zloty at Central Bank for 1927)	No
Soviet Union	1 gold rouble = 50 000 1923 rouble = 5 mill. 1922 r. = 50 bill. 1921 (pre-war) rouble	Yes?	No

Legal safeguards		Exchange rate regime	Real exchange rate, %
Central bank	Budget		
Yes (new and independent bank) (control by League of Nations)	Yes	100 kronen = 0.0014 \$ 9.1922 (exchange controls)	294.52 9.1923
No; but management and 2/3 of personnel exch.	No	Controlled floating	330.04 9.1986
Yes (currency board introduced by law)	Strict safeguards, limited fiscal reserve account	1 DM = 1000 lev 1.7.1997	
Yes (new and independent Rentenbank)	No (but credit limitation at Rentenbank)	1 \$ = 4.2 rentenmark, 20.11.1923	258.87 12.1924
Yes (treaty with and by control of UK and USA)	No (but credit limitation at Central Bank)	Gold convertibility at fixed rate	296.64 5.1947
Yes (independent Central Bank) (control by League of Nations)	Yes	Fixed exchange rate with £, implying 3800 pengoe = 1kg 9/10 fine gold	214.74 3.1924
Amount of domestic liquidity bound to foreign reserves	No	1 \$ = 5 gold cordoba	144.74 5.1992
Yes	Partly	1 \$ = 5.1826 zloty, 1924, devalued to 1 \$ = 8.91 zloty, 1926	368.14 12.1924
Yes (by decree)	Partly (by decree)	1 \$ = 5.14 chervonetz = 51.4 gold rouble (foreign trade monopoly of state)	174.84 3.1925

Note:
No figure for the Bulgarian real exchange rate as compared to its minimum is given. For this figure is not reliable since it implies a strong overvaluation with respect to the relative purchasing power parity, whereas an undervaluation of 0.74 was present even in 1999 if the absolute purchasing power parity is taken (Statistisches Bundesamt 2000, p. 7).

Sources: See Appendix

For Greece, with a huge remaining budget deficit, things seem to look much worse. In fact, a first currency reform had already been undertaken in November 1944 (Greece I). But no sufficient measures had been taken in this case to reduce the budget deficit. It is true that the deficit fell from 99 per cent to 71.1 per cent of Government expenditures in the first four months after this reform. But this was only the case since the population increased its demand for the national money because they believed in the success of the reform. Tanzi's Law worked in reverse. But as had to be expected, with a budget deficit of this size the reform proved to be a failure. The annual rate of inflation in 1945 rose again to 1177.76 per cent, and the second reform (Greece II) was introduced in January 1946, with substantial help from the United Kingdom (Delivanis and Cleveland 1949). As shown in Table 8.1 this proved to be successful in spite of a huge remaining budget deficit of 50 per cent of expenditures. The budget deficit was financed, at least partially, with the help of foreign grants and credits, mainly by the USA and the United Kingdom. For another part money creation was probably responsible (see the huge increase of the real stock of national money in Table 8.1). But complete stability was not reached, given that the problems of the budget deficit had not been completely solved even with the foreign help. As a consequence additional measures had to be taken to fight the reviving inflation during the next years (Delivanis and Cleveland 1940, Eliades 1954/55).

The case of Bolivia raises a different problem. Why did the annual rate of inflation in the year after the reform still amount to 19.4 per cent, though the budget showed a surplus (Table 8.1)? Even the decrease of the annual rate of inflation to about ten per cent in 1987/88 cannot remove these problems. I have argued in an earlier article (Bernholz 1988a) that a persistent doubt about the permanent success of the reforms was probably the reason for this development. The lack of confidence can be observed in the extraordinarily high real rates of interest and in the rather small rise of the real stock of money after the currency reform, compared to those in the other cases (Table 8.1, Sachs 1987). These doubts were probably caused by the political instability which Bolivia experienced over decades and the absolutely insufficient institutional safeguards for the reforms combined with controlled floating of the exchange rate instead of a fixed rate (Table 8.2).

In spite of these remarks concerning Bolivia, note that a great deal of confidence was restored in all these cases of most successful currency reforms. The rates of inflation were reduced drastically, while at the same time the real and nominal stocks of the national money rose substantially (Table 8.1) and while real exchange rates increased by a factor from 1.45 (Nicaragua) to 3.68 (Poland 1) (Table 8.2). This proves that the public were prepared to increase their real holdings of the national money, and that this was partly done by exchanging stable foreign into national currencies. That is, Thiers' Law worked in reverse. It follows that the creation of confidence is of critical importance for the success of reforms.

During a long-lasting high inflation or a hyperinflation, government and central bank have lost any public credibility. Only when confidence in the currency is restored as much and as soon as possible, given this unfavourable initial situation, will the public be prepared to expect a low rate of inflation or even a total end to it. And only then are people ready to hold increased amounts of the national currency. If this is the case, then a strong transitory increase of the nominal stock of the national money is possible together with a stable or very slowly rising price level. As a consequence Tanzi's Law will work in reverse, the budget situation will improve. A relatively stable level of prices and a strongly rising nominal and real stock of the national money are, moreover, necessary to prevent a strong recession or even a depression implying a substantial growth of unemployment. Furthermore, a reduction of the budget deficit is necessary to hinder future inflationary money creation to finance it and thus for the permanent success of the currency reform. And as we have seen, Bolivia had to make up for its limited success in restoring confidence by creating a budgetary surplus without being able to reduce inflation to the same degree as other countries.

Consequently, a fundamental change in the expectations of the population is a necessary ingredient of any currency reform in an advanced inflation or hyperinflation. To quote Thomas Sargent (1982, p. 42): The reforms have to imply an abrupt change of the *'policy regime'* and *'the fiscal regime'* in the sense of *'setting deficits now and in the future* [in a way] *that is sufficiently binding as to be widely believed.'*

From the point of view of public choice theory, however, we have to ask ourselves how the credibility of government and central bank can be restored, given the fact that it has been absolutely eroded. Certainly, a new tough government makes it easier to restore credibility. Also, the chances that a new government can take over are quite good. For as Paldam (1994, p. 149) states: *'In none of the four Central European countries that experienced a high inflation during the 1920s did the government survive the inflation, . . . The nine largest inflations in the eight largest Latin American countries during the last 50 years all led to several government changes . . .'*

Also, governments that stop inflation obtain a large popularity bonus. Thus opposition parties have a strong incentive to enter the government and to pursue successful reforms. And in fact, in most of the cases in Table 8.1 the decisive reforms were introduced by new governments.

Similarly, the introduction of a new central bank directorate is important. But both events happened in Bolivia (Table 8.2) without making the currency reform as successful as in most other cases. This can be explained by the fact that a new government and central bank directorate are no guarantee against adverse changes in the future, given the inflationary bias of governments (Chapter 2). The problem is exacerbated if the country in question or the general situation have shown a high degree of political instability.

A solution to this problem lies in binding the hands of government and central bank by institutional changes in such a way that they are no longer capable of financing the government budget deficit partially or completely by creating new money. To quote Sargent (1982, p. 89) again: *'The essential measures that ended hyperinflation in each of Germany, Austria, Hungary* [1], *and Poland were, first, the creation of an independent central bank that was legally committed to refuse the government's demand for additional . . . credit and, second, a simultaneous alteration in the fiscal policy regime.'*

Let us look from this perspective at the institutional changes introduced (Table 8.2). In the cases of Austria, Germany, Greece 2 and Hungary independent central banks and in that of Bulgaria a currency board were created which were not allowed to extend credit to the government except for a very limited amount. Note that a currency board can only create central bank money (notes and deposits at the central bank) in exchange for an inflow of a reserve currency like the dollar, DM and pound (see for example Hanke and Schuler 1994, Dornbusch 2001). Budget discipline was also enforced either by the limited credit line which was granted to the government at the independent central bank or by legal measures.

In the case of Austria and Hungary 1 protocols of agreement were signed with the League of Nations. The protocols obliged the two countries to balance their budgets and provided that a commissioner of the League monitored whether the performance of the central bank and of the fiscal authorities corresponded to the agreement (League of Nations 1946, Bordes 1924, Heilperin 1931, Sargent 1982). In the case of Greece 2 the currency reform was based on the Anglo-Hellenic Convention of 24 January 1946. This convention established a currency committee which had the statutory right to decide, by unanimous vote, on any increase of the volume of banknotes. Besides three members of the government an Englishman and an American belonged to the committee. As a consequence, a real control of the money in circulation and thus indirectly of the budget deficit had been institutionalised. In a similar way to the cases of Germany, Austria and Hungary 1, where the introduction of the gold (exchange) standard was a main ingredient of the reforms, Greece too introduced gold convertibility of the drachma at a fixed parity (Delivanis and Cleveland 1949, Makinen 1984a).

We have already seen how in the case of Poland the first reform left a loophole for money creation by the Treasury, which was successfully closed by the second reform. Moreover the newly independent Central Bank was not allowed to grant more than 50 million zloty to the Government in 1927. In Poland too, the discretion of the Central Bank was limited by a fixed exchange rate.

The case of Bolivia has already been discussed. Institutional safeguards were generally missing. This fact probably explains the remaining rate of inflation of 19.4 per cent in the first year after the reform in spite of a sizeable budget surplus. If we turn next to Nicaragua, we observe that the Central Bank was not made independent and that no institutional safeguards were introduced for fiscal policy. On the other hand, the amount of domestic liquidity was bound to foreign exchange reserves and a fixed exchange rate introduced. Both measures clearly restricted Central Bank and budgetary policies to a certain degree. But that they were not sufficient is shown by the fact that the cost of living index increased again by 20.4 per cent in 1993 and dropped only slowly to a growth of 8.7 per cent in 1999. Related to this, the gold cordoba was devalued by 20 per cent in January 1993, and a crawling peg maintained with a pre-announced 12 per cent rate of annual devaluation. The nominal anchor of a fixed exchange rate was removed.

Let us finally turn to the Soviet Union. In this case institutional safeguards were also not missing. The new State Bank was made independent and had to cover the amount of circulating banknotes by a 25 per cent reserve of precious metals (platinum, gold and silver) and foreign exchange. The remaining 75 per cent of banknote circulation had to be balanced by short-term assets and loans, which could easily be called back (Griziotti Kretschmann 1928, for the reforms compare also Bernholz 1996 and Siklos 1995b). However, in a dictatorship institutional safeguards are not very credible, since power holders can transgress or remove them at their discretion at any time. Nevertheless, they were probably accepted as trustworthy to a certain degree by the population of the Soviet Union. For in spite of the remaining budget deficit of 5.5 per cent of expenditures, the rate of inflation dropped to minus 0.5 during the ten months after the final reforms had been made. Some distrust seems, however, to have remained. For the real stock of the national money recovered less than in all other cases (Table 8.1).

After having discussed the importance of adequate institutional safeguards let us stress that they are not necessary conditions for successful reforms. This is proved by the examples of Bolivia and Nicaragua. But these cases show also that the absence of institutional safeguards leads to additional problems. The defeat of inflation is retarded, or even not fully accomplished. Perhaps more important, they imply higher real interest rates after the currency reform, which discourages investments, hinders real economic development and furthers unemployment. Of the countries in our sample Bolivia and Nicaragua show by far the highest real interest rates after the reform.

8.5   LESS AND LEAST SUCCESSFUL REFORMS

Let us turn now to the cases in which hyperinflation was stopped by reform measures which were less successful. In Tables 8.3 and 8.5 economic

Table 8.3 *Economic characteristics of less successful currency reforms*

Country	Date of reform	Annual rate of inflation in year after reform, %	Real stock of national money (100% = Normal) — Minimum before reform	After reform	Real interest rate (ex post), %	Unemployment (before reform = 100)	Govt. deficit/expenditure before reform %	after reform %
Argentina	1990/91; 3.1991	84 1991; 17.5 1992	15.07 2.1990	40.93 6.1992; 44.07 3.1993				7.72 1990; 10.12 1993
Brazil	1993/94; 2–7.1994	84.38 1995; 15.32 1996	13.4 3.1994	22.8 7.1995; 36.77 4.1997	58.18 DR 9.1994; −13.3 MMR 1995; 12.37 MMR 1996	87.23 1994; 87.5 7.1994–6.1995	25.05 1993; 18.04 1994	8.61 1996
Hungary 2	1.8.1946	40.91 till 7.1947	near zero 7.1946		−15.2 (planned rates & credit rationing) 10.1946–7.1947	248.57 8.1947	88.38 7.1945–5.1946	21.89 1946/47; 4.02 1947/48
Moldova	1993	83.3 1994; 23.81 1995	12.43 12.1992	20.6 IV.1995	60.6 RF 1994; 29.09 TBR 1995	146.2 1994; 173.76 1995	25.63 1993	22.65 1994; 14.93 1995
Peru	1990/91; 1.7.1991	73.33 1992; 48.64 1993	7.4 5.1991	18.91 11.1992	17.63 DR 1992; 96.47 LR 1992; 48.76 LR 1993	117.23 1992; 127.71 1993	28.16 1990	17.21 1993; −11.37 1994
Poland 2	From 10.1990; 9.1991	62.22 9.1991	24.66 2.1990	39.43 9.1990	−22.22 LR 9.1991		5.87 1989	
Taiwan	15.6.1949	82 6.1949–12.1949; 89 1950; 53 1951; 3.4 1952	3.85 5.1949	40 12.1950	Positive		High	19 1950; 13 1951; 2 1952; −2.72 1953

Notes:

Inflation measured with cost of living indices. 'till 7.1947' means year ending July 1947. '2.1990' and '7.1945–5.1946' refer to February 1990 and to the period from July 1945 to May 1946. 'Hungary 2' refers to the second Hungarian hyperinflation.

Peru: Unemployment as percentage of unemployment before reform: Rough estimate from industrial employment figures.

LR lending rate, DR deposit rate, MMR money market rate, RF refinancing rate, TBR treasury bill rate.

Sources: See Appendix

characteristics have been accumulated for all those hyperinflations in which the annual rates of inflation remained between 25 and 100 per cent, or surpassed 100 per cent, respectively, during the first year after the reforms. But since reforms were sometimes drawn out over more than one year, some judgement has had to be applied. Tables 8.4 and 8.6 add figures for the same countries on the development of real exchange rates after the attempted reforms and, more importantly, concerning the institutional changes undertaken in the reform process.

Let us first note that France and China can be dismissed at once, since their reform efforts failed (Table 8.5). Further, all other cases of least successful currency reforms reported in Table 8.5 refer to successor states of the former Soviet Union, with the exception of Yugoslavia and Serbia (together with Montenegro). And though the latter two cases did not result from the breakdown of so-called planned socialist economies, they both originated from 'socialist market economies'. Moreover, Poland 2, a case belonging to the less successful currency reforms (Table 8.3), arose also in the wake of the breakdown of a socialist planned economy. These facts are probably not unrelated to the limited success of the currency reforms in these cases. But note also that even under the conditions of 'transition economies' successful currency reforms can be undertaken, as demonstrated by the Bulgarian example (Table 8.1).

What then are the reasons which make the introduction of a successful currency reform much more difficult for countries in transition to market economies? At least three factors have to be mentioned. First, in planned economies prices are fixed by government agencies, usually without much regard for the scarcity of goods resulting from supply and demand. The planning of production relies on amounts of outputs and inputs prescribed to state-owned firms or collectives by government planning agencies. Prices and financing are subordinated to this process and enough money is created to prevent any binding financial budget restrictions on firms. Also, there is a tendency to set prices below market-clearing levels, first for ideological reasons. It has to be pretended that the people get the basic necessities of life at very low prices. Second, there is an interest of planners and functionaries in preventing any problems in motivating consumers to accept the goods produced according to plan. Third, prices below market-clearing levels grant functionaries the power to distribute goods at their discretion or to use them as scarce resources in exchange for goods they need, including necessary inputs to fulfil the over-ambitious aims of the output requirements prescribed to them by the planning authorities. Consumers and firms, on the other hand, are consequently often not able to spend the monetary income or revenue they earn, and have to put it into (mostly) short-term bank accounts at low interest rates. It follows that a monetary overhang, a so-called repressed inflation, is present at the beginning of the transition to a market economy.

Table 8.4   Institutional characteristics of less successful currency reforms

Country	New currency unit	Reform credits and grants	
		Domestic	Foreign
Argentina	1 peso = 10 000 austral 1.1.1992	Yes	Yes
Brazil	1 real = 2750 cruzeiro real 1.7.1994 (six months after first reform steps)	Yes	Yes (little)
Hungary 2	1 forint = $4*10^{29}$ pengoe = $2*10^8$ tax pengoe 1.8.1946	Yes (Credit limit 300 mill. forint at Central Bank)	Yes
Moldova	1 Moldovan leu = 1000 Moldovan roubles 29.11.1993	Yes	Yes
Peru	1 nuevo sol = 1 mill. inti (after first reforms 1.7.1991)	Yes	No (only 1990)
Poland 2	No	Yes	Yes?
Taiwan	1 new Taiwan $ = 40 000 taipi yuan 15.6.1949	No	No

Legal safeguards		Exchange rate regime	Real exchange rate, % (minimum = 100)	
Central bank	Budget			
Yes (mainly Currency Board; Law of 3.1991; Charter 9.1992)	Yes (financing of budget deficits by money creation excluded)	1 peso = 1 $	745.23	5.1993
No	No	Freely floating rate (from 10.94 to 1.1999 managed floating, 10% penalty on purchases of reals)	423	7.1995
Yes (Article 50 of Central Bank statutes revalidated)	No (except for limit at Central Bank)	1 $ = 11.74 forint, required gold reserve. No convertibility	1009	31.5.1947
No	No	Freely floating rate (no restrictions since 8.1995)	153.89 186.15	II.1995 I.1996
Yes Central Bank autonomy (1992)	Yes? (8.1990) (cash management committee)	Freely floating (since 8.1990)	366.33 Official 695.3 Black market rate 9.1992	
No	No	9500 zloty = 1 $ (devalued 5.1991)	256.39	9.1991
Note issue limited (but limits later extended)	No	1 $ = 5 new Taiwan $	314.15 Official exch. rate 6.1950 1155 Black market rate 6.1950	

Note:
Peru: The institutional safeguards for Central Bank and budget policies were weak, since they presumably depended on Presidential decree. The figures for the real exchange rate are not very reliable, since Peru had a system of multiple exchange rates until August 1991. But it seems that the exchange rate was overvalued after the reforms. It is thus not surprising that it fell sharply in the third year after the reforms.

Sources: See Appendix

Table 8.5(a)   Economic characteristics of least successful currency reforms

Country	Date of reform	Annual rate of inflation in years after reform, %	Real stock of national money (100% = normal) — Minimum before reform	Real stock of national money (100% = normal) — After reform	Unemployment (before reform = 100)	Government deficit/ expenditure % — Before reform %	Government deficit/ expenditure % — After reform %
Armenia	1993/94	177.78 (1995); 19 (1996)	5.5 (12.1994)	14.03 (12.1996)	126.42 (1994/95); 173.58 (1996)	46.78 (1993)	37.41 (1994); 31.09 (1995)
Azerbaijan	1995	222.2 (3.1996); 12 (3.1997)	5.07 (1.1995)	11.13 (12.1995)	119.9 (1996); 135.6 (1997)	27.37 (1993); 26.39 (1994)	21.83 (1995); 7.83 (1996)
Belarus (no real reform)	Early 1995	161 (1.1996); 66 (5.1997)	9.27 (2.1995)	14.24 (12.1996); 18.54 (12.1997)	144.44 (1996)	8.41 (1993); 8.05 (1995)	5.55 (1996); 4.63 (1997)
China	8.1948	11248955 (31.8.1948–25.4.1949)	19.09 (31.8.1948)	15.1 (11.1948); 1.16 (25.4.1949)		66.67 (1–6.1948)	78.25 (7–12.1948)
Congo (Zaire)	7.1994 to early 1995 (no real reform)	598.37 (till 3.1996)	12.04 (8.1993)	18.42 (8.1994); 14.57 (2.1995)		86.6 (1992); 75.46 (1993)	34.19 (1994); 73.62 (1995)
France	15.3.1796	235.44 (3–9.1796)	4.41 (3.1796)	11.16 (6.1796)		91 (1795)	
Georgia	Mid-1994	163 (1995); 39.41 (1996)	4.01 (9.1993)	28.56 (12.1995); 51.99 (5.1996)		76.63 (1994)	63.63 (1995)
Kazakhstan	1994/95	177.01 (1995); 39.2 (1996)	33.21 (1.1995); (2.77)	(4.33)	190.9 (1995); 372.72 (1996)	27.8 (1994); 54.55 (II.1994)	14.29 (1995); 16.67 (1996)
Kyrgyzstan	1993	383.77 (5.1994); 39.96 (5.1995)	5.53 (3.1994); (42.97)	7.91 (12.1994); (61.44)	433.33 (1994)	51.3 (1992)	36.76 (1993); 32.69 (1994)
Serbia	1.1994	20 (1–11.1994); 100 (1995); 58.6 (1996)	4.36 (9.1993)				

Notes:

Inflation measured with cost of living indices. 'till 9.1923' means year ending September 1923. '5.1987' and 'IV. 1986' refer to May 1987 and to the fourth quarter of 1986.

China and France: for inflation rates the wholesale price index and the exchange rate were used.

Belarus: the figures for the real stock of money are probably much too high, since calculated only from December 1994.

Congo (Zaire): budget figures for 1995 provisional. Expenditure for this year includes net financing, deficit = financing requirements.

Serbia: unemployment estimated higher than 40% in 1994.

Kazakhstan and Kyrgyzstan: the figures for the real stock of money are much too high, because they are based on periods too late in the development. Figures stemming from earlier base periods are given in brackets, but may be less reliable.

Sources: See Appendix

Table 8.5(b) *Economic characteristics of least successful currency reforms*

Country	Date of reform	Annual rate of inflation in years after reform, %		Real stock of national money (100% = normal) Minimum before reform		After reform		Real interest rate (ex post) after reform, %		Unemployment (before reform = 100), %		Government deficit/expenditure Before reform, %		After reform, %	
Tajikistan	1996	40.5	1996	5.05	3.1998	11.27	3.1997	60.72RF negative from II.97	8.1996	143.75	1996	46.46	1992	31.98	1-9.1997
		234	I-III 1997									38.35	1993		
												32.33	1996		
Turkmenistan	1996	179.6	8.1997	17.27	12.1996	28.7	12.1997	-119.4CB	8.1997			12.04	1994	4.22	1997
												11.2	1995		
												(+ Govmt. directed credit, tax arrears)			
Yugoslavia	12.1989	110.15	12.1990	24.66	2.1990	39.43	9.1990	-70.15DR	12.1990			-0.857	1988		
		82.3	II.1991			30.53	7.1991	-42.3DR	II.1991			-5.215	1989		
Ukraine	Late 1994	376	1995	5.69	2.1995	7	3.1996	-18TB	12.1995	433	12.1996	21.98	1992	11.08	1995
		80	1996			8.89	7.1996	22TB	12.1996			13.67	1993	7.99	1996

Notes:
Inflation measured with cost of living indices. 'till 9,1923' means year ending September 1923. '5.1987' and 'IV.1986' refer to May 1987 and to the fourth quarter of 1986.
Tajikistan: Unemployment figures not reliable.
Turkmenistan: Government directed credits not included in budget.
Yugoslavia: Deficit/expenditures figures are not credible. Presumably without deficits of states and losses of firms.

Sources: See Appendix

Table 8.6 Institutional characteristics of least successful currency reforms

Country	New currency unit	Reform credits and grants		Legal safeguards		Exchange rate regime	Real exchange rate, % (minimum = 100)	
		Domestic	Foreign	Central bank	Budget			
Armenia	1 dram = 200 rouble 22.11.1993 (sole legal tender 1.1.94)	Yes	Yes	Yes (independent by law of June 1996)	No	De facto but not legally stable nominal exchange rate with $ until mid-1996	280.32 368.47	12.1994 12.1995
Azerbaijan	1 manat = 10 rouble 15.8.1992 (sole legal tender 1.1.94)	Yes (small amount)	Yes	No	No	Floating exchange rate since 3.1995 (revaluation to $)	211.67 289.61	12.1995 12.1996
Belarus	1 rouble = 10 Belarussian rouble (as unit of account)	Yes	Yes (small)	No (autonomy strongly reduced)	No	Foreign exchange controls	309.42	12.1995
China	1 gold yuan = 1 mill. fapi	No	Yes (not related to reform)	Yes (note issue limited, but controlled by Government commission)	No	1 $ = 4 gold yuan (abolished 11.1948)		
Congo (Zaire)	1 new zaire = 1 mill zaire 22.10.1993 (before measures)	Yes	No	No (new governor)	No (new Government)	No control, nearly without value	168.18 146.13	8.1994 2.1995
France	1 mandat = 30 assignats	Forced loan (before)	No	No (no central bank)	No	Fixed exchange rate with real estate		
Georgia	1 lari = 1 mill. coupon 25.9.95 (sole legal tender 2.10.95)	Yes	Yes	No	No	Floating exchange rate (stable since 1995, inconvertible)	1259.88	12.1995

Kazakhstan	1 tenge = 500 rouble Nov. 1993 (before measures)	No	Yes	No	Floating exchange rate (relatively stable, 1995)	339.78	12.1995
Kyrgyzstan	1 som = 200 rouble 10.5.1993	Yes	Yes	Yes ('relatively high independence')	Floating exchange rate	352.74	12.1993
Serbia	1 new dinar = 12 mill. old dinar	No	No	No	1 new dinar = 1 DM Repegged to 3.3 dinar per DM 11.1995	Overvalued?	
Tajikistan	1 Tajik rouble = 100 rouble 10.5.1995	Yes	Yes (1996/1997)	Yes (12.1996, but effective 7.1997)	Floating exchange rate (for some time restrictions 1996/97)	343.62 282.97	5.1996 4.1997
Turkmenistan		Yes (1996)	Yes (1997)	No	Floating commercial bank exchange rate	289.91	12.1997
Yugoslavia		Yes	No	No	Exchange rate stabilised until IV.1990 as reform anchor	332.64	12.1990
Ukraine	1 hryvnia = 100 000 karbovanets 2.9.1996 (after reform)	Yes	Yes	No	Floating rate (relatively stable 1996/97)	3344.6	2.1996

Notes:

The real exchange rate figure for Armenia is somewhat doubtful, since it implies a huge overvaluation for 7.1995.

No real reform was undertaken in Belarus, where price controls were introduced to limit inflation. Monetary restraint only in early months of 1996.

Ukraine: Currency most strongly undervalued in July 1992, but overvalued in 1996.

In China and France currency reforms were undertaken, but failed.

Sources: See Appendix

Second, in planned economies with collectively-owned firms, there exists no need for a well-developed tax system with well-organised tax authorities. For the government can take the resources which it needs directly from the firms it owns or controls. Moreover, most of the social tasks faced by the government in other countries are taken over by the collective firms them-selves, from kindergarten, recreation, organising and providing the resources for holidays to caring for the sick. It follows that, when a country tries to move towards a market economy, the tax system as well as the tax administration are underdeveloped at a time when the government has to take up additional tasks, which can no longer be burdened on the firms which have to be privatised. Since the creation of a sufficient tax administration and the introduction of taxes take time, transition economies usually face a widening budget deficit which has to be financed by money creation. Moreover, many of the lower levels of government are faced with similar problems. Inefficient plants cannot be privatised and face losses, which are also financed by creating money, given the budgetary plight of the government. For politicians do not dare to close many of these firms because they are afraid of the higher unemployment which would result and thus threaten their chances of re-election, if the coun-try has moved towards democracy. Finally, it also takes time to create the necessary bankruptcy laws. Even the accounting procedures are usually not adequate and adequate ones have to be newly introduced.

For the purposes of our analysis we would need the budget figures of the consolidated general government, that is of the central, regional and local governments, and also of all state agencies not covered by the ordinary budget, for instance those responsible for social security systems. Moreover, all cred-its to state-owned or -directed firms used to finance losses should also be included. Unfortunately, the figures which are available and are presented in the tables often do not follow this procedure.

Third, the institutional preconditions for successful currency reforms have to be created. This is especially difficult under conditions in which most of the institutions characteristic of well-functioning democratic market economies are absent and an adequate legal system has to be re-established. Also, the functionaries of a command economy may have a very difficult time intro-ducing institutions which limit their own sphere of power. And the politicians belonging to the opposition usually lack the experience to proceed quickly with adequate institutional reforms. Finally, the banking sector is usually organised in one or only a few state-owned banks, which are not accustomed to the tasks expected of them in a market economy. The functions of a central bank have to be newly created and to be separated from other tasks of ordinary banking business.

Let us first analyse the case of Poland 2 from this perspective (Table 8.3). It is probable that this country just removed its monetary overhang by allowing liberated prices to increase until the real stock of money reached normal proportions. This is suggested by a deficit of the budget in 1989 of only 5.87 per cent of expenditures. But one may entertain some doubts concerning the size of the deficit in view of the high remaining annual rate of inflation one year after the reform and of the fact that a deficit of consolidated general government operations of 11.6 per cent of expenditures was still present in 1992. Unfortunately no such figures were available to the author for the years before 1992. The same deliberations have to be applied to the cases of Belarus (Table 8.5(a)), Turkmenistan and Yugoslavia (Table 8.5(b)). In Belarus *'Directed credits* [that is credits which had to be given at the command of the Government] *played a major role in the conduct of NBB's* [National Bank of Belarus] *policies'* (Wolf et al. 1997, p. 17) from March to December 1996. Some 90 per cent of the credits given at a low nominal interest rate below the refinancing rate were of this nature. Similarly, in Turkmenistan *'the government **resumed** directed credits on a large scale in 1997 after refraining from such credits in most of 1996'* (Guergen et al. 1998, p. 39).

Yugoslavia surprisingly even showed a small budget surplus, which is scarcely credible except for the central Government. For it is well known that sizeable credits were extended to the republics as well as to labour-managed firms, probably in many cases by direct orders of the republics. Finally, we have to take into account that in all other cases of hyperinflations we have deficits above 20 per cent of expenditures, a fact which casts a dark shadow of doubt on the figures available for these transition countries.

Let us now analyse the factors which seemed to be responsible, according to Section 8.3, for successful currency reforms. According to Table 8.4 Brazil, Poland 2 and Taiwan did not introduce any institutional safeguards concerning the limitation of budget deficits. Brazil and Poland 2 also introduced no measures to safeguard the independence of the central bank. And the Hungarian restriction on central bank credits could not be very convincing, given the dominance of the Communist party supported by the Soviet occupation forces. The same is true for the institutional independence of its central bank. Similar remarks apply to the institutional safeguards taken by Peru. They were also weak, since they were introduced not by law but by Presidential decrees. Taiwan introduced a limit on the amount of notes which could be issued by its central bank. But it suffered also from an authoritarian Government at that time, which did not hesitate to extend this limit at its discretion. It follows that only Argentina succeeded in getting sufficient institutional safeguards for the central bank and against deficit financing by introducing a currency board with the exchange rate of the peso fixed at the rate 1 peso = 1 dollar. It seems thus to be surprising that the annual rate of inflation remained at 84 per cent in 1991, instead of falling below 20 per cent at once as in the case of Bulgaria (Table 8.1). The answer may be related to two facts.

First, Argentina had suffered from high inflation for decades and several attempted currency reforms had failed before. As a consequence, a deep distrust in the population concerning the possibility of maintaining these institutions may have been present. Second, the reforms were not taken at one stroke, a fact which endangers or retards the creation of confidence. Still, inflation subsided more quickly in the following years than in most other cases in Table 8.3 (perhaps with the exception of Hungary 2).

If we next look at the institutional characteristics of the least successful currency reforms (Table 8.6), we realise that no safeguards at all were introduced concerning the independence of central banks or to prevent budget deficits. An exception seems to be the independence of the central banks of Armenia and Tajikistan. But note that the independence granted in Armenia was introduced only two years after the beginning of the reform efforts. And though central bank independence was introduced by law in Tajikistan in December 1996, the bank still followed directives by the Government to grant credits to the Government and state enterprises until its independence was reaffirmed by a Presidential decree in July 1997 (Saavalainen *et al.* 1998). Similarly, the control of the note issue by a Government commission established in China proved to be a failure, a fact which is not surprising, since the people in the commission were identical to those who had to care for the financing of the civil war against the communists. Finally, the substitution of the old central bank governor by a new one in the Congo in July 1994 was certainly insufficient to stem the tide of inflation. The old one refused to step down until the President had signed his dismissal. Thus a new governor took office only in January 1995 (Beaugrand 1997).

One can argue that the International Monetary Fund (IMF) tried actively to support the stabilisation efforts of the successor states of the Soviet Union, and that agreements as to the monetary and fiscal policies to be followed were signed. Such efforts are also reflected in the foreign credits and grants extended to these countries (Table 8.6). But it seems to be suggested by the facts presented that these agreements were not really binding; at best it took several years until they exerted some influence. Moreover, in most cases, that is with the exception of Bulgaria and Argentina (Tables 8.2 and 8.4), the IMF promoted restrictive monetary and fiscal policies. But, as argued in Section 8.2, the former is a very inferior measure for stopping hyperinflation, since the real stock of the national money has reached a level way below normal. In fact, the policies of the League of Nations in helping to end the Austrian and Hungarian hyperinflations in the 1920s were much better suited and effective than those of the IMF in the 1990s, again with the exception of Bulgaria and Argentina.

One institutional safeguard which has been much discussed in the literature (see for instance Dornbusch 1982, Bruno and Fischer 1990, and Calvo and

Vegh 1994) has been the 'anchoring' of monetary policies by the introduction of a fixed exchange rate with a stable currency, as in recent decades mostly the US dollar, or in some cases the DM. Besides such an exchange rate target a monetary anchoring by postulating a restrictive monetary growth rate is often debated as an alternative option (for a comparative analysis of the problems and consequences of the different 'anchors' see Paldam 1994, 153ff.). From our analysis above and in Sections 8.3 and 8.4 it follows, however, that this option is not an optimal measure. True, future monetary growth has to be restricted and the financing of budget deficits to be prevented. But presently the nominal stock of the national money has to be increased without financing a budget deficit, so that the real stock can approach its normal level without putting prices and thus real economic activity under severe downward pressure. For if expectations can be stabilised the real demand for the national money is bound to rise.

Fixing the nominal exchange rate as an anchor is often a better alternative. It is interesting to note that in all cases of the most successful currency reforms fixed exchange rates to stable currencies or gold parities were introduced (Table 8.2). Apart from the dubious value of such a policy in the Soviet Union, only the Bolivian case is an exception. In the seven cases of less successful currency reforms, exchange rates were fixed in four of them. But in the case of Hungary 2 this was meaningless, since its new currency remained inconvertible. On the other hand, in most cases of least successful currency reforms no fixed exchange rate regimes were introduced, except in the cases of China and Serbia. In the former case this proved to be of no consequence, since the reforms failed. In the latter, the official exchange rate of 1 new dinar = 1 DM had to be devalued to 3.3 new dinar = 1 DM as early as the end of the year following the currency reform. It seems to follow that a nominal exchange rate anchor can help to restore confidence and to end hyperinflation. But is has to be credible, for market participants must be convinced that the rate can and will be maintained. For this purpose the other institutional safeguards mentioned above are of the greatest importance. If the government is able to change the parity at its discretion and if no safeguards are taken to prevent the financing of budget deficits, a fixing of the exchange rate is of little permanent help. However, this does not imply that even a *de facto* stability of the exchange rate observed for some time may not help to restore some confidence, as in the cases of Armenia, Georgia, Kazakhstan, Yugoslavia and the Ukraine. But this alone can never be an optimal reform policy, for otherwise the countries just mentioned would not belong to the category of the least successful currency reforms.

Let us next look at the other indicators of success besides the annual rate of inflation after reforms. We turn first to the real stock of the national money before and after the reform measures have been taken. As can be seen from

Tables 8.1, 8.3 and 8.5 the real stock of money increased in all cases as a consequence of the reforms made, except for China. But there the reform measures failed and hyperinflation returned. It is also revealing that the real stock rose to higher levels in all cases of the most successful currency reforms, except for the Soviet Union, than in all the cases of the less or least successful reforms, except for Kazakhstan. But the Soviet Union as a totalitarian regime could not induce permanent confidence in the stability of the institutional measures taken. And the figures for the real stocks of money in Kazakhstan and Kyrgyzstan are probably much too high, since they are based only on late periods as a base (= 100). For if we take earlier years with base 1991 into account, the real stocks of money in May 1996 and December 1994, respectively, amount only to 4.35 per cent and 7.91 per cent. These figures seem to be rather too low, but they show that our statement is probably also valid for these two countries. Looking again at the figures, we note that the real stock of the national money increased to values greater than 44.5 per cent in all cases of successful currency reforms except for the Soviet Union. Figures between 18.91 and 44.07 per cent were reached in the cases of less successful reforms, and figures below 18.55 per cent for the least successful currency reforms (for Georgia the figure of 11.16 per cent has been taken, since this was the situation one year after the beginning of the reforms; and the higher figure for Kazakhstan is not credible). The different magnitudes of this reversal of the process of 'demonetisation' as it is often called, which is, however, mainly a reversal of the currency substitution which took place during the hyperinflation, supports again the hypotheses of how best to end a hyperinflation. The reversal of the currency substitution is the other side of the coin of the increase of the real stock of the national money. It is retarded or brought to an end when the institutional measures to guarantee the future stability of the national currency are not convincing enough. Moreover, the more currency substitution has proceeded during the hyperinflation, the more difficult it is to replace foreign currencies by the national money after the reforms. For the more people use a certain, here the foreign currency, the less motivation exists to move to another, here the national currency. It has for instance been estimated (Horvath et al. 1998, p. 25) that:

> *The ratio of foreign currency deposits in broad money declined to around a fifth by late 1995* [in Armenia] *and stayed at this level through end-1996. While this level is substantial, it is not excessive in a small, open economy at Armenia's stage of development. It is similar to the 15 per cent level experienced in Georgia, and compares favourably with Bolivia and Vietnam* [which experienced a high but not a hyperinflation], *where over 80 per cent of broad money is held as foreign currency deposits in spite of a stable economy.*

One may have grave doubts concerning the latter figure for Bolivia in view of the more successful currency reform. But the quote shows the difficulty in reversing the currency substitution in cases of less or least successful currency reforms.

If we look at real (ex post) interest rates after the reforms, a similar though less conclusive picture emerges than that for the real stocks of money. In most cases real interest rates were either negative or, if positive, higher in the cases of the less and least than in those of the most successful currency reforms. Negative real interest rates often point to higher rates of inflation than expected, so that the stabilisation effort was less successful than expected before. Very high positive real rates, on the other hand, point to a lack of confidence in the permanent success of the reforms. We forego studying the exceptions, especially since only interest rates for different types of credit were available.

Next, let us cast a look at the budget deficits after reforms. Again, the deficits were reduced in all cases, but no clear-cut differences emerge for the different categories (the Peruvian and Taiwanese budgets showed a surplus only years after the beginning of reforms), except for the fact that no surpluses are reported for the less and least successful countries after the reforms, whereas surpluses are characteristic for the most successful currency reforms. It is not surprising that no more definite results emerge, since the way of financing the deficit is also important. And as can be seen from Tables 8.4 and 8.6, foreign credits and grants were extended to all successor states of the former Soviet Union.

The real exchange rate recovered after the reforms in all cases for which data are available and in which the reforms did not fail. The degree of the recovery reported in the tables can, however, not be used to judge the relative success of the different reforms, since the minimal values of the real exchange rates during the hyperinflations, on which the comparison is based, were very different in the cases considered, though usually the lower the higher the rates of inflation.

Finally, unemployment rose in most cases after the reform measures. The only further conclusion which can be drawn from the available evidence is that reductions of unemployment only occurred in some cases of most and less, but not in cases of least successful currency reforms. This conclusion can however be only of a tentative nature, since the figures are not very reliable.

8.6 THE INFLUENCE OF WRONG EVALUATIONS OF REFORM PACKAGES BY THE PUBLIC

Let us begin this section by looking at a few cases in which the measures taken were inadequate, so that reforms failed, but which still had some short success in reducing inflation, since the population attached some credibility to them.

Sargent's hypotheses concerning a change of the monetary regime with the purpose of ending a hyperinflation at one stroke (Sargent 1982) presuppose that market participants and the general public can form a correct judgement on whether the reforms taken are adequate or not. The general public and even more sophisticated market participants are, however, only knowledgeable in a rather limited way concerning the relevant relationships. Mostly, they even lack the education necessary to form an adequate judgement. As a consequence it may happen that they either distrust reforms which should prove successful, or on the other hand, believe in the future success of inadequate measures. In the latter case the majority of the public must have supposed, that, with a certain probability, the unsuccessful reform measures would lead to success. Or, as expressed by Makinen and Woodward (1989, p. 103):

> *In Taiwan the public appears to have believed in a non-existent regime change – based on the kind of evidence used by Sargent. And Taiwan is not an isolated instance. Makinen (1984b) has shown that in Greece the public reacted favourably to two reforms* [one of them is not contained in Table 8.7 below] *that failed to contain elements necessary to stabilise prices. Thus the public may have difficulties in distinguishing regime changes from superficial changes in economic policy.*

Here the authors obviously interpret the reform steps undertaken in the case of Taiwan (Table 8.4) as not a regime change. This is certainly warranted, since the limitation of the note issue was not binding and no institutional safeguards against budget deficits were taken. Still, the real stock of money increased to 40 per cent of normal in December 1950 from a minimum of 3.85 per cent in May 1949 (Table 8.3). The wrong interpretation of events on the part of the public may even have helped to finally defeat inflation in the following years. And even in the case of France, where the reform measures failed, the annual rate of inflation went down during the months immediately after they were introduced.

The following examples (Table 8.7) are also cases in which unwarranted confidence has been created. In the case of Poland 1, which has already been discussed above (Section 8.5), it is doubtful whether we should speak of a failure of the reforms. It might perhaps have belonged to the category of successful or at least of less successful reforms even without the second reform. In spite of this it has been included here again since the Polish authorities themselves were not satisfied with the results and introduced additional reform measures (Section 8.4). The other three cases all ended in failure, as already mentioned for Greece (Section 8.4). When we look now at the figures, we observe that the rates of inflation and the budget deficits were reduced in all four cases, even in the three in which the reforms failed and which later became hyperinflationary or nearly so (Greece suffered a very high but not a hyperinflation in December 1945, before the second reform package was

Table 8.7 Cases of high inflations in which inadequate reform measures failed

Item	Argentina	Brazil	Greece 1	Poland 1
Date of reform	14.6.1985	27.2.1986	10.1944	11.1.1924
New currency	1 austral =	1 cruzado =	1 new drachma	1 zloty = 1.8
unit	1000 pesos Arg.	1000 cruzeiros	= 50 mill. dr.	mill. Pol. mark
Inflation rate:				
before	1036 per annum	289 per annum	8896 per month	158 per month
after	50.9 per annum	69.8 per annum	1118 per annum	24.5 per annum
Deficit/GNP				
(GDP Argentina):				
before	11.9 (3–6.1985)	27.5 (1985) w.CB		
after	3.2 (7.1985–3.1986)	10.8 (1986) w.CB		
Deficit/expend.:				
before			99 (1.4.–10.11.1946)	61.92 (2.1923–1.1924)
after			71 (11.11.1944–31.3.1945)	12.49 (1924)
Reform credits:				
domestic	No	No	Yes (credit limit w.CB)	Yes (credit limit w.CB)
foreign	No	Yes	Grants in kind	No
Real interest rate	107 (IV.1985)	194.27 (3.1987)		
after	(for firms)	(Overnight money)		

Note:
w.CB: with Central Bank. For the deficit this means that the Central Bank is included.

Sources: See Appendix

191

introduced in January 1946). But real interest rates were exceptionally high in Argentina and Brazil a few months after the inadequate reform steps had been undertaken. This seems to suggest that the participants in financial markets formed a clearer perspective of the results to be expected than the general public.

It should be obvious that not only a mistaken interpretation concerning insufficient measures to end high inflation may be influential, but that there may also exist unfounded doubts concerning sufficient steps to end a hyperinflation. And these wrong perceptions may influence the results of even well-conceived reforms. The high real interest rates which usually prevail for about one year after the currency reform (compare Germany and Hungary 1 in Table 8.1) even for the most successful regime changes, and the fact that the real stock of the national money remains for months below its normal level (Table 8.1), seem to support the correctness of this hypothesis. For note that in these cases the budget deficit had been successfully reduced or even turned into a budget surplus and that the reforms had been institutionally safeguarded. For example, Bordes (1924, pp. 226f.) explains concerning Austria: *'The interest on mortgage credit is still so high . . . that farmers cannot get sufficient credit for intensive cultivation. . . . The* [National] *Bank is attempting to bring down the extremely high rate of interest, which forms a severe handicap on Austrian industries.'*

It is true also that a different interpretation as to the reasons responsible for the subnormal real stock of the national money and the very high real interest rate has been given. According to this alternative explanation these developments have been caused by a too restrictive policy of the central bank which prevented the real stock of the national money reaching its normal level (Dornbusch and Cardoso 1987). It seems, however, that this hypothesis cannot be maintained for the cases just discussed. For we have mentioned already that some circulation of foreign currencies, or 'dollarisation', as it is called in more recent cases, was present even after the reforms. This provides an argument against the thesis of a general scarcity of the money supply. Second, we know, for instance, that the interest rate in Germany on bonds denominated either in units of wheat, coal or gold showed a normal level. How can the 7.87–13.34 per cent nominal interest on bonds denominated in gold in comparison to interest rates ranging from 30–26.32 per cent for monthly money between January and June 1924 be explained, if not by the remaining inflationary expectations (Bernholz 1988b)? Finally, it has to be mentioned that unemployment rose substantially, even in the three most successful cases of currency reforms (Table 8.1, compare also Wicker 1986).

Taking into account the evidence adduced, one can agree with Sargent (1982) that a change of the monetary and fiscal regime taken at one stroke will change expectations much more quickly and strongly than gradual and (or) incomplete reform measures. It will thus usually lead to a smaller recession and a smaller increase of unemployment than the latter. But the assumption that adequate currency reforms can bring about an immediate and complete change of inflationary expectations is contradicted by the empirical evidence.

8.7 CONCLUSIONS

The following results have been derived in this chapter:

1. The political conditions to end a high inflation are most favourable during hyperinflations. For in such a situation the government is in the process of losing its monetary authority and the revenue earned from the inflation tax because of increasing currency substitution. Moreover, only a few people are still deriving benefits from the inflationary process.
2. A necessary condition to stop hyperinflations is to end money creation for the purpose of financing budget deficits of the government, its agencies and the losses of firms owned or controlled by it. For this purpose a strict limitation of these deficits is necessary.
3. Since the real stock of the national money has fallen well below its normal level, the nominal stock of money should be increased to prevent a pressure on the price level and on the activity level of the real economy. The latter would lead to strongly rising unemployment and thus possibly to a defeat of the government at the next elections, with the consequence of a high probability of abolishing the reform efforts.
4. To increase the real stock of the national money the demand for it has to increase. For this purpose the reforms have to re-establish the confidence of the public in the currency. This stage can best be reached by adequate and visible institutional reforms guaranteeing a strict and narrow limit for budget deficits of the general government (including the losses of firms owned or controlled by it), an independent central bank or a currency board and a fixed exchange rate as a nominal anchor. Control of these provisions by an independent and trustworthy foreign or international authority is helpful.
5. Foreign financial help can help to finance government expenditures until the measures to increase taxes and (or) lower expenditures are felt.
6. The fewer of these institutional reforms are introduced, the less successful the reforms, as measured by a smaller rise of the real stock of the national money, the remaining circulation of stable (foreign) money, often called the degree of 'dollarisation', negative or very high real interest rates and the remaining annual rates of inflation.

7. Since the general population is not well informed concerning the underlying relationships and mostly lacks the necessary education, even inadequate reforms which eventually lead to a failure may for some time restore confidence. In such cases the real demand for the national money rises. Inflation subsides for some time. As a consequence the budget deficit is reduced, since Tanzi's Law works in reverse. But in the end high or hyperinflation returns, because the underlying budgetary problems of money creation have not been solved and the confidence of the public is thus eroded again.
8. Unemployment increases in most cases in the wake of currency reforms, though a weak tendency is observed, that this is less or not at all the case if currency reforms are fairly successful.
9. Since the general public and even many participants in financial markets have only an insufficient or incomplete understanding of whether the reform measures taken are adequate, they may either expect the success of inadequate reforms, or doubt the success of a reform package sufficient to end high inflation. These wrong perceptions can substantially influence the course of events.

REFERENCES

Agenor, P.-R. and Taylor, M. (1992), 'Testing for Credibility Effects', *IMF Staff Papers*, International Monetary Fund, September, 545–71.
Beaugrand, Philippe (1997), *Zaire's Hyperinflation, 1990–96*. IMF Working Paper 97/50, April, International Monetary Fund.
Bernholz, Peter (1986), 'The Implementation and Maintenance of a Monetary Constitution', *Cato Journal*, 6 (2), 477–511.
Bernholz, Peter (1988a), 'Hyperinflation and Currency Reform in Bolivia: Studied from a General Perspective', *Journal of Theoretical and Institutional Economics (JITE)*, 144, 747–71. Reprinted in Pierre Siklos (ed.) (1995), *Great Inflations of the 20th Century: Theories, Policies and Evidence*, Aldershot: Edward Elgar, pp. 227–54.
Bernholz, Peter (1988b), 'Inflation, Monetary Regime and the Financial Asset Theory of Money', *Kyklos*, 41, 5–34.
Bernholz, Peter (1996), 'Currency Substitution during Hyperinflation in the Soviet Union, 1922–1924', *The Journal of European Economic History*, 25 (2), Fall, 297–323.
Blanchard, Olivier Jean (1997), 'Comment on Stopping Inflations, Big and Small', *Journal of Money, Credit and Banking*, 29 (4), Part 2, November, 778–82.
Bordes, J. van Walras de (1924), *The Austrian Crown*, Westminster: P.S. King & Son.
Bruno, M., Tella, G. di, Dornbusch, R. and Fischer, S. (eds) (1988), *Inflation Stabilization. The Experience of Israel, Argentina, Brazil, Bolivia, and Mexico*, Cambridge (Mass.) and London: MIT Press.
Bruno, M., Fischer, S., Helpman, E. and Liviatan, N. (eds) (1991), *Lessons of Economic Stabilization and Its Aftermath*, Cambridge (Mass.) and London: MIT Press.

Cagan, P. (1956), 'The Monetary Dynamics of Hyperinflation', in M. Friedman (ed.), *Studies in the Quantity Theory of Money*, Chicago: Chicago University Press.

Calvo, G. and Vegh, C. (1994), 'Inflation Stabilisation and Nominal Anchors', *Contemporary Economic Policy*, 12, 35–45.

Delivanis, D. and Cleveland, W. C. (1949), *Greek Monetary Developments 1939–1948*, Bloomington, Indiana: University of Indiana Press.

Dornbusch, Rudiger (1982), 'Stabilisation Policies in Developing Countries: What Lessons Have We Learnt?', *World Development Report*, 9, 701–8.

Dornbusch, Rudiger (1992), 'Credibility and Stabilization', *Quarterly Journal of Economics*, 106, 837–50.

Dornbusch, Rudiger (2001), 'Exchange Rates and the Choice of Monetary Regimes. Free Monies, Better Monies', *American Economic Review*, 91 (2), Papers and Proceedings, 238–42.

Dornbusch, Rudiger and Cardoso, E. A. (1987), 'Brazil's Tropical Plan', *American Economic Review*, 77, Papers and Proceedings, 288–92.

Eliades, E. A. (1954/55), 'Stabilisation of the Greek Economy and the 1953 Devaluation of the Drachma', *IMF Staff Papers*, 4, 22–72.

Griziotti Kretschmann, Jenny (1928), 'La Reforma Monetaria Bolsevica', *Giornale degli Economista e Rivista di Statistica*, 168, 693–713.

Guergen, Emine, Snoek, Harry, Zavoico, Basil, Izvorski, Ivailo, Schaetzen, Bruno de and Lighthart, Jenny (1998), *Turkmenistan: Recent Economic Developments*, IMF Staff Country Report 98/81, August, International Monetary Fund.

Haffner, Sebastian (2000), *Geschichte eines Deutschen: Die Erinnerungen 1914–1933*, Munich: Deutsche Verlagsanstalt.

Hanke, Steve H. and Schuler, Kurt (1994), *Currency Boards for Developing Countries: A Handbook*, San Francisco: ICS Press.

Heilperin, M. A. (1931), *Le Problème Monétaire d'Après-Guerre et Sa Solution en Pologne, en Autriche et en Tchecoslovaquie*, Paris: Recueil Sirey.

Horváth, Balázs, Thacker, Nina and Hemming, Richard (1998), *Achieving Stabilization in Armenia*, IMF Working Paper, 98/38, March, International Monetary Fund.

Ireland, Peter N. (1997), 'Stopping Inflations, Big and Small', *Journal of Money, Credit and Banking*, 29 (4), Part 2, November, 759–75.

Kalter, Eliot, Terrones, Marco, Barajas, Alfonso, Nyawata, Obert, Ronci, Marcio and Rizavi, Syed (1998), *Nicaragua: Statistical Annex*, IMF Staff Country Report 98/48, May, International Monetary Fund.

League of Nations (1946), *The Course and Control of Inflation: A Review of Monetary Experience in Europe after World War I*, Geneva: League of Nations, Financial and Transit Department.

Makinen, Gail E. (1984a), 'The Greek Stabilisation of 1944–46', *American Economic Review*, 74, 1067–74.

Makinen, Gail. E. (1984b), 'The Greek Hyperinflation and Stabilisation of 1943–6', *Journal of Economic History*, XLVI, 795–805.

Makinen, Gail E. and Woodward, T. G. (1989), 'The Taiwanese Hyperinflation and Stabilization', *Journal of Money, Credit and Banking*, 21, 90–105.

Miller, Marcus and Zhang, Lei (1997), 'Hyperinflation and Stabilization: Cagan Revisited', *Economic Journal*, 107, 441–57.

Paldam, Martin (1994), 'The Political Economy of Stopping High Inflation', *European Journal of Political Economy*, 10, 135–68.

Rostowski, J. (1992), 'The Benefits of Currency Substitution During High Inflation and Stabilization', *Revista de Analisis Economico*, 7, 91–107.

Saavalainen, T., Wakeman-Linn, J., Ma, J., McGettigan, D., Nielsen, L. and Young, H. (1998), 'Republic of Tajikistan: Recent Economic Developments', IMF Staff Country Report, 98/16 International Monetary Fund.

Sachs, Jeffrey (1987), 'The Bolivian Hyperinflation and Stabilisation', *American Economic Review*, 77, Papers and Proceedings, 279–83.

Sargent, Thomas (1982), 'The End of Four Big Inflations', in Robert Hall (ed.), *Inflation: Causes and Effects*, Chicago: University of Chicago Press.

Sargent, Thomas (1997), 'Comment on Stopping Inflations, Big and Small', *Journal of Money, Credit and Banking*, 29 (4), Part 2, November, 776–7.

Siklos, Pierre (1995a), 'Hyperinflations: Their Origins, Development and Termination', in Pierre Siklos (ed.), *Great Inflations of the 20th Century: Theories, Policies And Evidence*, Aldershot: Edward Elgar, 3–34.

Siklos, Pierre (1995b), 'Tales of Parallel Currencies: The Early Soviet Experience', in J. Reis (ed.), *The History of International Monetary Arrangements*, London: Macmillan, 237–68.

Vegh, Carlos A. (1995), 'Stopping High Inflation: An Analytical Overview', in Pierre Siklos (ed.), *Great Inflations of the 20th Century: Theories, Policies and Evidence*, Aldershot: Edward Elgar, 35–81.

Wicker, E. (1986), 'Terminating Hyperinflation in the Dismembered Habsburg Monarchy', *American Economic Review*, 76, 350–61.

Wolf, Thomas, Zamaróczy, Mario de, Arvanitis, Athanasios, Mercer-Blackman, Valerie, Tareen, Mohammed and Haas, Richard (1997), *Republic of Belarus: Recent Economic Developments*, IMF Staff Country Report 97/111, November, International Monetary Fund.

Appendix: Sources for historical data not identified in the text and literature relating to different cases of hyperinflation

1. DATA AND WORKS ON HYPERINFLATIONS WHICH OCCURRED UP TO 1960

For France:

Data for prices and paper money (currency) in circulation:

Falkner, S.A. (1924), Das Papiergeld der Franzoesischen Revolution, 1789–1797, *Schriften des Vereins fuer Socialpolitik*, Munich and Leipzig: Duncker & Humblot.

Harris, Seymour E. (1930), *The Assignats*, Cambridge, Mass.: Harvard University Press.

Data for exchange rates:

Bailleul, Antoine (1797), *Tableau Complet de la Valeur des Assignats, des Rescriptions et des Mandats*, 11th ed., Paris.

For most countries with high inflations in the 1920s data have been extracted from:

Statistisches Reichsamt, *Statistisches Jahrbuch fuer das Deutsche Reich*, 1921/22, 1924/25, 1928.

For Austria:

For banknotes in circulation until December 1921:

Bordes, J. van Walras de (1924), *The Austrian Crown*, London: P.S. King & Son.

For most other Austrian and American figures:

Young, John Parke (1925), Foreign Currency and Exchange Investigation, Serial 9, 2 vols, *Commission on Gold and Silver Inquiry, US Senate*, Washington: Government Printing Office, vol. 2, pp. 292–4.
Statistisches Reichsamt (1936), *Statistisches Handbuch der Weltwirtschaft*, Berlin, pp. 513–16.
Heilperin, Michel A. (1931), *Le Problème Monetaire d'Après-Guerre*, Paris: Sirey.

Garber, P.M. and Spencer, M.G. (1994), *The Dissolution of the Austrian-Hungarian Empire: Lessons for Currency Reform*, Essays in International Finance, 191, February, Department of Economics, Princeton University.

For China:

Kia-Ngau, Chang (1958), *The Inflationary Spiral: The Experience in China, 1939–50*, New York: MIT Press and John Wiley & Sons.
Shun-Hsin Chou (1963), *The Chinese Inflation, 1937–49*, New York and London: Columbia University Press.

Butler, J.S. and Liu, Jin-Tan (1989), 'Money, Prices and Causality: The Chinese Hyperinflation 1946–49 Reexamined', *Journal of Macroeconomics*, 11, 447–53.

For Germany:

Statistisches Reichsamt (1925), *Zahlen zur Geldentwertung in Deutschland, 1914–1923*, Sonderhefte zu Wirtschaft und Statistik, Berlin: Reimar Hobbing.

For figures on budget, 1914–1919:

Roesler, K. (1967), *Die Finanzpolitik des Deutschen Reiches im Ersten Weltkrieg*, Berlin: Duncker und Humblot, pp. 196ff.

For figures on budget, 1920–1923:

Statistisches Reichsamt (1924), *Deutschlands Wirtschaft, Waehrung und Finanzen*, Berlin: Reimar Hobbing, p. 32.

Michael, P., Nobay, A.R. and Peel, P.A. (1994), 'The Demand for Money During the German Hyperinflation Revisited', *International Economic Review*, 35, February, 1–22.
Webb, S.B. (1989), *Hyperinflation and Stabilization in Weimar Germany*, Oxford and New York: Oxford University Press.

For Greece:

Delivanis, Dimitrios and Cleveland, William C. (1950), *Greek Monetary Developments, 1939–1946*, Bloomington, Indiana: Indiana University Press.
Palairet, M. (2000), *The Four Ends of the Greek Hyperinflation of 1941–1946*, University of Copenhagen: Museum.

For Hungary in the 1920s:

Figures beginning for the US in 1924 and for Hungary in January 1925 are from:

International Conference of Economic Services (1934), *International Abstract of Economic Statistics, 1919–1930*, London.

Boross, Elizabeth A. (1984), 'The Role of the State Issuing Bank in the Course of Inflation in Hungary between 1918 and 1924', in Gerald D. Feldman et al. (eds), *The Experience of Inflation: International and Comparative Studies*, Berlin and New York: Walter de Gruyter, pp. 188–227.
Siklos, P.L. (1994), 'Interpreting a Change in Monetary Regimes: A Reappraisal of the First Hungarian Hyperinflation and Stabilization, 1921–28', in M.D. Bordo and F. Capie (eds), *Monetary Regimes In Transition*, Cambridge: Cambridge University Press, pp. 274–311.

For Hungary in the 1940s:

Ecker-Racz, L. Laszlo (1946), *Hungarian Economic Developments, January 1945–June 1946*, Budapest: US Legation.
Kemeny, Gyoergy (1952), *Economic Planning in Hungary, 1947–49*, London: Royal Institute of Economic Affairs.
Paal, B. (2000), *Measuring the Inflation of Parallel Currencies: An Empirical Reevaluation of the Second Hungarian Hyperinflation*, Working Paper, Stanford, Cal.: Department of Economics, Stanford University.
Siklos, P.L. (1991), *War Finance, Hyperinflation, and Stabilization in Hungary, 1938–48*, London and New York: Macmillan and St Martin's Press.

For Poland:

Heilperin, Michel A. (1931) (see above, 'For Austria').

For the Soviet Union:

Katzenellenbaum, S.S. (1925), *Russian Currency and Banking, 1914–1924*, London: P.S. King & Son.
Young, John Parke (1925) (see above 'For Austria'), pp. 359–60.

For cost of living indices (1923 roubles), November 1922–October 1923:

Griziotti Kretschmann, Jenny (1928), 'La Riforma Monetaria Bolscevica', *Giornale degli Economista e Rivista Statistica*, LXVIII, August, 693–713.

For November 1923–February 1924:

Griziotti Kretschmann, Jenny (1924), 'Les Salaires et la Reforme en Russie des Soviets', *Revue International du Travail*, LXVIII, 693–713.

For Taiwan:

For exchange rates between taipi and fapi, 1946–1949:

Shun-Hsin, Chou (1963) (see above, 'For China').

For exchange rates of fapi and gold yuan with the US dollar, 1937–May 1949:

Kia-Ngau, Chang (1948) (see above 'For China').

For a report on conversion rates at reform and some exchange rates:

Liu, Fu-Chi (1970), 'Taiwan's Experience of Transition from Inflation to Stability', in Fu-Chi Liu (ed.), *Studies in Monetary Development of Taiwan*, Taipei: Nankang.

For money stock and wholesale price index for Taipei:

Liu, Fu-Chi (1970), 'The Single Equation Estimation of the Demand for Money', in Fu-Chi Liu (ed.), *Studies in Monetary Development of Taiwan*, Taipei: Nankang.

For conversion rates and new exchange rates for the US dollar, and the subsequent exchange rates for the US dollar from June 1949 to 1952:

American International Investment Corporation (1977), *World Currency Charts*, 8th edition, April, San Francisco.

For additional exchange rates:

Yu, Tzong-Chian (1991), Private communication by fax of 3 October, from Chung-Hua Institution for Economic Research, Taipei, Taiwan, 75 Chang Hsin Street: '*The data you need have never appeared in any statistics or any book. However, thanks to the help of the Central Bank of China, I got them.*'

Burdekin, Richard C. K. and Whited, Hsin-hui I. H. (2001), *Exporting Hyperinflation: The Long Arm of Chiang Kai-shek*, Claremont Colleges Working Papers, 18 (June). http://econ.claremontmckenna.edu/papers/2001–19.pd

2. DATA AND WORKS ON HYPERINFLATIONS OCCURRING SINCE 1960

For most countries suffering from high inflation during this period many data have been extracted from:

International Monetary Fund, *International Financial Statistics*, *Monthly Reports* from 1980 to 2000.

For the successor states of the Soviet Union, moreover, data have been used from:

International Monetary Fund (1993), *International Financial Statistics, Supplement on Countries of the Former Soviet Union*, Supplement Series, 16.
World Bank (1994 and 1996), *Statistical Handbooks, States of the Former Soviet Union*.

Melliss, Chris and Cornelius, Mark (1994), *New Currencies in the Former Soviet Union: A Recipe for Hyperinflation or the Path to Price Stability*, Working Paper, 26, London: Bank of England.

Data for some of the successor states:

Personal communications by Dr Guy Pfeffermann, International Finance Corporation.

For Argentina:

Cost of living indices from January to March 1990, for February and March 1991 and for January to May 1992 calculated from inflation rates in several numbers of the:

Argentinisches Tageblatt (1990–1992), Source: INDEC.

Kiguel, M.A. and Neumeyer, P.A. (1995), 'Seignorage and Inflation: The Case of Argentina', *Journal of Money, Credit and Banking,* 27 (3), August, 651–86.

For Armenia:

Horvath, Balazc, Tucker, Nita and Ha, Jiming (1998), *Achieving Stabilization in Armenia,* IMF Working Paper, 98/38, March, International Monetary Fund.

For Azerbaijan:

Owen, D., Fanizza, D., Jones, D., Chami, S. and Parry, T. (1998), *Azerbaijan Republic: Recent Economic Developments,* IMF Staff Country Report, 98/83, August, International Monetary Fund.

For Belarus:

Wolf, Thomas, Zamaróczy, Mario de, Arvanitis, Athanasios, Mercer-Blackman, Valerie, Tareen, Mohammed and Haas, Richard (1997), *Republic of Belarus: Recent Economic Developments,* IMF Staff Country Report 97/111, November, International Monetary Fund.

For Bolivia:

For most data and black market exchange rates since 1982:

Morales, A. (1987), *Estudio, Diagnostico, Debate: Precios, Salarios y Politica Economica Durante la Alta Inflacion Boliviana de 1982 a 1985,* La Paz: Ildis.
Mueller, H. and Machicado, Flavio (1987), *Estadisticas Economicas,* La Paz: Idea.

Morales, A. (1991), 'The Transition from Stabilization to Sustained Growth in Bolivia', in Michael Bruno, Stanley Fischer and Nissan Liviatan with Leora Meridor (Rubin) (eds), *Lessons of Economic Stabilization and Its Aftermath,* Cambridge, Mass. and London: The MIT Press, pp. 15–47.

For black market exchange rates until 1981:

World Currency Yearbook 1985 (published 1986), formerly *Pick's Currency Yearbook.*

For budgetary figures see also:

Machicado, Flavio (1986), *Estudio, Diagnostico, Debate: Las Finanzas Publicas y la Inversion*, La Paz: Ildis.

Pastor, M. (1991), 'Bolivia: Hyperinflation, Stabilization and Beyond', *Journal of Development Studies*, 27, January, 211–37.

For Brazil:

Banco Central do Brasil, *Boletim*. Several years until March 1994, then 'International Monetary Fund, International Financial Statistics', *Monthly Reports*, Washington, D.C.: IMF.

For black market exchange rates:

World Currency Yearbook (see above 'For Bolivia').

Blumenschein, F. (1995), 'The Positive Economics of Inflation in Brazil', *Development and Change*, 96(4), October, 651–86.
Bresser Pereira, L.C. and Nakano, Y. (1991), 'Hyperinflation and Stabilization in Brazil: The First Collor Plan', in Paul Davidson and J. Kregel (eds), *Economic Problems of the 1990s*, Aldershot: Edward Elgar.
Calomiris, C.W. and Domowitz, I. (1989), 'Asset Substitutions, Money Demand, and the Inflation Process in Brazil', *Journal of Money, Credit and Banking*, 21, February, 78–89.
Franco, Gustavo H.B. (2000), *The Real Plan and the Exchange Rate*, Essays in International Finance, 217 (April), Princeton: International Economics Section, Princeton University.
Sachs, Jeffrey, and Zini, A. Jr (1996), 'Brazilian Inflation and the Plano Real', *The World Economy*, 19 (1), January, 13–37.

For Bulgaria:

Gulde, Anne-Marie (1999), 'The Role of the Currency Board in Bulgaria's Stabilization', *Finance and Development*, 36 (3), September.

For Congo (Zaire):

Beaugrand, Philippe (1997), *Zaire's Hyperinflation*, IMF Working Paper 97/50, April, International Monetary Fund.
Kabuya Kalala, F. and Matata Ponyo, Mapon (1999), 'L'Espace Monétaire Kasaien: Crise de Légimité et de Souveraineté Monétaire en Période

d'Hyperinflation au Congo (1993–1997), *Le Cahiers Africain,* 41, Institut Africain-CEDAF and L'Harmattan.

For Georgia:

Shadman-Valaxi, Tsinleata, Monroe, Andrews and Verhoeven, (1995), *Republic of Georgia: Recent Economic Developments,* IMF Staff Country Report, 95/112, December, International Monetary Fund.
Castello Branco, Maria de (1996), 'Georgia: From Hyperinflation to Growth', *IMF Survey,* September.
Tsikata, Taida (1996), IMF Economist, Southern Division, European II Department, Personal communication of 26 April.
Wang, Jian Ye (1999), *The Georgian Hyperinflation and Stabilization,* IMF Working Paper, 99/65, May, International Monetary Fund.

For Kazakhstan:

Hansen, Leif, Figliuoli, Lorenzo and Panth, Sanjaya (1998), *Republic of Kazakhstan: Recent Economic Developments,* IMF Staff Country Report, 98/84, August, International Monetary Fund.

For Kyrgyzstan:

IMF (1995), *Kyrgyz Republic: Recent Economic Developments,* IMF Country Staff Report 95/38, May, International Monetary Fund.

For Moldova:

IMF (1995), *Republic of Moldova: Recent Economic Developments,* IMF Staff Country Report, 95/73, August, International Monetary Fund.

For Nicaragua:

For black (parallel), free and official market exchange rates:

Pick's (World) Currency Yearbook.

Banco Central de Nicaragua. Kindly transmitted by William Taylor by intervention of Dr Guy Pfeffermann, International Finance Corporation.
Dijkstra, Geske (2000), 'Structural Adjustment and Poverty in Nicaragua', Paper prepared for delivery at the 2000 meeting of the Latin American

Studies Association (LASA), Miami, 16–18 March 2000, Draft, Institute of Social Studies, The Hague, Erasmus University, Rotterdam.

For Peru:

Quimica Suiza SA, Nicaragua kindly provided many data for 1987–1989.

For Poland:

Daseking, A., Doyle, P., Jiang, G. and Summers, V. (2000), *Republic of Poland: Statistical Appendix*, IMF Staff Country Report 00/61, August, International Monetary Fund.

Wescott, R., Christoffersen, P. and Stotsky, J. (1998), *Republic of Poland: Selected Issues and Statistical Appendix*, IMF Staff Country Report, 98/51, May, International Monetary Fund.

For Serbia and Montenegro (Yugoslavia):

For most figures:

Petrovic, Pavle (1994), Personal communication by fax, 11 July, Belgrade: Center for Economic Studies, CES MECON.

US State Department (1997), *FY 1998 Country Commercial Guide: Serbia and Montenegro*, Report prepared by US Embassy, Belgrade, released August 1997.

Petrovic, Pavle and Vujosevich, Zorica (1996), 'The Monetary Dynamics of the Yugoslav Hyperinflation', *European Journal of Political Economy*, 12, 467–83, with erratum in this journal, 1997, 13(2), 385–7.

For Tajikistan:

Saavalainen, Tapio, Lorie, Henri, Wang, Jian-Ye, Jafarow, Etibar, Jacobs, Davina and Bakker, Bas (2000), *Republic of Tajikistan: Recent Economic Developments*, IMF Staff Country Report, 00/27, March, International Monetary Fund.

Wakeman-Linn, J., Ma, J., McGettigan, D., Nielsen, L. and Young, H. (1998), *Republic of Tajikistan: Recent Economic Developments*, IMF Staff Country Report, 98/16, February, International Monetary Fund.

For data on money supply M2, 1991–1995:

US State Department (1995), *Country Reports: Tajikistan: Economic Policies and Trade Practices*.

For Turkmenistan:

Guergen, Emine, Snoek, Harry, Zavoico, Basil, Izvorski, Ivailo, Schaetzen, Bruno de and Lighthart, Jenny (1998), *Turkmenistan: Recent Economic Developments*, IMF Staff Country Report, 98/81, August, International Monetary Fund.

For Ukraine:

For most figures until early 1993:

PlanEcon Report (1993), 10 June.
Bogomolov, Oleg T. (1993), Fax of 9 November, Moscow: Russian Academy of Sciences.

For figures until early 1996:

CEPS (1996), Letter of 7 July, Brussels: Centre for Economic Policy Studies. The figures originate from the Ukrainian Ministry of Statistics.

Havrylegshyn, Oleh, Miller, Marcus and Perraudin, William (1994), 'Deficits, Inflation and the Political Economy in Ukraine', *Economic Policy*, 19 (2), 353–401.
Knoebl, Trines, Wang, Arvanitis, Dunn, Al-Atrash, MacArthur and Wolfe (1997), *Ukraine: Recent Economic Developments*, IMF Staff Country Report, 97/109, October, International Monetary Fund.
Kravchuk, R.S. (1998), 'Budget Deficits, Hyperinflation, and Stabilization in Ukraine, 1991–96', *Public Budgeting and Finance*, 18(4), 45–70.

For Yugoslavia:

Exchange rates and retail prices since January 1987, and money supply M1 since May 1987:

Petrovic, Pavle (1994), Personal communication by fax, 11 July, Belgrade: Center for Economic Studies, CES MECON.

Bogetic, Z., Dragotinovic, D. and Petrovic, P. (1994), *Anatomy of Hyperinflation and the Beginning of Stabilization in Yugoslavia 1991–1994*, Working Paper. Washington, DC: The World Bank.
Frenkel, J.A. and Taylor, M.P. (1993), 'Money Demand and Inflation in Yugoslavia', *Journal of Macroeconomics*, 15, Summer, 455–82.

Index

Alexander the Great 21
American Civil War 1, 50, 53, 107, 117
American War of Independence 40, 47, 61, 65, 84, 107, 114
Argentina 9, 13, 15, 92, 109, 146, 164, 248, 185, 192
Aristophanes 1, 24
Armenia 186
assignats 8, 66, 69, 118, 131, 163
Augustus 21, 35
Austria 9, 23, 68, 76, 82, 98–101, 103, 107, 116, 118 , 127, 149, 169, 174, 186, 192
autocratic government 13, 44, 175, 185, 188

balance of payments 23, 45, 105, 114, 120–24, 130, 147, 150, 165
Bank of England 40
Belarus 65, 71, 163, 185
Belgium 10, 142, 148
Bodin, J. 21
Bolivia 9, 12, 71, 106, 109, 164, 166, 169, 172–5, 187
Brazil 9, 13, 94, 109, 163, 185, 192
Bretton Woods System 6, 15, 17, 105, 151
budget deficit 10, 41, 45, 53, 55, 58, 66, 69–72, 74, 77, 80, 92, 104, 110, 114–19, 121–9, 131, 160, 164, 169, 172, 174, 184–7, 189, 192
Bulgaria 15, 86, 164, 174, 177, 185

Cagan, P. 2, 48, 160
Capie, F. 8, 13
capital markets 7, 92–4, 105, 110, 161
Castile 21, 28, 32, 35, 37
central bank independence 6, 10, 15, 19, 136, 151, 157, 165, 174, 185, 193
Cesar 21
Charlemagne 27

China 1, 41, 72, 74, 77, 84, 87, 118, 163, 177, 186
Ming dynasty 41, 52–6, 59, 114
Chile 14, 109
Christiernin, P. N. 41, 44
coins 1, 5, 21, 24–7, 29, 35, 40, 45, 51, 53, 55, 59, 67, 76, 118, 141, 160, 162, 169
denarius 25, 35
florin 27, 31, 137
real de a ocho (piece of eight) 31, 137
vellon 29, 32–5, 37
solidus 27, 31
Congo, *see* Zaire
convertibility 5, 9, 14, 18, 40, 42, 44, 51, 53, 55, 61, 107, 116, 136, 141, 145, 150, 157, 174, 187
currency board 15, 19, 136, 151, 157, 166, 174, 185, 193
reform 32, 46, 50, 53, 69, 71, 74, 77, 84, 87, 98, 100, 103, 107, 109, 114, 148, 161–4, 166, 168, 172, 175, 177, 184–9, 192
substitution 33, 50, 53, 56, 58, 61, 68, 71, 76, 79–82, 89, 92, 96, 103, 110, 114, 130, 162, 164, 188, 193
Czechoslovakia 148

death penalty 33, 37, 58
debasement 24, 28, 31, 34–7, 106
debt, public 12, 31, 117, 146, 165, 238
deflation 32, 35, 44, 58, 119, 138, 148
democracy 11, 44, 108, 184
Denmark 138
depression 44, 61, 108, 138, 164, 173
devaluation 15, 18, 28, 44, 46, 48, 51, 66, 93, 138, 151, 153, 175, 187
Diocletian 26, 32, 36

Egypt, Roman 21, 25
employment 12, 16, 18, 44, 101, 104, 143

England, *see* Great Britain
Estonia 15
Euro Currency zone 153
European Monetary System 7, 18, 151,
     153
European Snake 18, 151, 153
exchange rate, 16, 27, 30, 33, 42, 44, 51,
     59, 61, 67, 79, 82, 85–8, 91, 93,
     96, 101, 110, 114, 117, 120, 125,
     129, 138, 140, 143–51, 153, 158,
     172, 177, 187, 189
   fixed 5, 10, 15–19, 36, 40, 45, 55, 62,
     105, 115, 123, 145, 151, 153, 157,
     166, 172, 174, 185, 187, 193
   flexible 6, 11, 16–19, 41, 50, 53, 77,
     131, 158
   overvaluation of 16, 45, 49, 51, 61,
     84–8, 138, 143, 145, 147, 153, 157
   undervaluation of 16, 27, 30, 37, 42,
     46, 49, 59, 68, 82, 85–91, 110, 117,
     131, 138, 140, 143, 147, 150, 153,
     157, 160
   undervaluation, relative 43
expectations, rational 129, 133

Federal Reserve System 15
fiscal policies 12, 146, 163, 174, 186
Fisher equation 92, 131
Florence 27, 30, 137
France 4, 8, 10, 15, 18, 23, 31, 35, 46,
     65, 71, 74, 77, 99, 127, 131, 147,
     157, 163, 177, 190
Franklin, B. 45

Gaul 21
Georgia 72, 187
German Bundesbank 144, 151
Germany 4, 15, 17, 23, 65, 68, 71, 77,
     85, 93, 97–104, 105, 107, 118, 127,
     131, 144, 151, 153, 160, 174, 192
Goethe, W. 78
gold exchange standard 150, 174
gold standard 5–10, 14–19, 41, 51, 65,
     107, 136, 138, 141, 147, 157
gold parity 5, 8, 14, 136, 145, 148, 150,
     157, 187
gold rush, in California 23
   in Alaska 23
Great Britain 4, 8, 14, 17, 23, 35, 40,
     47, 51, 65, 137, 145, 148, 157, 172

Great Depression 8, 14
Great French Revolution 8, 10, 19, 40,
     48, 65, 107, 118
Great Price Revolution 21, 35
Greece 71, 77, 169, 172, 174, 190
greenbacks 1, 51, 117
Gresham's Law 24, 29, 32, 35, 45, 50,
     55, 62, 67, 69, 77, 114, 123, 132
growth 2, 12, 16, 23, 42, 46, 48, 51,101,
     109, 110, 132

Haffner, S. 160
Hamburg mark banco 9, 45
Hemingway, E. 82, 85, 93
Hong Kong 15
Hungary 2, 65, 72, 99, 108, 127, 149,
     169, 174, 185, 192
hyperinflations in history 13

income distribution 104, 107
indexing 93, 97, 110, 165
India, British 150
inflation, in 3rd and 4th centuries AD
     25, 32, 35, 37
   definitions 2
   imported 18, 105, 141
   tax 77, 79, 92, 125, 127, 131, 162,
     193
inflationary bias of government 11, 14,
     18, 27, 41, 104, 135, 166, 174, 248
   cycle 53, 55, 61, 114, 168
interest parity, open 121, 131
interest rates, real 16, 92, 119, 131, 172,
     175, 189, 192, 277
International Monetary Fund (IMF) 164,
     186
interventions 6, 18, 123, 144, 150
Italy 4, 10, 15, 18

Jevons, W. S. 23, 135

Kazakhstan 65, 187
Keynes, J. M. 138
Klemperer, V. 64, 96, 99, 108
Kyrgyzstan 188

Law, J. 40, 116
law of one price 23
Latin Monetary Union 10
League of Nations 138, 169, 174, 186

Ligeti, G. 99
Louis XIV of France 40
Lydia 1

Mariana, J. de 33
Massachusetts 40, 45, 143
Mexico 21
Mises, L. von 14, 135, 150
monetary approach to the balance of
    payments 23, 114, 123
  disorder 27, 30, 35, 37
  reforms 26, 27, 50, 53, 56, 64, 162
  regime 1, 5–8, 10, 14, 19, 24, 26–30,
    41, 64, 77, 114, 135, 138, 140, 145,
    151, 157, 162, 190, 192
  policy 6, 10, 15, 26, 33, 37, 105, 145,
    163, 186
money, quantity theory of 22,
  as a means of payment 21, 23, 27, 31,
    56, 59, 62, 77
  as a medium of exchange 53, 55, 58,
    77, 88, 125
  as a store of value 77, 162
  as a unit of account 32, 66, 77, 162
  real stock of 2, 42, 46–9, 51, 68, 74,
    92, 110, 120, 127, 131, 135, 148,
    160, 162, 164, 169, 172, 175,
    185–90, 192
  normal real stock of 75, 135, 165,
    187, 192
  velocity of circulation of 76, 110

Napoleonic wars 7, 9, 14, 40, 137
Navarro, M. Azpilcueta de 21
Netherlands 8, 35, 138, 149
Nicaragua 72, 86, 159, 169, 172, 175
Norway 138, 153

paper money 1, 6, 10, 14, 16, 18, 26, 30,
    40, 42, 45, 50–56, 58, 61, 64, 69,
    98, 107, 114–131, 147, 150
  Continental Currency 40, 47, 53
  discretionary standard 6–11, 14,
    16–19, 26, 40, 96, 138, 151
  parity 5, 33, 40, 51, 55, 60, 114, 116,
    121, 124, 131, 136, 140, 147–51,
    157, 174, 187
  of foreign exchange rate 5
Peloponnesian War 1, 24
Persia 21

Peru 13, 21, 85, 117, 185, 189
Philip II of Spain 31
Pinochet regime 14, 109
Poland 71, 77, 108, 127, 148, 166, 169,
    172, 174, 184, 190
political business cycle 12
price controls 33–6, 98, 100, 110
price revolution 2, 21, 35
Punic Wars 1, 24
purchasing power parity 16, 19, 30, 42,
    45, 51, 84, 86, 89, 115, 121, 131,
    145, 151
  definition 42
  relative 43
  absolute 151, 153

Quincy, J. 50

Rational expectations 129
reserve currencies 7, 105, 151, 174
Ricardo, D. 138
Rome 1, 21, 24, 35, 106
Russia 9, 84, 127

Sargent, T. 173, 190, 192
seignorage 31, 37
Septimius Severus 25
Serbia (with Montenegro: Yugoslavia)
    65, 72, 162, 177, 187
share prices 99, 108, 160
silver standard 5, 7, 9, 14, 19, 41, 44,
    47, 65, 107, 116, 205
  parity 5, 8, 14, 136, 141, 145, 157
Soviet Union 79–82, 84, 106, 110, 161,
    169, 174, 177, 185–9
Spain 23, 30, 33, 35, 106, 137
Storch, H. F. von 16, 116
Subercaseaux, G. 114
Sweden 35, 40–45, 61, 117, 138, 153
Swiss National Bank 144
Switzerland 4, 8, 10, 15, 17, 105, 138,
    144

Taiwan 87, 109, 185, 189
Tajikistan 186
Tanzi effect, Tanzi's Law 71, 92, 110,
    162, 164, 172, 194
taxes 12, 31, 33, 47, 50, 55, 58, 66, 71,
    77, 80, 92, 106, 147, 162, 184,
    193

Thier's Law 41, 61, 76, 79, 110, 114, 130, 132, 172
Turkey 16
Turkmenistan 71, 185

unemployment 11, 101, 103, 108, 110, 140, 148, 163, 173, 175, 184, 189, 192
Ukraine 72, 187
United Kingdom, *see* Great Britain
United States 4, 7, 8, 15, 18, 40, 47, 105, 117, 215, 172

Venice 30, 137

wages 10, 60, 97, 100, 104, 110, 140, 145, 147, 160
Wagner, A. 7, 135
World War I 8, 10, 14, 76, 106, 137, 147
World War II 2, 15, 118

Yugoslavia 65, 71, 177, 185, 187

Zaire (Congo) 72, 79, 163, 186
Zweig, S. 76, 83, 98, 100, 104, 107, 109